BEYOND NEOCLASSICAL ECONOMICS

Beyond Neoclassical Economics

Heterodox Approaches to Economic Theory

Edited by

Fred E. Foldvary

Lecturer, California State University, Hayward, California
John F. Kennedy University, Walnut Creek, California
University of San Francisco, California

Edward Elgar
Cheltenham, UK • Brookfield, US

Published by
Edward Elgar Publishing Limited
8 Lansdown Place
Cheltenham
Glos GL50 2HU
UK

Edward Elgar Publishing Company
Old Post Road
Brookfield
Vermont 05036
US

A catalogue record for this book is available from the British Library

Library of Congress Cataloguing in Publication Data
Beyond neoclassical economics : heterodox approaches to economic
    theory / edited by Fred E. Foldvary.
      Includes index.
      1. Neoclassical school of economics. 2. Economics. I. Foldvary,
    Fred E., 1946– .
    HB98.2.B49 1996
    330.15'7—dc20   96–602
                                                                                        CIP

ISBN 1 85898 395 9

Printed in Great Britain at the University Press, Cambridge

Contents

List of figures   vi
List of contributors   vii
Foreword   x
   Warren J. Samuels
Introduction   xx
   Fred E. Foldvary

1 Comparative economic theory   1
   Fred E. Foldvary
2 What is wrong with neoclassical economics (and what is still
   wrong with Austrian economics)?   22
   Peter J. Boettke
3 Geo-economics   41
   Kris Feder
4 The Virginia school of political economy   61
   Charles K. Rowley and Michelle A. Vachris
5 The institutional approach to political economy   83
   Charles J. Whalen
6 Feminist economics: let me count the ways   100
   Ulla Grapard
7 Humanist economics: from *homo economicus* to *homo sapiens*   115
   Gerald Alonzo Smith
8 Nondeterminist Marxism: the birth of a postmodern tradition in
   economics   134
   Jack Amariglio, Antonio Callari, Stephen Resnick, David Ruccio,
   and Richard Wolff
9 Foundational economics   148
   Fred E. Foldvary
10 Dialogues in economics   163
   Kris Feder, Charles J. Whalen and Fred E. Foldvary

Index   177

Figures

7.1   A spectrum of knowledge   117
7.2   The empty- and full-world scenarios   118

Contributors

Jack Amariglio teaches at Merrimack College, **Antonio Callari** teaches at Franklin and Marshall College, **David Ruccio** teaches at the University of Notre Dame, and **Stephen Resnick** and **Richard Wolff** teach at the University of Massachusetts in Amherst. All economists, they are among the founders and editors of the interdisciplinary journal *Rethinking Marxism: A Journal of Economics, Culture, and Society*.

Peter J. Boettke teaches economics at New York University, where he is also a faculty in the Austrian Economics Program. Boettke is a specialist in comparative economic systems and the history of economic thought. He is the author of *The Political Economy of Soviet Socialism: The Formative Years, 1918–1928* (Kluwer, 1990) and *Why Perestroika Failed: The Politics and Economics of Socialist Transformation* (Routledge, 1993). Boettke was also the editor of *The Elgar Companion to Austrian Economics* (Elgar, 1994). He has been a National Fellow at the Hoover Institution on War, Revolution, and Peace at Stanford University (1992–3); a visiting scholar at the International Institute for Political and Economic Studies of the Russian Academy of Science; and a visiting professor at the Central European University.

Kris Feder is Assistant Professor of Economics at Bard College in Annandale-on-Hudson, New York. She earned her BA in Philosophy at the University of Pennsylvania and her PhD in Economics at Temple University. Her 1992 dissertation is 'Issues in the Theory of Land Value Taxation'. She has taught at Westchester State University and at Franklin and Marshall College. She is co-author of *A Philosophy for a Fair Society*, with Michael Hudson and G.J. Miller (London: Shepheard-Walwyn, 1994), and has contributed a chapter to *The Corruption of Economics*, by Mason Gaffney and Fred Harrison (London: Shepheard-Walwyn, 1994). She is currently engaged in research on land policy in association with the Jerome Levy Institute of Bard College.

Fred E. Foldvary received his PhD in Economics from George Mason University. He has taught economics at the Latvian University of Agriculture, the University of Latvia, Mary Washington College, Virginia Polytechnic Institute and State University, California State University at Hayward, the John F. Kennedy University, and the University of San Francisco. He is the author of *The Soul of Liberty* (Gutenberg, 1980), *Public Goods and Private*

Communities (Elgar, 1994), chapters in several books, and of articles in the fields of ethical philosophy, public finance, land economics, monetary policy, economic reforms, and economic theory.

Ulla Grapard teaches economics at Colgate University in Hamilton, New York. She is active in the International Association For Feminist Economics (IAFFE) and has recently published research on economic methodology in the organization's new journal, *Feminist Economics*.

Charles K. Rowley is General Director of The Locke Institute in Fairfax, Virginia and Professor of Economics at George Mason University. He received his higher education at the University of Nottingham and the London School of Economics. He is author *inter alia* of *Welfare Economics: A Liberal Restatement* (Wiley & Martin Robertson, 1975) (with Alan Peacock), *The Right to Justice* (Elgar, 1992), *Property Rights and the Limits of Democracy* (Elgar, 1993) and *Trade Protection in the United States* (Elgar, 1995) (with William Thorbecke and Richard E. Wagner). He has published 125 scholarly papers. He is co-editor of *Public Choice* (with Robert D. Tollison). His specialist fields are classical liberal political economy, public choice, and law and economics.

Warren J. Samuels is Professor of Economics at Michigan State University. He specializes in the history of economic thought, methodology, and the economic role of government. He is co-editor of *Research in the History of Economic Thought and Methodology* (JAI Press, 1983) and of *The Elgar Companion to Institutional and Evolutionary Economics* (Elgar, 1994). His principal current research is on the use of the concept of the invisible hand.

Gerald Alonzo Smith received his PhD from Louisiana State University, where he studied under Herman Daly. He has co-edited *Morality of Scarcity* (Louisiana State University, 1979) and was the primary editor of the *Human Economy Newsletter* from 1984 to 1994.

Michelle A. Vachris graduated with a PhD in Economics at George Mason University in 1991. She holds the position of Assistant Professor of Economics at Christopher Newport University, Virginia. Her specialist areas of research are public choice analysis and the economics of antitrust. She has published several papers in these fields.

Charles J. Whalen is Resident Scholar, The Jerome Levy Economics Institute of Bard College. He has served on the faculty of both Cornell University and Hobart and William Smith Colleges, and his contributions to institutional economics have appeared in a number of academic journals and research volumes. He is editor of *Political Economy for the 21st Century* (M.E. Sharpe, 1996).

Foreword

Warren J. Samuels

The hegemony of neoclassical economics in the period since the Second World War has, not surprisingly, given rise to some arguable misconceptions: that its conception of the economy is the only, or only correct, one; that its definition of the central problem of economics is the only, or only correct, one; that its practice of economic theory is the only, or only correct, one. None of these ideas are either empirically or conceptually correct. The economy is more than a process of resource allocation. The economy is more than the market. Markets in the real world involve more than the operation of abstract price mechanisms. The practices of formalist techniques and of reaching unique determinate optimum equilibrium solutions are not the only mode of theorizing open to the human mind. In short, there are more ways of doing economics than are sanctioned by neoclassical economics.

That is not to say that neoclassical economics is either uninteresting or uninstructive. It does have much to offer by way of deep insights into how economies operate. But there is much which neoclassical economics omits or on which it presents arguably myopic and/or stylized versions. Moreover, properly practiced, neoclassical economics is more sensible and less objectionable than its extremist or improper uses, but that is true of all schools of thought.

Actually, neoclassical economics is not monolithic. It is comprised of a number of diverse formulations. As with all schools of thought, the short, three-by-five card summary of its doctrines – often enough, alas, that which is presented in the standard textbooks – neither fully nor accurately represents the diversity of its practice. Economics, even neoclassical economics alone, is more diverse and richer than is typically recognized. That, too, is true of all schools of thought.

As for the truth of the doctrines of neoclassical economics, we know, I believe, from both positivist and post-positivist epistemology that all deductive and inductive conclusions are highly constrained, and that it is improper to fail to appreciate the range and importance of the constraints. Indeed, contemporary work on the rhetoric and/or discourse of economics suggests, if not conclusively demonstrates, that neoclassical economics is a set of stories, stories whose conclusions are driven by the design strategies established by the general paradigm and attendant assumptions of neoclassical economic theorists. Some naive people may believe, or want to believe, that, for example, the constrained-maximization rational-agent self-interest story is both self-subsistent and accurately descriptive in a complete and meaningful way of economic behavior. Others, whom I would consider more sophisticated, know (believe?) that that story is but an instrumentally useful technique – perhaps following John R. Hicks in the view that all concepts, theories, models, etc., are but conceptual tools.

But all that too is true of all schools of economic thought, not solely neoclassical economics.

The reasons for the hegemony of neoclassical economics reside much more in ideological compatibility with the dominant mind-set and in the sociology of small groups driven by exclusivist status emulation than in its putative exhaustive truth, however analytically useful its theories may be. The fact of the matter, however, is that from the earliest period in which the discipline of political economy/economics was self-consciously practiced, and including the period of self-conscious neoclassicism, the discipline has been comprised of multiple schools of thought. Some of these were ideologically and/or conceptually close to neoclassical economics; others were not. During the twentieth century, the heyday of neoclassicism, a variety of schools have existed. Indeed, the situation at the end of the twentieth century is no different than it was at the end of the nineteenth. There is now, as there was then, controversy over the name of the discipline; over the status of its founding fathers and other putatively great names; over the central problem and paradigm of the field; over its relationship to the existing economic system(s); and, *inter alia*, over its methodology(ies).

Of all the social sciences, only economics has a hegemonic school, only economics is driven by a seeming desire to pursue singular paradigms. Why this is the case – perhaps the desire for the putative uniqueness and precision of the natural sciences, perhaps the desire to present singular and unequivocal policy recommendations – need not detain us here. What is important is the historical and contemporary fact of multiple schools of economic thought. From the viewpoint of the open-minded, eclectic or heterodox economist, the feast is vast indeed.

The essays comprising this collection present a variety of alternatives to neoclassical economics. Perhaps the term 'alternatives', with its connotation of complete mutual exclusivity, is not apposite, and for at least two reasons. First, one or more schools is, relative to the others, somewhat close to neoclassical economics, at least from the standpoint of those furthest removed from neoclassicism. Second, so far as I can see, not one of the approaches included here presents theories which are *completely* contradictory with those of neoclassicism. Each of these schools presents pictures and explanations of what is going on in the economy – as each school defines the economy – more or less different from those offered by neoclassical economics.

Some heterodox economists would dismiss neoclassical economics out of hand as being irremediably flawed or entirely wrong and useless, ontologically, epistemologically and substantively. This is not the view which I take or which is, I think, taken by the contributors to this volume. On the one hand, the writers identify and challenge neoclassical economics as the product of one interpretive community, as one view of the economy, as one set of conceptual and interpretive tools. On the other hand, they welcome conversation among economists of different schools, including neoclassicists and among themselves – even if some have doubts about the commensurability of theories.

The reader should be aware that it is not possible to rely on 'reality', or 'the facts', to settle the issues which emerge in these inter-school conflicts. The definition of reality itself is the point at issue, and, following Immanuel Kant, it is not possible to confront reality directly. We approach reality willy-nilly through schools like these. It is also possible, indeed quite likely, that the object of study, the economy, is multifaceted, so that more than one theory or paradigm can apply to it; most likely, no one universal absolute theory can exhaustively describe and/or explain the economy. And as for 'the facts', they are socially constructed and theory- and preconception-laden; no facts speak only for themselves alone.

It is my view that what is important is not which one of these schools, including neoclassical economics, is the right school, or presents absolute truth, if indeed such exists. What is important are (1) the fact and substance of the issues on which the different schools take positions, and (2) the matrix formed by the issues and the positions. It is exceedingly presumptuous to think that one school, and one school only, asks the right questions and poses the correct answers, or that only one paradigm or one theory can answer all the questions in which we might be interested. It is also presumptuous to define economics as coextensive only with the paradigm, doctrines and theories of one school, and to rule out of disciplinary bounds the theories, etc., of other schools.

It is also my view that, because of the continued turmoil within economics – yes, even among neoclassicists – there is some likelihood of a post-neoclassicism, another 'new' economics emerging within the next decade or so. This new systematization would, and certainly should, encompass the breadth and depth of substantially all schools of economics and not be limited to a myopic, stylized story which omits inconvenient or ideologically sensitive topics and lines of reasoning. For example, various forms of evolutionary economics already have opened up the study of topics which have hitherto been treated within neoclassical economics as static and/or outside economists' purview, such as the formation of preferences, the formation of institutions, the role of power, and so on.

Such a new economics would explore both the factors and forces actually at work in the economy and the operation of adjustment mechanisms, and not be unduly narrowed by a quest for unique determinate optimum equilibrium solutions. Notice that the mathematicization of economics (formalism) is not at issue; nonlinear and other mathematics can be used to open analysis, rather than, as is so much the case today, invoke assumptions which prematurely narrow, finesse, and foreclose analysis in order to accommodate deterministic tools.

Interestingly, a major inroad has already taken place: despite the conventional invocation of 'competition' as an assumption, analytical activity is increasingly utilizing game theory. Game theory does not go far enough to open up economics, but it does introduce forms of inter-agent interaction and thereby considerations of power and interest-formation which go beyond the standard analysis. (On both of these points, see the essay by Ulla Grapard.) This may prove to be a significant step on the way toward analyses which deal directly with the questions of (1) power and power play, which govern whose interests count in the actually achieved non-unique Pareto optimum results, and (2) with the formation of preferences, including the formation of a firm's objective function and thereby what 'profit maximizing' is taken to mean, worked out, in part through power play, within and for the firm. The work of Douglass North, Robert Frank, Ronald Coase and many others has already moved in these directions, whether or not they are considered to be modifications within or departures from standard neoclassicism.

But, again, I remind the reader that historical neoclassicism was never as narrow and myopic as too many of its devotees and of course many of its critics have made it out to be. One would think, therefore, that the 'new' economics of which I write will undoubtedly include much of neoclassicism, though without the self-serving machinations which, unfortunately, characterize all schools of economic thought.

Fred Foldvary's chapter on comparative economic theory is a contribution to a wide array of topics and diverse bodies of literature which so far have eluded systematic integration. These topics include the problems of: (1) the comparison of theories, especially the grounds and range of their complementarity and substitutability relationships; (2) the noncommensurability of theories; (3) the criteria of theory choice; (4) the operation of the filtration system(s) by which paradigm, theory, model and concept-definition choices actually are made; (5) the criteria of epistemology and of meaningfulness; and so on.

My own view is that one can form a matrix of the different positions (e.g., schools) on any subject, including their diverse views of each other, which can help identify the issues with respect to which different positions are taken. Among other things, the matrix approach can be seen as a solution to the problem of incommensurability and as the construction of a different level of meaning. Foldvary's analysis of comparative economic theory, outlined in his essay, is consistent with the matrix approach. Finally, it should be noted that Foldvary's analysis (as well as the matrix approach) can be applied to the relations of both (1) varieties of heterodox schools and (2) orthodox neoclassical and heterodox schools, as well as (3) varieties of neoclassical economics. It is not too much to contemplate the eventual construction of a synthetic and synoptic truly general economics.

Peter Boettke's contribution demonstrates a dual heterogeneity. Insofar as Austrian economics agrees with neoclassical economics on some matters, it strongly dissents therefrom on other matters, thereby arguably illustrating the heterogeneity within neoclassicism. Insofar as it agrees on some matters with the critique and/or agenda of other quite demonstrably heterodox schools, it disagrees with those schools on other matters, thereby illustrating the heterogeneity among heterodox schools. Both respects combined thereby illustrate the heterogeneity within economics as a whole, defined to include all schools of economic thought. In pursuing all this, Boettke also illustrates how different schools can agree (or disagree) on the general objective of study yet disagree as to the particulars of how to go about pursuing that objective.

Much of Boettke's chapter is devoted to a critique of mathematical formalism and its seemingly correlative quest for determinate solutions, both at the considerable expense of neglecting, indeed avoiding, the actual economy. Boettke takes aim at the conception of a pure, abstract, institutionally empty economy. He prefers an economics which pays suitable attention to the actual institutions, processes and path dependency of actual economies. Overall, however, his espousal of Austrian economics is as an 'alternative conception *of* the entire neoclassical project', not an alternative *to* it.

Boettke's alternative, as one would expect, pursues methodological individualism and subjectivism, and process analysis in aid of a general theory of human action, market processes, and institutional evolution. It is in this connection that he acknowledges the disagreements within the ranks of the Austrian economists. A solid and pregnant intimation of what his Austrian variant of neoclassicism would involve is given by Boettke's statement calling for 'A clearer understanding of how institutions not only emerge as the unintended outcome of individual efforts to improve their lot in the world, but also how institutions shape the individual's perception of what improving their lot in the world means'.

Kris Feder's chapter introduces the reader to what may be both the most dramatic and the most venerable school – indeed movement – of heterodox economics, that following Henry George. In the late nineteenth century, Henry George, an autodidact, advanced an idea that became treated as radical by both its opponents and its advocates. It was an idea that was both premised upon one of the most established theories in political economy, the theory of Ricardian rent, and nested within a set of doctrines otherwise quite conservative. George argued that land values (representing the capitalization of rent) were due to the growth of society and not to the efforts of its nominal owners. He further argued that such values were a fit subject of taxation, because, on the one hand, rent was a residual and its taxation would have no adverse effect on production, and, on the other hand, its imposition would permit the lowering (if not removal) of other taxes which did have adverse incentive and other effects.

Although opponents often treated his ideas as an attack on property, George and his followers argued that the establishment of private property in land – with its ability to capture privately what the owner had not created – had been a mistake and that the imposition of a tax on land, especially unimproved land, would promote socially productive property rights. To them, George's 'single tax' was entirely consistent with the work ethic and income distribution by productivity. Feder's contribution applies Georgian thinking to a wide range of topics, from issues in theoretical economics to questions of economic policy, including the still pregnant matter of capitalism and socialism.

Charles Rowley and Michelle Vachris's contribution is, in effect, a survey of a considerable literature which together makes the case for the non-efficiency of results under democratic political markets. Their article raises or illustrates several important matters. One is diversity within neoclassical economics, at least the problem of whether certain work is an extension of, but conducted largely within, neoclassical economics or is a departure therefrom. Is neoclassicism to be identified with Pigouvian rather than Paretian welfare economics, and is the paradigm within which the present essay is written neoclassicist on other terms? Another is the question of how much economic theory is driven by the debate, often conducted on *a priori* terms, over the economic role of government, at least the problem of the degree to which economic theory is a result of the desire to construct a propaganda for economic freedom (to use Frank Knight's felicitous expression), the principal issue centering on the meaning of economic freedom. Another is the protean and inconclusive nature of 'efficiency' in either economic or political markets; that is, the issue of the limits of presumptive optimality reasoning in both economics and politics. Another is the importance of institutions, the degree to which 'institutions matter', the proposition that the story is in the institutional details. Still another is the question whether the issues raised both in and by their essay can be settled in any meaningful way by the 'detailed empirical analysis' called for in the essay's concluding sentence.

Charles Whalen articulates the institutionalist approach to economic heterodoxy in several steps. He first traces the early history of institutionalism and identifies the interests and analytical themes of several generations of institutional economists. These writers were very different from one another and in the work they undertook but they generally shared certain ideas. One shared idea is the evolutionary character of the economic system. For all of them this involves an emphasis on the problem of the organization and control of the economic system *qua* system. Economic evolution also implies the correlative concept of the economy as comprising more than the market and price system, and of the market as more than a pure conceptual construct – an economy is also the product of the institutions which form and operate through it. Still other ideas include the pecuniary nature of the modern business system and the dynamic force of technology in the modern industrial system.

These writers have been critics of both the existing economic system and of the mainstream economics which emanated from it as both explication and legitimation. They have been attentive to social problems, such as business cycles and poverty, and were social reformers, some as theorists, some as activists, and some in both capacities. They emphasized the on-going social construction of the economy and rejected mainstream practices which reified and legitimized status quo arrangements as the natural order of things. Institutionalists have therefore attended to considerations of process, going far beyond market process and in a rather non-teleological open-ended manner; of values, going beyond market prices; of the study of actual economies and not extraordinarily abstract and esoteric conceptual realities, including, for example, the structures of actual markets and how prices are in fact formed.

Ulla Grapard's exposition of feminist economics makes a number of critical points and identifies that approach as a credible school of economic thought. She indicates that mainstream economics can be interpreted as highly gender-specific, as giving effect to the male rather than the female component of gendered alternatives. In this view, the definition of the economy and the pursuit of economic knowledge reflects male-specific categories and views of the world. What is deemed natural is comprehended in male-specific terms; humanity is taken to be homogeneous but defined in male-specific terms. Grapard argues that ontological, epistemological and substantive aspects of economic analysis, down to the most fundamental concepts, have been masculinized.

It is clear that any 'new economics' which was responsive to the claims of feminist economics would be more diverse and richer, if less (misleadingly) determinist, than is presently the case. Until that happens, a central hermeneutic lesson must be learned and given effect: insofar as the mind-set of western civilization has been constructed in masculine terms and treated as the natural order of things, saying that that is so and only the work of a particular (if vast) interpretive community, will appear counter-intuitive and heretical. An analogy is instructive: from the feudal point of view, bourgeois civilization seemed to conflict with the natural order of things, in much the same way. And, indeed, one of the feminist points is that modernity's treatment of women may be seen as more feudal than free.

Gerald Smith's chapter on humanistic economics is a complex treatment of a vast subject. As Smith appreciates, economics *is* humanistic by almost any reckoning. But there are varieties of arguably humanistic economics, all pretty much in the post-Enlightenment tradition. Neoclassical economics is humanistic, though its mechanistic, deterministic and positivistic characteristics are considered objectionable to other variants of humanistic economics. Spiritual and pragmatic (in the sense of Charles Saunders Peirce and John Dewey) variants of humanism also exist. Smith's *Homo sapiens* approach centers on several key topics: (1) the importance of values in the social construction by mankind of economic reality; (2) a critique of neoclassical economics as a blueprint for such social reconstruction, in part on the grounds that wider issues exist than can be handled by neoclassicism, including the moral foundations required in order to have a business society (which include the role of economics itself in nurturing certain behavior and in diminishing compassion and sacrifice in personal life); (3) the problems of non-reproducible resources and of environmental degradation, especially on a massive scale (a theme which echoes considerations raised in Feder's chapter); (4) a critique of a civilization gone excessively materialist; in short, the relevance to human welfare of factors beyond those coming within the domain of neoclassical economics.

Somewhat more narrowly, the attentive reader will see a distinction between 'rational' constrained maximization decision-making and wealth maximization; the former can be instrumental to the latter but need not be. Smith's humanistic economics queries: which values is post-Enlightenment economics to promote? For some values will necessarily be presumed and advanced, positivist pretensions to the contrary notwithstanding.

'Nondeterminist Marxism' is the designation of both a postmodern variant of Marxism and a further school of heterodox economics. It is treated in the chapter by Stephen Resnick and Richard Wolff, the chief creators of the school, and three of their former students, Jack Amariglio, Antonio Callari, and David Ruccio. 'Nondeterminist', by their own account, might be better named 'overdeterminist', for their emphasis is on variables which are simultaneously both causes and effects – in a process called by the institutionalists 'circular and cumulative causation'. Overdeterminism, as simultaneously a technique of analysis and an hypothesis about economic 'reality', helps its users from becoming wedded to singular interpretations of the relationships between variables, thereby foreclosing both the possibility of multiple relationships and questions of the origins of certain variables. What is rejected is unidirectional determinism, in favor of overdetermination.

Thus, the present writers are prepared to treat economic actors as active agents and as complex (multiple) socially constructed selves; to see capitalist firms as the product of many forces, and not homogeneous; to envision the spheres of production and circulation as overdetermined; to read commodity fetishism in a number of ways, evidencing the complexity of capitalist systems; to see capitalism itself as anything but homogeneous; to relate race and gender interactively (that is, overdeterministically) with class, and most notably class itself as both a dependent and independent variable; to model society itself as an overdetermined complexity, including both class and nonclass processes; and so on. In all these and other respects, the non- or overdeterminist theoretician is able to get multiple handles on variables that function, as both dependent and independent variables, in various ways in the processes (which are themselves overdetermined) of working out systemic, organizational, and operating solutions to foundational problems, including that of the organization and control of the economic system.

Fred Foldvary's chapter on foundational economics deals with methodological, or epistemological, considerations and thereby with the nature of economics as a science and the relation of its epistemological foundations to the theories and propositions putatively constituting economic knowledge. Foldvary starts with the fundamental inconclusivity of particular methodologies and attempts to take a macroscopic or holistic view of the work actually done by economists (and other scholars). In this catholic view, he demonstrates how the methodologies and techniques of axiomatics in deduction and in induction, hypothetical deduction, and interpretive understanding, among other things, each interactively contribute to the development of conjectures, hypotheses and testing (of various sorts). Foldvary's analysis suggests (1) the diversity of actual practice, (2) the limits of actual methodological positions and techniques, (3) the fatuity of mutually exclusive, antinomian positions, and, *inter alia*, (4) the relevance of Charles Saunders Peirce's concept of abduction.

I presume to neither dictate nor predict the future of economics, especially the relationship and conversation among heterodox schools and between them and mainstream neoclassicism. I can, however, identify some themes about which the conversation can usefully center. These include: the non-uniqueness of so-called determinate optimal equilibrium solutions in relation to both the equilibrium mode of analysis and the existence of variables conventionally excluded from neoclassical economics; the considerations of power and structure in conjunction with both the foregoing non-uniqueness and the problem of the organization and control of the economy; the technical limits of economic theory and analysis; the inevitable presence and operation of values in economic theory; the propriety of evolutionary variables in the formation and operation of particular organizations and general economic systems; the relevance of multiple forms of rationality; and, as in the words of Frank H. Knight, a recognition that the principal product of the economy is man him- and herself.

Introduction

Fred E. Foldvary

The March 1995 conference of the Eastern Economic Association at New York City had the theme 'Dialogues in Economics'. I proposed a panel encompassing various schools of thought, in which the central ideas of each school would be presented, and then the presenters would engage in a dialogue with one another. The panel was entitled 'Comparative Economic Theories: A Foundational Approach', with two sessions which met on 18 March. The particular schools at the panel and this book were not as comprehensive as I had wished, but perhaps the result was fortuitous in keeping the sessions and length of the book manageable.

The authors of these chapters also took part in the panel, with Charles Rowley presenting the paper on the Virginia school, Antonio Callari presenting nondeterminist (postmodern) Marxism, and Michael Hudson also speaking on 'What's Wrong with Economics?'. There is a growing interest in heterodox approaches to economics and the schools represented in this collection. There has also been a continuing concern with the limitations of the neoclassical mainstream. The aim of the panel was not only to understand the thought, methodology, and approach of various economic schools, but to critique the state of economic science today, understand why there are different approaches to economics, and obtain insights on how the different schools can learn from one another.

In this book, each school of thought is represented by one chapter, and, in keeping with the conference theme, there is a chapter on 'Dialogues in Economics', in which the authors were invited to comment on the other chapters. A related aim of the panel and book is to further the understanding of the foundations of economic theory and a better understanding of comparative analysis. My chapters on comparative economic theory and foundational economics address these topics.

It is hoped that this work will help spur further dialogue among the schools of thought and also contribute to a broader and deeper understanding of economics.

1 Comparative economic theory

Fred E. Foldvary

Comparative Economic Theory (CET) is defined here as the analysis of two
or more schools of economic thought, or contending bodies of theory, to
determine and judge how they develop their theory and how their theory
determines their treatment of economic problems. As discussed in Chapter 4,
Dennis Mueller (1985) specifies three characteristics of 'schools' as methodology, world view, and an ardor for the idea, especially in a home institution
or place. Mueller identifies only a few schools of thought. Here, a 'school' is
broadly defined such that all bodies of theory fall within at least one school.
Neoclassicism is thus a school, even though it may not satisfy Mueller's third
criterion. A 'school of thought' is defined here as (1) a group of scientists
who adhere to a distinct body of beliefs, and (2) the set of beliefs of that
group.

A school of economic thought encompasses a methodology, a social philosophy (*Weltanschauung* or world view) and set of questions, a body of
theory and research agenda, and a set of economic policy prescriptions. By
this conception, the beliefs of a school need not be comprehensive to economics. A school can have a unique belief regarding macroeconomics or
political economy while using the microeconomics of another school. It is
sufficient that some set of beliefs be different from those of any other school.

The research questions that characterize a school are often motivated by its
belief in a Great Problem, a key source of social evil, the great obstacle to
examine and overcome. A school's research agenda is motivated by the Great
Problem and its Remedy, although this may not be the case for the institutionalist school (which perhaps may also be one of its strengths).

The Great Problem for Austrian economics is government intervention; for
geo-economics it is poverty and the taxation of labor instead of land rent; for
the Virginia school it is rent seeking; for humanists, self-gratification; for
Feminists, male domination; for postmodern thought, the pretention of absolute and universal truth; for Keynesians, market failure; for Marxists, capitalist exploitation; for the classical school, trade barriers; for the neoclassical
school, suboptimality; for foundational economics, ignorance.

CET is related to the history of economic thought, which studies the
development of economic theory, and to comparative economic systems,
which compares actual and hypothetical ways in which economies are structured as well as the underlying theories of economic systems. But CET is

distinct from either field, since it is concerned with theory itself rather than its history and personages, and it is not directly concerned with actual economies. Another field similar in name but not much related in substance is comparative economics, which compares differing applications of economics or the organization of production, such as different ways of manufacturing a product.

The recent anthologies on heterodox economic theory and comparative schools of economic thought have contained chapters presenting various schools of thought, and some commentary and analysis regarding these approaches. Among recent works, Mair and Miller present *A Modern Guide to Economic Thought: An Introduction to Comparative Schools of Thought in Economics* (1991), and Warren Samuels has published his *Essays in the History of Heterodox Political Economy* (1992a). However, comparative economic theory as a topic has itself not been widely presented. This chapter is an attempt to analyze comparative economic theory as a subject of its own, and then to show briefly how CET can be applied to the various schools presented in this book.

Elements of comparative economic theory
A comparison of different schools of economic thought includes an analysis of the premises of the various schools, of whether a school of thought is logically derived from its foundations, and of the extent to which different approaches to economic theory are complementary or substitutive. Mair and Miller (1991, p. 6) state that economics needs 'some rational or "scientific" way of choosing between schools, or between theories from different schools'. That is the task of CET, which provides the tools of such analysis, and applies the tools to make judgments about bodies of theory.

Some theorists doubt that there can be conclusive or definitive judgments about the schools. Thomas Torrance (1991, p. 33) states, 'there is no completely unambiguous way to distinguish prudent dismissals of erroneous evidence from a "reactionary" refusal to countenance inexplicable findings of a noteworthy kind'. Mair and Miller (1991, p. 6) claim that 'there is no clear or unambiguous way in which we can compare theories from different schools, or even accept or reject any theory in economics with complete confidence'.

But comparative economic theory does posit some principles with which contending theories can be evaluated, even if not with 'complete confidence' or 'completely unambiguous'. The theory of CET can in principle use the same scientific methods used by other economic topics. Nevertheless, although it is the contention here that theories can be significantly compared and evaluated, there are aspects to being attached to a school that involve criteria beyond logical analysis, such as being inculcated in a certain tradition, or having particular subject interests or ideological viewpoints, so that warranted schools of thought can continue to exist even when they present theory with different perspectives.

Comparative economic theory includes, among other themes, three related topics: (1) economic taxonomy; (2) axiomatic economic analysis; (3) theory description and analysis. It is linked to foundational economics (in Chapter 9), which analyzes foundations of economic theory. When describing a body of theory, to be fair to the school of thought, CET must accurately portray the school's major principles in the context presented, and not project ideas beyond the meaning and context of the analyzed texts. The 'ethics of conversation' described by McCloskey (1985), such as being truthful and open minded and not sneering, apply to CET.

CET should abide by the principle of charity in reasoning, assuming the most reasonable and intelligent interpretations of a school's theory. One technique of doing so is to present textual evidence from one or more sources, especially for critiques which may be disputed by members of the school. Schools of thought which critique orthodoxy or other schools are in effect doing comparative theory and should thus also abide by the principle of charity and textual context.

I agree with Mair and Miller (1991, p. 19) that 'No individual, no school of thought has a monopoly on the truth in economics'. CET and foundational economics offer the opportunity to make economic theory more comprehensive, by merging the truths found in the various schools. A task of foundational economics is to determine a comprehensive set of axioms, the intersection of the sound axiomatic propositions of all known schools of thought, and then synthesize a comprehensive theory of economics that combines in an integrated fashion the sound theorems and insights of all the schools. But even a 'foundational school' would not have a monopoly of truth in the sense that in proper science, there is always unrestricted entry and competition from dissenting and contending approaches. Thus, both foundational and comparative theory seek ultimately to know the reason for having differing schools and approaches as a subject in itself, and no doubt there will be disagreement there too.

The meaning of economics
One topic of CET is the examination of comparative definitions of what economics is. Classical economists considered economics to be the science of wealth. Neoclassical texts now define it, following Robbins (1973), as the relationship between ends and the allocation of scarce resources with alternative uses. Institutionalists regard it as 'social provisioning'. The classical definition treated economics as a physical topic, whereas the neoclassical definition is that of a human process, that of rational allocation, or as a method of analysis. John Maher (1969, p. 22) states that 'it is not *what*

economics deals with that makes it a distinctive science. Instead, it is *how it organizes and analyzes* its materials, the perspective from which it views the world, that make it a special field of study' (emphasis in the original).

However, if one looks at the table of contents of a typical economics principles text, one sees topics such as consumption, production, exchange, labor, and interest rates, rather than family relationships, international relations, religious practices, or personality types. Clearly, some topics are regarded as more 'economic' than others. But since, for example, economists do study family relationships from a different angle than a sociologist would, the defining characteristic is not topics such as production versus families, but something more subtle. Economists study the utility generated by relationships, and the economizing in obtaining such utility, whereas sociologists are concerned with the relationships for their own sake. Similarly, political scientists study the pursuit of power, whereas economists study how politicians economize in obtaining utility from power. And the reason production and consumption are major economic topics is that people obtain much of their utility from consuming, which requires production.

Robbins' process-based definition permeates all human activity, as recognized by Wicksteed (1967), since all human relationships, power structures, and psychological motives are involved in allocating resources. And yet it retains the classical notion of wealth in the centrality of resources in its definition.

McKenzie and Tullock (1978, p. 5) define economics as a mental skill plus 'a special view of human behavior'. The skill set includes abstractions, amoral analysis, having the individual person as the focal point, the premise of rational behavior, and treating costs as foregone opportunities. Some of these features are not only skills but also premises and concepts. Some economists would take issue with the exclusion of collectivist or (holistic or 'organic') methodology. Abstraction is a skill common to all scientists, as is amoral analysis for positive theory. The concept of rational behavior itself has various meanings and interpretations, and some economists posit non-rational behavior within the realm of economic study.

A topic-type definition therefore seems better suited to delimit economics from its sister social sciences than the definitions using means-ends or analyst skills. But 'wealth' is too narrow. A broader topic definition is utility, which includes the institutionalist-school 'social provisioning'. Economics as 'the science of utility' would include the production and distribution of (utility-generating) wealth, the allocation of resources to maximize utility (or economize in the generation of utility), and the creation of utility functions, or wants. Physical constraints such as diminishing returns would be included as involved in the process of generating utility. To the extent that human relationships generate utility, the cultivation of utility with relationships would be included in this definition, but cultural and psychological aspects of relationships would be excluded, hence leaving non-economic fields excluded by the definition of economics. The exchange of goods and factors would be subsumed by the utility it generates.

Economic taxonomy
Comparative economic theory analyzes the taxonomic foundations of various schools, but also seeks to analyze the taxonomy of economics itself. The taxonomy of economics is then a tool for studying comparative theories, since one can determine the scope of a particular school. Many schools of thought are confined to particular topics or methodologies, while others seek to be a comprehensive treatment of economic science.

Here is one possible taxonomy (the sequence of topics is somewhat arbitrary, and the topics are not necessarily complete):

An anatomy of economic theory

(A) Structure The field of economics, the set of propositions that constitutes economic science, has a fuzzy boundary. The *Journal of Economic Literature*, for example, includes business economics among its fields, although this topic is generally taught in business schools and departments distinct from economics, which is not generally concerned with the internal operation of organizations. In the taxonomy presented here, internal household and business management is excluded. Also excluded are topics related to the field of economics but not inherently part of economic theory, such as the teaching of economics. No endorsements are implied in the listing of any topics.

Economic theory is typically divided into the two subfields, microeconomics and macroeconomics. But since many economic concepts do not fall neatly into either of the two fields, another field, mezoeconomics, is entered into the taxonomy of theory. The role of government, for example, is both microeconomic and macroeconomic, filling as well the spectrum in between. Also, the analysis of factors such as land, labor, and capital goods spans the scope from firms to economy-wide analysis. Such topics that transcend the micro/macro distinction are placed in the category of 'mezoeconomics'.

I.   Philosophy and methodology
    A.   Methodologies
        1.   Methodological individualism
        2.   Methodological holism or collectivism
        3.   Non-envalued (value free) science
        4.   Envalued science
        5.   Axiomatic-deductive
        6.   Hypothetical-deductive

       7. Observation and description
       8. Inductive
       9. Case study
      10. Experimentation
      11. Introspection
      12. Interviewing
      13. Deconstruction
  B. Mathematics
  C. Game theory
  D. Statistics and econometrics
  E. Rhetoric
  F. Interpretive understanding
  G. Taxonomy
  H. Verbal logic
  I. Simulation

II. Theory

  A. Pure (universal)

      1. Foundational propositions
         a. Physical; b. Biological; c. Psychological;
         d. Knowledge
      2. Praxeology (Misesian)
      3. Microeconomics
         a. Utility and demand
         b. Cost and supply
         c. Sectors (households, firms, government)
         d. Market structure, competition, monopoly
         e. Partial equilibrium
         f. General equilibrium
         g. Disequilibrium
      4. Mezoeconomics
         a. Theory of institutions
         b. Government in economics
         c. Process analysis
         d. Factor analysis and distribution
         e. Expenditure analysis (e.g. consumption)
         f. Land economics
         g. Labor economics
         h. Capital-goods theory
         i. Economic anthropology and culture
         j. Demographics and gender
      5. Macroeconomics
         a. Money and banking

    b. Interest and time
    c. Business cycles
    d. Aggregate models
    e. Forecasting
   6. Political economy
   7. History of thought
   8. Comparative theory
  B. Specific (to time, place, culture dependent)
   [the same subgroups as pure theory]
  C. Fields, topical subsets
   1. Public economics
    a. Public goods
    b. Public finance
    c. Social choice
    d. Public choice
    e. Budgeting
    f. Law and economics
    g. Jurisdiction levels
   2. Industrial organization
   3. Industries
    a. Agricultural economics
    b. Natural resources
    c. Transportation
   4. Urban and regional economics
   5. Economic growth and development
   6. Economic systems
   7. International economics
   8. Finance
   9. Welfare
    a. Health economics
    b. Education economics
    c. Poverty
    d. Unemployment
    e. Crime
   10. Intersection with non-economics fields
    a. Bioeconomics
    b. Information and computer science
    c. Socioeconomics
    d. Physics applied to economics
III. Empirical studies
  A. Institutions
  B. History and current description

       1. By geographic region
       2. By topic
   C. Data, description
       1. Archival
       2. Numeric
   D. Persons
   E. Bibliographies

(B) *Schools of thought*   The following list of schools is not exhaustive:
1. Mercantilism
2. Physiocracy
3. Classical economics
4. Neoclassical (mathematicized) economics
5. New classical macroeconomics
6. Geo-economics (Georgist)
7. Austrian economics
8. Virginia political economy
9. Chicago school macroeconomics and political economy
10. Keynesian and New Keynesian macroeconomics
11. Post-Keynesian/neo-Ricardian economics
12. Historicist economics
13. Institutional/evolutionary economics
14. Feminist economics
15. Humanist economics
16. Ecological economics
17. 'Radical' (socialistic) economics
18. (Determinist) Marxian economics
19. Nondeterminist (post-modern) Marxian economics
20. Foundational economics

Comparing economic theories

Foundational economic analysis is the study of the premises on which an economic theory and methodology are based, and the derivation of the theory from the premises. It is based on the principle that science is founded upon axiomatic propositions (see Chapter 9). The two key questions that foundationalism asks are: (1) how do you know, and (2) what do you mean? 'How do you know' traces theory down to foundational observations, and 'What do you mean' reduces ambiguity in expression to clearly defined terms and metaphors, or else exposes terms and propositions as ambiguous.

A major element of analyzing a body of theory is the analysis of the definitions of the key terms used. The analysis includes (1) whether key terms are given explicit definitions; (2) whether the definitions are clear and distinct; (3) whether the definitions, if clear, are meaningful and consistent with their usage.

The taxonomy, or division of a field into categories, is a key element of a school of thought and a major influence on its theory. For example, the division of expenditure categories into consumption and investment implies a different theory than if a third category were added, waste. The inclusion of waste would imply some way of distinguishing useful consumption and investment from the destruction of value without corresponding utility, a line of inquiry which may not take place if that category is absent.

The classical school laid great importance on the taxonomy of production and distribution, with three factors of production: land, labor, and capital. The neoclassical school, in contrast, blurs and homogenizes the factors in its marginal, especially mathematical, analysis. While the classical school simplified models to the original factors land and labor, the neoclassical model uses labor and capital, often with labor as the variable and capital as the fixed factor. Marxist economics also typically blends land and capital, distinguishing between proletarian labor and the capitalist class. The geo-economics school, presented in Chapter 3, has preserved three-factor economics.

In CET, a body of theory is analyzed to determine the axioms it is based on, but also to determine which parts of it lack such foundations, but are based on unwarranted assertions, errors in logic, or personal and cultural predilections. The premises upon which a school of economic thought are based consist of ethical as well as economic propositions. A school of thought typically includes normative policy theory. But even its positive theory implies an ethical basis in its theory of markets and the role of government. The market process implies rules within which agents legitimately operate; the theory of consumer behavior, for example, involves choice among purchases rather than the choice to commit theft, which would be treated rather in the economics of crime.

Joan Robinson proposed that one function of economics was to facilitate social control (Samuels, 1992b). An economic ideology thus permeates the theory, and the foundational propositions, explicit or implicit, will include these ideological elements. In the command economies, economic study was clearly ideological, and in mixed economies, geo-economists, for example, point to the exclusion of land from contemporary factor analysis as a means to keep land rent out of significant academic discourse (Gaffney, 1994), and neoclassical price theory masks underlying interventions that create distortions that are then used to justify further intervention. CET thus also examines the often tacit ideological foundations of schools, in the context of the economic system in which they are located.

Another task of CET is to examine the premises of a school of thought for lateral as well as vertical reasoning. The foundations are analyzed to determine whether they are comprehensive, i.e. whether there are missing axioms for the field of study. Vertical reasoning is defined here as that used in deriving conclusions from premises. Lateral reasoning examines the set of premises to determine whether they are comprehensive for their field of study. (A third type of reasoning analyzes the depth of individual propositions to determine their meaning and warrantedness.) Lateral reasoning has been a topic of study by scientists and philosophers (e.g. de Bono, 1968; 1969). Much peer criticism of theory consists of pointing out errors in lateral reasoning, such as missing premises or incomplete treatment of topics. Many insights in science consist of finding new lateral connections among topics. De Bono (1969, p. 245) states the relationship between vertical (deductive) and lateral reason as follows:

> Lateral thinking is a generative type of thinking. Once a new arrangement of information has come about then it can be examined by the usual selective processes. Lateral thinking as a process can never justify the outcome, which has to stand by itself. Lateral thinking in no way detracts from the efficiency of vertical thinking. On the contrary, as a generative process it can only add to the over-all effectiveness of any selective process.

An example of missing premises is an analysis of various types of taxes for reform policy which omits one or more categories. If some significant type of tax has not been considered, no valid conclusion can be derived regarding the 'best' tax system. As another example, in considering various monetary policy options under a central bank, no valid conclusion can be derived for stabilizing policy in general, since other alternatives include banking under a currency board or free of any central authority.

Policy analysis often focuses on treating social problems without a foundational analysis of the root causes. For example, schools critical of markets typically ascribe economic woes to deficiencies of markets without acknowledging that the outcomes of a mixed economy depend on the mix of market and government action. Conversely, a critic of a particular intervention may not realize that there is some cause which causes the problem the second intervention was enacted to remedy, hence the elimination of an immediate intervention without remedying the basic problem will lead to political pressure to reinstate the intervention. Theory and policy can be analyzed to determine whether they address causes or only effects, or whether they only deal with immediate elements to the exclusion of more fundamental or related aspects.

Lateral reasoning also extends to 'contextual reasoning', in which theory is analyzed with respect to its context within the school and in relation to other schools and economics as a whole. Warren Samuels (1992a, pp. 2–3) characterizes one aspect of the history of thought as the 'intellectual form or character' of a school of thought, whose meaning resides 'in the context of the matrix formed by the entire set of formulations' of economic thought.

When CET examines the reasoning of a body of theory, the analyst examines whether propositions are warranted by logic and evidence. There are degrees of warranting. Mere assertions have no warrant, no logical argument or evidence. Speculations are guesses made about some data for which there is a plausible explanation but not yet any logical argument. For example, an economist may observe a sudden decrease in the income of a community and speculate that it may be caused by some structural shift in production, but not yet have any further evidence, nor lateral analysis to rule out other causes.

A conjecture goes a step beyond speculation. There is enough evidence to make a tentative proposition, and some logical analysis has been done. But more analysis remains, and possibly more evidence needs to be obtained. The proposition becomes a hypothesis when the initial analysis has been completed, but the proposition remains to be thoroughly tested against evidence and against peer review.

A theorem is a proposition fully warranted by logic and evidence. The warrant might be deductive reasoning from premises, or hypothesis testing by evidence that is deemed to be conclusive, or a back-and-forth cumulative refinement of the proposition in which the data leads to a better proposition which is then further tested by more data, so long as the process yields returns.

To the extent that some of the propositions in a school of thought are conjectures and hypotheses, rather than theorems, with controversy over their warranting, the schools can remain distinct bodies of theory without being reconciled or synthesized into a more universal body of theory. Comparative economic theory thus judges the warrantedness of schools' propositions. There is no aspersion to a school's having a body of conjectures, since evidence may be lacking or a body of thought may be in the process of evolving warrants. But it is useful to recognize which propositions are relatively more warranted and which are less so.

Warren Samuels (1992c, p. 8) has noted the four basic economic problems as resource allocation, income distribution, aggregate-income determination, and the organization of an economic system. Samuels divides economics into economic theory that treats the first three problems (the domain of typical neoclassical thought), and the theory of economic policy, which deals with the fourth (a domain emphasized by institutional economists and analysts of comparative systems). One aspect of CET is thus the study of how various schools of thought deal with such problems.

Substitution and complementarity

Suppose there are two schools of thought, A and B. A has a proposition A1, and B has B1. One can compare them to determine whether they are alternative explanations for the same phenomenon. If both A1 and B1 cannot both be true, then they are substitute propositions, and at least one must be unwarranted. In contrast, if both A1 and B1 may be true because they apply to different topics, ask different questions about a topic, or they depend on different conditions, then they are possibly complements. Two intersecting bodies of theory can be partly complementary and partly substitutive. In the language of set theory, A and B can intersect, and the intersection would be substitutive (either A or B can be valid but not both) while the union outside the intersection can be complementary.

At the foundational level, the axiomatic propositions of two or more schools can be analyzed. If propositions are substitutes, then one can determine which is more warranted. If both are conjectures, we then are left with alternative conjectures, and leave it at that. If, however, one proposition is well warranted and the substitute is not, the analyst can then make a judgment that the foundation of one school is better warranted.

If the propositions of two or more schools are complements, especially if their foundational axioms are not substitutes, then the two schools are candidates for a synthesis among them.

Synthetic theory construction selects sound complementary theories from various schools and approaches to economics and synthesizes their premises and consequent propositions into an integrated theory, with the object of generating theories that are more comprehensive than prevailing theory. Unwarranted propositions are rejected, and warranted ones are included in the synthesis. Conjectures are labeled as such, and there may be several contending bodies of conjectural propositions in the synthesis. But the synthesis itself is not an eclectic mix of propositions, but should be itself warranted as an organized, integrated and consistent body of theory that derives logically from its synthesized foundations.

Applications

Neoclassical economics
Peter Boettke in Chapter 2 criticizes the predominant methodology of the neoclassical school, in which mathematical modeling and econometric testing have dominated over other rigorous abstract methods such as verbal logic, a critique also made by other heterodox schools as well as some neoclassical scholars, such as McCloskey (1985). This constricted methodology limits theory to mathematically tractable models with determinate

solutions, often hypothetical constructs with little connection to actual economies. As Brian Loasby (1991) stated, in neoclassical optimality, there are no unintended consequences, as there are in Austrian process theory.

The implicit foundational premise in positivist neoclassicism is that legitimate theory is necessarily expressed as mathematical or game models (Beed, 1991), and that legitimate empirical evidence in rigorous economic science consists principally of numerical data amenable to statistical and econometric techniques. But explicit defenses or even expressions of this methodological prescription are rarely, if ever, made. The exclusively mathematicized neoclassical paradigm is thus logically unwarranted, being scientifically optimal only within its own arbitrary self-constraint.

Austrian economics – Chapter 2
Peter Boettke designates the Austrian project as explaining the undesigned regularities of market orders. That is an end product of the school's paradigm. Starting with Carl Menger in 1871, the Austrian school has held to methodological individualism, the use of realistically discrete units of goods, and an axiomatic-deductive methodology of understanding human action (a body of theory called 'praxeology' by Ludwig von Mises), in which pure theory is deduced from realistic universally-valid premises. The Austrian School, however, has so far not developed a set of explicit axiomatic premises from which its theory is deduced. Mises (1949) put forth 'human action' as a foundational premise, but as discussed in Chapter 9, human action is a complex phenomenon that itself can be deduced from more basic propositions.

Austrian economics places great emphasis on subjective values, purposeful human action in the face of uncertainty, the role of the entrepreneur, and the decentralized and incomplete nature of economically-relevant knowledge. As a consequence, Austrian economists have critiqued central planning as well as intervention as deficient in economic calculation, hence the interest of members of the school in spontaneous orders and market processes which create a market order without central direction, but within a rule of law, and with an important role for entrepreneurship. This is a positive analysis, separate from any normative preference for or against market orders.

In contrast to prices being simultaneously determined as in general equilibrium (and in nondeterminist or postmodern) theory, Austrian economics uses logically sequential causation; the prices of capital or 'higher order' goods, for example, are imputed from the prices of lower order or consumer goods. Prices may be set simultaneously, but their logical determination is imputation at the margin.

Another premise of Austrian economics is that for many phenomena, such as capital goods, the heterogenous aspects dominate homogenous treatments. The heterogenous capital structure, with a structure of ever more roundabout or higher-order capital goods in turn fuels the Austrian business cycle in which money injection artificially reduces interest rates and induces malinvestments in capital goods. Austrian theory also disaggregates the money injection by emphasizing the effects of shifts in relative prices in addition to the increase in average prices. Austrian theory complements neoclassical theory by focusing on the internal heterogeneity of neoclassical aggregates, and can also substitute for it if the heterogenous aspects dominate.

To a large extent, Austrian theory thus is complementary to neoclassical theory in providing theory as well as methodology that the mathematicized neoclassical paradigm with exogenous inputs leaves out. But in presenting a richer and more realistic theory, Austrian economics also presents substitutive theory for the understanding of market processes and in implications for policy.

Geo-economics – Chapter 3
The normative foundations of orthodox neoclassical economics are usually implicit in its literature. Price theory normally presumes a theory of consumer behavior rather than misbehavior. The implicit normative basis of neoclassical price theory is that a free market consists of voluntary acts in some context; force is external to the market.

Although private force is implicitly regarded as illegitimate, in conventional public economics, force is considered to be proper if it is used for certain ends, namely to provide public goods and to redistribute income to those deemed to deserve it. Theories of optimal taxation based on ability-to-pay implicitly presume that rights to income and wealth are shared by government and private agents. This in turn implies that resources, including labor, have a joint ownership by government and those holding nominal title, with government as the dominant owner which can set the ratio of returns between government and the private title holder. Since in orthodox theory the ethic of joint government/private ownership is implicit, arguments are seldom provided to warrant it.

Geo-economics therefore has a refreshingly explicit alternative normative premise. As Kris Feder puts it, the geo-economic ethic states that individual effort is properly private and natural resources are properly common property. The foundation for this ethic is a moral equality among human beings, which then both endows each person with an equal right to the yield of natural opportunities, and also an equal right of self ownership. Any ownership claim on one person by another would make the owning person a superior or master, which is inconsistent with moral equality. Since self ownership does not extend to natural resources, the Lockean proviso applies: homesteading endows title of possession, but rental yields are to be shared equally.

The positive element of geo-economics is its proposition that the abolition of taxation on human effort and the shift of taxation instead to land rent, would result in much more efficiency and productivity, substantially reducing unemployment and poverty, and the associated social problems and government expenses.

That the use of land rent to finance public goods and government is efficient, eliminating tax wedges and excess burdens, is not disputed by orthodox texts. But typical textbooks give the concept a brief mention without deriving the implications for both public finance and macroeconomic reforms. Orthodox theory has thus not refuted geo-economics, although there is a body of literature which argued against Henry George's theory and policy, and a literature rejecting these arguments (Andelson, 1979). Hence, although orthodoxy may accept the efficiency properties of taxing land rent, its macroeconomic and public finance theory does not adopt the logical conclusion of using a substantial amount of that rent to finance public goods and of reducing other taxes accordingly. As mentioned in Feder's Chapter 3, there is a 'Henry George theorem' that is now part of the literature in which the optimal amount of public goods is equal to the land rent, but this has not altered the prevailing paradigm of orthodox fiscal policy.

Conventional theory thus fails to be comprehensive. First, its taxonomy of labor and capital does not take into account the classical distinction that land had; the fact that its marginal product has the same type of derivative as that of labor and capital does not invalidate the distinctive features of land as immobile, inelastic, and independent of human effort, a point also recognized by the Austrian economist Menger (1871, p. 169). The classical concept of a rent-free margin has thus also disappeared from neoclassical theory. In retaining it, geo-economics also recognizes Henry George's theory of the determination of the wage level as that set at rent-free margins (Foldvary, 1994a).

Finally, recent theory (Foldvary, 1994b) has rebutted the market-failure argument in orthodox neoclassical theory, which largely ignores the spatial aspect of typical public goods. Once the real-world context of land and community are introduced, market-failure theory is turned on its head; users do not ride free, since they pay for the goods in land rent, as Feder has also indicated.

Although geo-economics can be integrated into mainstream neoclassical theory with little methodological problem, its integration would fill serious lacunae in neoclassical thought, and, as Feder notes, its implications for policy would be profound.

Virginia political economy – Chapter 4
As described by Rowley and Vachris, the Virginia school uses the self-interest premise to study public choice, focusing on the question of political-

market or government failure. The school also emphasizes comparative institutions, especially constitutions and governmental structures, in analyzing
public choice and seeking remedies for government failure. The Virginia
school's theory, using neoclassical as well as Austrian analysis, concludes
that institutional structures determine political outcomes, in contrast to the
Chicago view that purely economic phenomena, such as competition, dominate. In particular, the Virginia school's analysis states that contemporary
political institutions, particularly majoritarian representative democracy, is
infected by wasteful transfer seeking, a cost that needs to be taken into
account by those advocating government action.

Although the Virginia school at first glance seems to focus on one particular topic, public choice, it has potential links to other schools in subjecting
their policy prescriptions to the possibility of government failure as well as in
examining the outcomes of alternative structures. The Virginia school in turn
has theory complementary with the critique of intervention of the Austrian
school and the analysis of the tax alterative offered by geo-economists in its
potential to reduce rent seeking. On the other hand, the Virginia and Chicago
approaches to political economy are substitute theories, Rowley and Vachris
providing arguments to show that the Virginia school has a more realistic
body of theory.

Institutionalist economics – Chapter 5

In the above taxonomy, I have listed the institutionalist school and also
institutions under empirical studies and in theoretical analysis. This is because 'new' institutionalists also study and include institutions (e.g. Williamson,
1985). Conventional money and banking theory typically examines the institution of a central bank, while Virginian public choice theory studies the
consequences of various structures of government.

The institutionalist school, depicted here by Charles Whalen, goes deeper
than such applications to incorporate institutions (as well as values) more
fully as a paradigm of economics and also in presenting critiques of neoclassical as well as Marxian thought. Institutionalists argue that neoclassical
analysis focuses on pure economic mechanics such as supply and demand,
profits, and utility maximization, leaving out as exogenous important elements such as culture, power, and institutions. Institutionalism encompasses
a whole range of methodologies and readily adopts theory from other disciplines. With roots in historicism and empiricism, the institutionalist school
posits economics as holistic, historically grounded and evolving, as opposed
to the ahistorical neoclassical price theory.

The institutionalist 'processual' evolutionary perspective encompassing innovation in an environment of uncertainty is shared by the Austrian school
and is a contrast (and a complement) to the static equilibrium constructs of

neoclassical analysis. In its holistic approach, institutionalism fills areas neglected by neoclassical orthodoxy, such as administered pricing, the inclusion of status as a goal, and family provisioning, with the entire institutional structure of society included in resource allocation. By including descriptions of behavior and institutions, such as case studies and interviews, the school widens the scope of empirical studies, and, as noted by Whalen, documents economic phenomena that is overlooked by statistical studies. Much of anthropology and biology is descriptive, e.g. in depicting a new species. Yet the study of community economies does not carry much prestige in academic economics.

In its taxonomy, institutional economics distinguishes between instrumental and ceremonial activities. Institutionalists also posit a dual economy with a 'center' of large firms with great economic power and a 'periphery' of small firms, with behavioral theory that complements and substitutes for neoclassical industrial organization as well as macroeconomic policy analysis.

Institutional thought shares with foundational economics a comprehensive approach to theory, seeking to encompass the whole range of phenomenon. As Whalen states, institutionalism offers a broader perspective that reflects reality more accurately than the more limited scope of conventional theory. But Whalen also notes the need for more institutional theory. I would add that the school does not yet seem to have analyzed and presented an explicit set of foundational propositions for theory, which would in turn be founded on its methodological propositions such as holism. This would facilitate the efforts of institutionalists such as Foster (1987) and Hodgson (1988) for a synthesis of the institutionalist and process-oriented approaches of various schools.

Feminist economics – Chapter 6
Feminist economics challenges orthodox theory for not taking into account gender, i.e. aspects of economics dealing with socially as well as biologically determined maleness and femaleness. Some applied neoclassical theory and empirical studies do deal with the role of women in the economy and delve into issues such as the status of women in less developed countries. But feminist economics criticizes orthodoxy for not making gender a more fundamental part of theory, yet at the same time criticizes the implicitly gendered bias of economic theory. Feminist economics thus appears to be both a complement to orthodox theory, which can broaden economic inquiry, and a substitute, challenging some of its theory and assumptions.

The feminist challenge to neoclassical orthodoxy extends to its foundational premises about human nature or behavior. Ulla Grapard contests what feminists regard to be the tendency to base such assumptions on male behavior. For example, neoclassical *homo economicus* is not concerned with the 'reproductive labor' of bearing and raising children. It is not clear, however, whether gendered assumptions consist of understudied applications rather than a biased, gendered view of basic economic behavior. The foundations of economics, as discussed in Chapter 9, for example, do not appear to be dislodged by the feminist challenge. Both males and females presumably economize in attaining their ends, and both have self-oriented as well as sympathetic or altruistic ends. It would be quite useful to present a set of explicit premises on which feminist economics is based; as yet, there does not seem to be such a foundation for analysis. But feminist economics does challenge implicit biases in much of basic theory, such as labor economics, and it can contribute to synthetic theory construction to achieve a more comprehensive and sounder economics.

Feminists might note ways in which the paternalistic power structure of government can be reduced by the reforms analyzed by the Virginia school and also how geo-economic policy would enhance female options by increasing the after-tax wage level.

Humanist economics – Chapter 7
Humanist economics brings important moral and social-philosophic considerations to economics, which other schools leave implicit, compartmentalize in welfare economics, or leave out in an attempt to be value-independent. Humanist economists posit the general goal of well being for economic science, although the school has apparently yet to provide an explicit logical derivation of a humanist ethic. Still, humanist economics presents an alternative theory conditional on an alternative value system of limited material desires, and they point out that self-interest can mean more than self-gratification.

In common with feminist economics, humanist economists claim to have a different conception of human nature than is typical in neoclassical economics. Gerald Smith states that the humanist *homo sapiens* strives for 'excellence of being', thus positing an Aristotelian end as part of human nature, in contrast both to the allegedly mainstream premise that people strive for power or that human ends are purely subjective, i.e. that desires determine value (on this, see the Foldvary discussion in Chapter 10). Smith also rejects the premise of human nature that desires, at least for material goods, are unlimited.

In placing economics in a spectrum of knowledge, humanists are in accord with institutionalists and feminists in viewing knowledge from related fields as important for economics. The inclusion of the experience of the economist in humanist methodology has links to Austrian introspective methodology.

Nondeterminist Marxism – Chapter 8

Nondeterminist Marxism analyzes topics of the old determinist Marxism, such as class, surplus value, and exploitation, but in its postmodern vein denies historic teleology and unidirectional cause-effect relationships. Elements of postmodern thought are found in other schools as well, including the feminist chapter in this book. The nondeterminist concept of a decentered, endogenous subjectivity resonates in Austrian economics with Hayek's (1952) study of the mind, and also with the Austrian rejection of fixed, given preferences. The Austrian emphasis on uncertainty and disequilibrium also accords with nondeterminist or overdeterminist analysis, despite sharply different policy conclusions.

Significant substitutive principles of postmodern thought include the rejection of universal truths and standards for truth and the rejection of foundational determinants. But even if the more determinist schools successfully defend themselves from the postmodern challenge, a more complex synthetic theory may develop.

Foundational economics – Chapter 9

Foundational analysis is not (yet) an established school of thought, but it is an approach to economics which some schools have engaged in and it potentially can be a field if not a school in itself. It has relevance to the study of basic theory, to history of economic thought, to comparative theory and comparative systems, and to economic methodology.

Universalist economics   Just as there are individuals who are bi-national or bi-cultural, there can be economists who are bi-paradigmatic or bi-theoretic, adhering to two compatible paradigms or bodies of theory which are not integrated in conventional thought. As Ulla Grapard indicated, for example, there are feminist economists in various other schools of thought. Some schools are not comprehensive paradigms, and thus necessitate at least a bi-paradigmatic approach, e.g. a geo-economist may be a neoclassical or else a geo-Austrian. This intersecting can be extended to multi-paradigmism, in which a pan-theoretic or universalist economist does not confine himself to one approach or school of thought, but seeks to integrate several paradigms, for example one could be an Austrian institutionalist geo-economic adherent of the Virginia school.

Universalist theory cannot adopt all propositions of all schools, since many schools offer contending, substitutive theory; using the language of set theory, the schools may offer a union of theory, but not a compatible intersection. One would have difficulty favoring a paradigm of massive government direction and also one of unhampered markets. But some conflicts in theory may be only apparent; it is possible that the theories are conditional on disjoint premises, and can thus be unified, the empirical question then being which premise most closely approximates perceived reality. For example, school A may posit self-oriented *homo economicus*, and school B posits *homo sympaticus*, human beings who sympathize with others. Theory A and B are not substitutes but complements, both being conditional on different premises, it being an empirical matter which premise predominates in a particular culture or for a particular circumstance.

In addition, just as ethnic identifications are often retained in multi-ethnic societies and religious differences persist, schools of thought as interests and economists' sub-cultures will likely persist indefinitely even if economists become more open to a comprehensive universalist approach to their science.

Dialogues in economics – Chapter 10

A conclusion that can be drawn from the heterodox schools presented in this book is that, though most of the schools are critical of neoclassical thought, much of the theory complements it by expanding the methodology and the restricted premises of neoclassicism. The title of this book implies that the heterodox schools exist 'beyond' neoclassical analysis, modifying and extending it, not necessarily eliminating it. As Boettke states, neoclassical thought is a special case, but this turns the neoclassical treatment of heterodoxy on its head. Economic theory is a giant pie, with each school part of the pie. Neoclassical economics is a major slice, but economic reality can be understood only if one takes in the whole pie. And although economists specialize in their research and adhere to various traditions, their basic education should devour the whole pie. This book presents some slices which have been heretofore untasted by much of the mainstream.

References

Andelson, Robert (ed.) (1979), *Critics of Henry George*, London, and Cranbury, N.J.: Associated University Presses, Inc., and Fairleigh-Dickinson University Press.

Beed, C. (1991), 'Philosophy of science and contemporary economics: an overview', *Journal of Post Keynesian Economics*, **13** (4), 459–94.

De Bono, Edward (1968), *New Think: the Use of Lateral Thinking in the Generation of New Ideas*, New York: Basic Books.

De Bono, Edward (1969), *The Mechanism of Mind*, New York: Penguin.

Foldvary, Fred (1994a), 'Poverty and the Theory of Wages: a "Geoclassical" analysis', in Nicolaus Tideman (ed.), *Land and Taxation*, London: Shepheard-Walwyn Ltd, 141–56.

Foldvary, Fred (1994b), *Public Goods and Private Communities*, Aldershot, UK: Edward Elgar.

Foster, John (1987), *Evolutionary Macroeconomics*, London: Allen & Unwin.

Gaffney, Mason (1994), 'Neo-classical Economics as a Stratagem against Henry George', in Mason Gaffney and Fred Harrison (eds), *The Corruption of Economics*, London: Shepheard-Walwyn, 29–163.

Hayek, Friedrich (1952), *The Sensory Order: an inquiry into the foundations of theoretical psychology*, London: Routledge & Paul.

Hodgson, Geoffrey (1988), *Economics and Institutions: A Manifesto for a Modern Institutional Economics*, Cambridge: Polity Press.

Loasby, Brian J. (1991), 'The Austrian School', in Douglas Mair and Anne Miller (eds), *A Modern Guide to Economic Thought: An Introduction to Comparative Schools of Thought in Economics*, Aldershot, UK: Edward Elgar, 40–70.

Maher, John E. (1969), *What is Economics?*, New York: John Wiley & Sons.

Mair, Douglas and Miller, Anne G. (1991), Introduction to *A Modern Guide to Economic Thought: An Introduction to Comparative Schools of Thought in Economics*, Douglas Mair and Anne Miller (eds), Aldershot, UK: Edward Elgar, 1–20.

McCloskey, Donald (1985), *The Rhetoric of Economics*, Madison: University of Wisconsin Press.

McKenzie, Richard B. and Tullock, Gordon (1978, 1975), *The New World of Economics*, Homewood, IL: Richard D. Irwin.

Menger, Carl (1871, 1976), *Principles of Economics*, trans. James Dingwall and Bert Hoselitz, New York: New York University Press.

Mises, Ludwig von (1949, 1966), *Human Action*, New Haven: Yale University Press and Henry Regnery Company.

Mueller, D. (1985), *The 'Virginia School' and Public Choice*, Fairfax: Center for Study of Public Choice

Robbins, Lionel (1930, 1973), *The Nature and Significance of Economic Science*, 2nd edn, New York: Macmillan.

Samuels, Warren J. (1992a), *Essays in the History of Heterodox Political Economy*, Washington Square: New York University Press.

Samuels, Warren J. (1972, 1992b), 'In Praise of Joan Robinson: Economics as Social Control', in *Essays in the History of Heterodox Political Economy*, Washington Square: New York, University Press, 340–48 (originally in *Society*, **26**, 73–6).

Samuels, Warren J. (1972, 1992c), 'The Scope of Economics Historically Considered', in *Essays in the History of Heterodox Political Economy*, Washington Square: New York, University Press, 8–36 (originally in *Land Economics*, **48**, 248–68).

Torrance, Thomas S. (1991), 'The Philosophy and Methodology of Economics', in Douglas Mair and Anne Miller (eds), *A Modern Guide to Economic Thought: An Introduction to Comparative Schools of Thought in Economics*, Aldershot, UK: Edward Elgar, 21–39.

Wicksteed, Philip (1967), *The Common Sense of Political Economy*, New York: Augustus M. Kelley.

Williamson, Oliver E. (1985), *The Economic Institutions of Capitalism*, NY: The Free Press.

2 What is wrong with neoclassical economics (and what is still wrong with Austrian economics)?

Peter J. Boettke

A discipline, a region of the world of thought, should seek to *know itself*. Like an individual human being, it has received from its origins a stamp of character, a native mode of response to the situations confronting it. Right responses, 'responsibility', will require of the profession as of the individual an insight into the powers and defects of the tool which history has bequeathed to it.

G.L.S. Shackle (1972, p. 24)

Introduction

In the late 1970s and early 1980s video recorders burst on the scene of home entertainment. It is a now familiar story how the Sony Beta machine was outcompeted in the market by the VHS format despite apparent technological superiority. Both machines provided the same service, but due to a network externality Beta was eliminated from the market. This elimination from the market was due to the poor management decision of refusing to share technology. Apple Computer supposedly made a similar mistake with its operating software and has lost valuable market share to the less user-friendly DOS operating system of Microsoft. Such is the stuff that explains the rough and tumble of the dynamic market competition we have seen in the last decade as the Information Age has engulfed us all. Faster, better, lower-cost machines that run on smaller and smaller chips dominate our lives. But the notions of path dependency, technological lock-in, network externality, etc., cast doubt on the ideal efficiency of all the changes we are living through. Perhaps there would be an even more efficient path, but once derailed, the cost of getting back on that path is prohibitive.

My purpose in relaying these oft-repeated stories is not to debunk them, but rather to borrow from them to explain developments in modern intellectual history. My hypothesis is that economics made a fateful choice in the 1930s and 1940s and chose an intellectual development path which has generated a bifurcation in economic thinking between theoretical systems and the real world these systems are supposed to represent, a bifurcation not easily repaired. Formalistic precision was (and is) followed, and the cost was (and is) a loss of relevance of the discipline of economics for the messy world in which we live. Even on the empirical front, fine estimation techniques were developed, but the richness of the empirical world remains hidden from scientific view. Theoretically and empirically, I assert, the technology chosen for the task at hand led (*ex post*) to an intellectual dead-end.

The task at hand – as I see it – was a neoclassical one: to explain market regularities as the outcome of the rational choices of individuals subject to constraints. In this sense, I am not challenging the marginalist revolution of the 1870s. Nor would I challenge the universalistic project of rational choice theory. The problem is not in the aspirations of these inter-related projects, but in the way the project proceeded and was thus transformed. (Just as in the Sony-Beta story nobody contends that the market for VCRs was wrong-headed in general, though the choice of VHS was 'wrong' from a technological perspective.)

In comparing neoclassical economics with Austrian economics it is important to recognize first and foremost that Austrian economics *is* historically a school within the broader tradition of neoclassical economics. Austrian economics, unlike institutionalism or Marxism or Post-Keynesianism, is not heterodox in certain fundamental respects. On the other hand, with regard to what neoclassical economics has become and the way that the original marginalist project is now understood within the mainstream, Austrian economics is every bit as heterodox as any of the alternative schools of thought mentioned above. This two-sided aspect of Austrian economics leads to many tensions within the school (on an intellectual level [both theoretical and empirical], strategic level [which professional alliances to pursue], and institutional [in terms of departmental location and in terms of funding support]). I will limit myself here, however, to a discussion of those tensions felt on an intellectual level leaving for more appropriate venues discussions of a strategic or institutional concern. In doing so I hope not only to present what are the limitations to mainstream neoclassical economics, but also to suggest what are some of the lingering problems which haunt Austrian economics and prevent the school from developing its potential as a framework for the theoretical and empirical examination of the world.

What is wrong with neoclassical economics?

The answer to the question 'What is wrong with neoclassical economics?' can be summed up in a few words: it is precisely irrelevant. But that answer takes some explaining. The neoclassical project that was begun in the 1870s sought to derive economic laws from the foundational proposition that economic agents base their decisions on their subjective evaluation of the situation. Choice is never about totals, but always choices at the margin. Individuals strive to obtain ends, and in doing so they arrange (and rearrange) the means available to them to achieve those ends.

As this program was translated into mathematical form certain simplifying assumptions were made to ease the translation of essentially a philosophical/ logical set of propositions about human choice and social interaction into a determinate system of equations. Neoclassical economics evolved to the point where it could be defined by the following research strategy: (a) maximizing behavior, (b) stable preferences, and (c) market equilibrium (Becker, 1976, p. 5). This evolution of the scientific program of neoclassical economics progressed slowly but steadily over a one-hundred year period, with each successive generation weeding out the use of natural language (just as VHS format did not immediately out-compete Beta). The younger practioners found that to pursue this research program 'relentlessly and unflinchingly' and in order to 'talk' with their colleagues, they had to 'speak' the language of mathematical models. Unless their ideas could be stated in formal proof, it was understood that the idea remained simply an interesting idea and not a contribution to science. This was a marked departure from the earlier view of economic reasoning found in say, Alfred Marshall. As A.C. Pigou wrote about Marshall:

> Though a skilled mathematician, he used mathematics sparingly. He saw that excessive reliance on this instrument might lead us astray in pursuit of intellectual toys, imaginary problems not conforming to the conditions of real life: and further, might distort our sense of proportion by causing us to neglect factors that could not easily be worked up in the mathematical machine (Pigou, 1925, p. 84).

I do not wish to stress the Mengerian essentialist critique of mathematical economics, but rather the consequentialist critique. Marshall limited mathematics to the footnotes; by the time Milton Friedman published his provisional text in price theory, the footnotes in Marshall had become the text and the text in Marshall had become the footnotes, so to speak. Still, Friedman's price theory was connected to the real world in a fundamental sense and was a powerful engine of inquiry into economic life. One could, at that time, still study for an economics exam by taking a trip to the local grocery store to examine inventory policies or ponder the 99¢ pricing rule.[1] The same is true for the economic teaching of neoclassical economics that took place at UCLA, Washington University and the University of Virginia (the birthplaces of property rights economics, new economic history, and public choice theory in the 1950s and 1960s).

By the next generation of graduate text-books on price theory, however, the footnotes containing Marshall's text are gone and all we have is an instructional book on the mathematical techniques and models. Gone is the concern with the everyday business of living that Marshall sought to understand. Successive generations of our brightest students are taught to play with their intellectual toys and solve imaginary problems not conforming to the conditions of real life. With that comes a distorting of our professional sense of proportions by turning a cold shoulder to any problem that cannot be presented in mathematical form.

As mathematics became the standard language of economic science there was a network externality effect on the entire profession. The profession became 'technologically' locked-in. The fateful moment of decision, I would argue, was with Paul Samuelson's *Foundations* (1947). Samuelson's obvious intellectual brilliance and his strategic astuteness (within a decade Samuelson came to dominant both the undergraduate education with his *Principles* and graduate education with his *Foundations* – and his dominance in this regard lasted at least two decades) led to a convergence of professional opinion on how economic *science* was to be done even if differences on a policy level remained. Galbraith (in books such as *The Affluent Society* 1958) or Hayek (in books such as *The Road to Serfdom* 1944) might provide food for thought, but one wasn't supposed to confuse this exercise with science – we had moved beyond that. The concerns of scholars such as Kenneth Boulding that 'Conventions of generality and mathematical elegance may be just as much barriers to the attainment and diffusion of knowledge as may contentment with particularity and literary vagueness' were dismissed (1948, p. 247).

Economists had forgotten that what mathematical modeling promised was fairly limited. Stating arguments in mathematical form does ensure syntactic clarity, but it does not guarantee semantic clarity – the very thing that Marshall was concerned about.[2] If one combines the philosophy of science arguments for a positivistic image of science that were circulating in mid-century, with the formalistic demand for mathematical representation, then the shift to instrumentalism as the dominant practice among economists is readily explained.[3] The only way to operationalize positivism in economics was to shift to 'as-if'ism and indirect testability. But once permission was granted to abandon all concern with realism of assumptions, theoretical thought experiments could and did run wild. Scientific exercises can as easily be seen as peculiar forms of escapism as contributions to knowledge.[4]

The evolution of the profession in this direction has not gone unnoticed. The exposé of graduate education in economics by Arjo Klamer and David Colander (1990) brought to attention what many believed. Graduate training in economics had lost sight of the substantive logic and 'art' of economics. As the *Report of the Commission on Graduate Education* states it, the general concern is that with each successive generation 'We might teach the language of mathematics but not the logic of economics, and end up valuing the grammar of the discipline, rather than its substance' (Krueger, et. al., 1991, p. 1041). The *Report* is too conservative and guarded, because the future is already upon us. The grammar has, for at least a decade, been more important that the substance of economics, as Klamer and Colander documented with their interviews with students at leading graduate institutions. Even the authors of the *Report* had to admit that 'It appears that mastery of technique has supplanted mastery of the kind of intuitive economic analysis that was once called "Chicago-style micro"'. The AEA Commission – in an unguarded moment – even stated that their 'fear is that graduate programs may be turning out a generation with too many *idiots savants*, skilled in technique but innocent of real economic issues' (ibid., pp. 1044–5).[5]

Since economics is what economists do, as Frank Knight said, the systematic weeding out of a certain type of scholar transforms the discipline. It is not just a question of science progressing one gravestone at a time. The problem is our understanding of the central questions which have occupied economics since its founding. The obsession with the language of mathematics has divorced the discipline from the world of everyday life.

Ronald Coase has argued forcefully against the misuse of formalism in economics.[6] The formal structure of an argument, Coase warned, can mask underlying contradictions in the project. The Coasian critique of the Pigovian analysis, for example, really was directed to pointing out that economists pursuing this type of analysis were 'engaged in an attempt to explain why there were divergences between private and social costs and what should be done about it, using a theory in which private and social costs were necessarily always equal' (1988, p. 175). The assumptions required to make the analysis tractable formally precluded the necessity of analysis. The policy recommendation that emerged out of the Pigovian framework required a level of detailed knowledge of the circumstances that were it to exist would render the policy recommendation redundant, because agents within that economy would already have acted upon the knowledge to eliminate the said problem. Moreover, if we grant that the logic of the analysis is impeccable, but admit we do not know how to calculate the required taxes and subsidies or approximate them through a process of trial and error, then we must admit that our formal tax analysis is nothing more than the 'stuff that dreams are made of'. The frustration with the twisting of the concept of theoretical economics to justify whatever mental experiment one can think up led Coase to state: 'In my youth it was said that what was too silly to be said may be sung. In modern economics it may be put into mathematics' (1988, p. 185).

The critics I've cited would defend the importance of abstraction and theory in economic analysis. What is wrong with modern economics is an issue of judgment and research direction. The skills required to survive PhD training and advance up the academic ladder ensure that those that survive are quick of mind, analytically astute – in a word, smart. But there are no guarantees that 'smart' translates into 'good' when it comes to the art of economics (McCloskey, 1995).

My point is simply to suggest that the 'medium is the message', so to speak. The language of modern economics, due to the demands for determinacy, crowds out questions of subjective assessment, institutional context, social embeddedness, knowledge (as opposed to information), judgment, entrepreneurship, creativity, process, and history (see Samuels, 1989). Some may be attempting to employ the tools of modern economics to analyze these questions, but in the process the questions are transformed. Institutions, for example, can be treated as formers of preferences, or as constraints. Maximizing models inevitably transform the treatment of institutions into constraints only, and questions about institutions as formers of preferences are pushed aside as intractable. Do mathematical models of learning, creativity, and information acquisition really connect to the problems which gave rise to our concern with these concepts in the first place?

Austrian economics as a general theory

Austrian economics promises a way out of the problems of neoclassical economics.[7] It does so not by jettisoning the neoclassical project, but by pursuing it in an alternative language – that of natural language – that affords us the possibility to explore social processes that defy determinate solutions. Natural language allows us to deal with the imprecise world of real time and ignorance, yet not have to either abandon the aspiration of universal theory, nor define the problem away in the search for determinacy. The Austrian project has always been one of attempting to explain the undesigned regularities of the market order as the outcome of the meaningful choices of individuals. This problem was a central mystery of economic life precisely because the individual's problem situation was one which admitted to the potential trap of solipsism that could engulf the individual as a subjective perceiver of the world. What *must* be explained is how institutions and various habits of living emerge that allow the individual to transcend the confines of his own mind and interact with others.[8]

One way to answer the problem is to deny it, that is treat the individual's problem situation in a simpler manner, the way modern economists have gone. In the modern text-book, the individual is assumed to possess all the relevant information necessary to maximize his utility subject to given constraints. The prices observed in the market are assumed to contain all the relevant information about relative scarcities, and reflect equilibrium values, and through price mediation profit-maximizing producers perfectly coordinate their decisions with utility-maximizing consumers to generate an optimal allocation of resources. The logic of this approach is sound, but it answers the question posed only by trivializing it. Theory in this fashion can proceed without concern for any particularity of the situation.

Another way to approach the problem is to deny its solution. Allow the problem of subjective perception to engulf economic actors and deny that they could ever coordinate their plans. Economic life, the stuff of subjective expectations and unique historical contingencies, defies solution. Sure, consumers have a bewildering array of choices, but many are left at the bottom of the economic ladder (or even unable to get on the ladder, but instead are 'free' to wallow in the streets without hope). Solutions to the social dilemma are not to be found, from this perspective, in the 'invisible hand' of market processes. This does not automatically translate into confidence for the 'visible hand' of government, because recognition of the 'hidden hands' of interest groups and problems with democratic governance may undermine the policy solutions proposed. But the normative issue is not what I want to stress. By denying the solution, social science proceeding this way will not pursue the analytical project of unlocking the mystery of economic order because the idea of ordered regularity is denied. Instead, the focus will be on the historically contingent.

Instead of either trivializing the problem or denying its solution, there is an alternative program of research that has motivated social scientists for centuries. The classical approach, especially in its mature Ricardian manifestation (with its focus on the objective long-run conditions), came close to steering the analytical exploration of the invisible hand in the direction of triviality. German historicists, especially of the younger school, denied the solution. The Austrian program – immersed as it was in the continental philosophical and scientific debates – promised to deal with the problem of unplanned order in its full mysteriousness. The German sociologist Georg Simmel (1908), influenced by similar intellectual trends, raised the question: 'How is society possible?' Once the problem situation of the individuals is complexified, the Austrian economists, from Menger on, focused on a subset of that question, namely 'How is market coordination possible?' Menger argued that perhaps the most noteworthy problem in the social sciences was:

> How can it be that institutions which serve the common welfare and are extremely significant for its development come into being without a common will directed toward establishing them? (Menger, 1883, p. 146)

In fact, Menger argued that 'The solution of the most important problems of the theoretical social sciences in general and of theoretical economics in particular is thus, closely connected with the question of theoretically understanding the origin and change of "organically" created social structures' (ibid., p. 147).

Without denying the potential trap of solipsism and the imperfections of our human existence, the question was to illuminate how the institutions and various habits of living evolved to escape the traps of subjective valuation, the passage of time, and the limitations of our knowledge.[9] Money, within the

Austrian analytical framework, represents both the exemplar of the compositive methodology they sought to pursue and the key social institution of coordination that allows us to bridge the gap between solipsism and social order.[10] Menger's depiction of the evolution of a medium of exchange out of the barter exchange situation shows how individuals pursuing only their own interest can generate an outcome that serves the common welfare even though that was no part of their intention.[11] In addition, recognizing the centrality of money (one half of all exchanges) to the system of production and the functions which money came to serve within economic life (the facilitator of exchange and economizer of information) led to an analysis of the social dilemma that differed from either the classical or historicist forerunners to Austrian economics.

Austrians rejected the historicist challenge by asserting the epistemological necessity of theory in social analysis. There is, according to the Austrians, no choice. There is either analysis in which theory was made explicit and defended, or there is inarticulate theory. There is no such thing as theory-free social science. One cannot possibly engage in social science without a guiding theory; the world is too complex (see Böhm-Bawerk, 1891).

But why not simply stick with the classical economic theory of Ricardo? Why muddy the analytical waters with concerns of the subjective nature of individual decision making and the particularity of the context of choice? The issue here, as we have seen, was one of the problem situation in which the individual was placed – and it is this issue which today still separates Austrian economists from their neoclassical brethren.[12] In this regard, the Austrians would join Keynes in claiming that classical and the other traditions of neoclassical economics (Marshallian and Walrasian) represent at best a special theory as opposed to a general theory (1936, p. 3).

The reason for the special nature of neoclassical theory is the problem situation so conceived. If we lived in a world of perfect information, zero transaction costs, infinite number of buyers and sellers, then perhaps the core model of neoclassical economics would depict our social plight.[13] But we obviously do not live in that world; our general situation is one filled with imperfections, misperceptions, costly transactions, and utter ignorance of lurking opportunities. Where Austrians differ from Keynes (and from other heterodox writers) is in the implications for economic science of the problem situation once appropriately complexified. Keynes sought some form of aggregate analysis, but Austrians denied that aggregate techniques of analysis would permit an examination of the underlying forces at work.[14] Austrians sound a bit like neoclassical economists when it comes to issues of microfoundations of macroeconomics, though they also sound a little like Keynes and many other heterodox scholars when it comes to the problem situation that must be studied.

Neoclassical writers agree that the world is not like the core model, but they insist that the model is useful and that abstraction is necessary. I am not denying the necessity of abstraction, nor that the economic project must begin with a firm microeconomic foundation. The question is whether parsimony favors the neoclassical model. I am willing to admit that if Austrian analysis ended with the same analytical propositions about human interaction as neoclassical analysis does, then the scientific burden of proof would have to be on the Austrians. Why worry about such issues as time and ignorance if in the end we can get the same result with a much simpler (and more elegant) model? Maybe some realist philosophical argument could be made, but good old American pragmatism would compel us to side with the neoclassical project. But the Austrian claim was not limited to Menger's essentialistic critique (though that is what has been stressed), as it included a consequentialist claim that the analysis of the simplified situation does damage to our understanding of the complex situation and turns our intellectual efforts in the wrong direction on both a theoretical and empirical level. It is not scientifically pragmatic to focus on the simplified situational logic of neoclassicism. Even an Austrian economist as wedded to the neoclassical mainstream as Oskar Morgenstern commented that:

> The abstraction made would be faulty if it bypasses a fundamental feature of economic reality and if the analysis of the radically simplified situation will never point towards its own modification in such a manner that eventually the true problem can be tackled. ... Radical simplifications are allowable in science so long as they do not go against the essence of the given problem (1964, p. 255).

If we admit that the tools of neoclassical theory have been developed with the aid of radical simplifications of the problem situation, then the questions that remain are whether these simplifications can be relaxed and what remains of neoclassical theory if they are.[15] And, what I mean by remains is not simply that the formal language of neoclassical economics is retained, but that the theoretical propositions about the world are retained. That is precisely where the difficulty lies. The modern research strategy of information economics and/or New Keynesian economics is one which retains the formal language of neoclassical economics, but introduces *selective realism* into the analysis. The conclusion of this sort of analysis overturns many of the core propositions of standard neoclassical analysis (such as market clearing) and the two fundamental welfare theorems associated with the concept of Pareto optimality (see Stiglitz, 1994). Generalized market failure theory (with missing markets and suboptimal allocations) substitutes for the theory of general equilibrium and the efficient market hypothesis.

The Austrian claim is not against abstraction, but challenges the selective realism[16] of modern information economics and questions whether the techniques employed in modern information economics undermine the analyst's ability to deal with knowledge and the informational role of the price system (see Thomsen, 1992). As such, modern Austrian economics offers an alternative theory of economic life, significantly more general in its applicability to the real world. The neoclassical mainstream of microeconomics (of both the perfect and imperfect market sense) is limited in scope precisely because it violates the principle of adequate abstraction in science. Furthermore, instrumentalist appeals cannot salvage the theoretical system given the lack of empirical findings to support the models of utility maximization and profit-maximizing as these models are understood in the standard text-book. Modern models may be logically coherent and formally elegant, but they *do not work* in illuminating basic questions of economics such as the formation of price, the path toward equilibrium or between equilibrium positions, and the nature of innovation.

This failure is generally recognized across the various subschools of mainstream neoclassical economics, but the general retort is two-fold: (a) so what?; and (b) what is the alternative? The second question presupposes that an acceptable alternative be couched in the same form as existing theory. This, however, is precisely where the two questions link up and get at the basic non-neutrality of the choice of language in the science of economics. For example, the prime mover of economic progress – the entrepreneur – has been systematically weeded out of formal economic theory, as Machovec (1995) and others have persuasively documented. If the meaning of 'theory' in economics has been so transformed as to tolerate any and all free-floating abstractions, then there is no compelling reason why the lack of a prime mover should be mourned. But failure to mourn the loss of the prime mover in economic activity should be understood as an abandonment of the main intellectual quests of economic science since Adam Smith: the explanation of how individual behavior influencing price adjustments generates an overall order that tends to coordinate the decisions of the most willing suppliers with those of the most willing demanders in the market. Equilibrium theories (independent of whether they describe an optimal or suboptimal situation) do not explain the activity that brings the situation about, but rather simply postulate the point so derived.[17]

Austrian economics focuses on those questions which neoclassical models do not formally allow – in this regard Austrian economics often appears to be nothing more than the appreciative theory underpinnings of the formal theory of the mainstream.[18] But what if appreciative theory outdistances formal theory in dealing with issues that matter for understanding market processes and the social structures that sustain or thwart the operation of these processes? This question does not occur to a formalist because the span of vision of the scientific enterprise is restricted by the language of analysis, but to the

Austrian (and various other heterodox schools of thought) the question represents the reason for dissent from the conventional scientific wisdom of the day in economics.

If what we demand out of an economic theory is realism, then Austrian economics strives to deal seriously with the real social conundrum in which human actors are placed. If economic theory is also supposed to strive for universality, then Austrian economics claims to offer logical derivations of analytical propositions that meet that aspiration to universal principles of human action and interaction. By consistently and unflinchingly pursuing methodological individualism (understood in its phenomenological as opposed to atomistic sense), methodological subjectivism (or intersubjectivism), and process analysis, Austrian economists have developed a general theory of human action, of market processes, and of institutional evolution. By recognizing the complex problem situation which is our social world, the individual and collective coping mechanisms that allow us to live with one another are highlighted and explored.

It may be, as some assert, that all the talk of schools of thought is counterproductive to an extent because what really matters is whether someone is pursuing good economic or bad economic analysis. Putting aside the obvious fact that the definition of 'good' or 'bad' is a function of the school of thought which one is privileging at the moment of assessment, it does seem plausible to argue that *if* one is to deal with the everyday world in which human beings live, then one must not distort their situational environment beyond recognition simply for formal tractability.[19] If the tools are not flexible enough to deal with the problem, then rather than turning away from the problem, perhaps it is time to choose new tools of analysis. Seriously grappling with the implications of time and ignorance, rather than ever more refined exercises in constrained optimization, may provide the foundation for a humanistic (yet logically sound) and policy-relevant economics.[20]

What is still wrong with Austrian economics?

Those committed to the Austrian paradigm do firmly believe that the analysis offered is both more realistic and more relevant than any of the alternative theoretical systems of inquiry in economics. As such, the claim is that on a positive level Austrian theory provides a more accurate description of the social world and, thus, a better understanding of the forces at work in that world. On a normative level, combined with some moral philosophical statements, the Austrian positive analysis can generate a deep appreciation for certain institutional configurations and how these configurations generate prosperity, peace, and liberty.[21]

Nevertheless, it must be admitted that Austrian economics is plagued with many thorny issues of an epistemological, theoretical, empirical, and political nature. Disagreement within the ranks of Austrian economists still persists over such issues as the role of equilibrium within the theory of the market process, the treatment of expectations from a subjectivist perspective, the incorporation of cultural factors (and social embeddedness) in the analysis of choice and preference formation, and the how and why of knowledge (its conveyance and use). Within the literature of contemporary Austrian economics, questions of the standard of refutation, the issue of empirical subsidiary assumptions, the recognition of empirical magnitudes still have not been dealt with in the sophisticated manner required. In fact, the relationship between theory (conception) and history (understanding) must be rethought in the wake of modern philosophical developments. The philosophical debates of the 1920s and 1930s that so influenced Mises and Hayek in their methodological pronouncements have progressed, and this progression in the argument for a non-positivistic and non-mechanistic social science must be incorporated. In my opinion, the effect of this incorporation will not be benign in terms of the self-understanding of the Austrian social-scientific project.

Analytically, Austrians must develop a more subtle understanding of the social infrastructure within which market processes operate and a clearer understanding of how institutions not only emerge as the unintended outcome of individual efforts to improve their lot, but how institutions shape the individual's perception of what improving their lot means. The institutionally contingent domain of theoretical economics must be developed more clearly in Austrian theory. Too much rhetoric in the history of the tradition has been on the exact or pure theory level – even when dealing with the empirically contingent area of applied theory. The pure logic of choice may be a necessary component of any successful research program in economics, but it is not sufficient. The logic of choice must be supplemented with a richer understanding of the epistemic properties of alternative institutional arrangements. This would also include an explicit treatment within the Austrian literature of alternative political institutions and their epistemological and motivational impact on human behavior and interaction.

Unlike the problems I have stressed concerning the neoclassical project, the lingering problems with Austrian economics are signs of a progressive research program capable of growth (see Rizzo, 1995). Neoclassical economics, by artificially restricting the problem situation, has become a stagnant research program. The mainstream has been able to escape the implications of stagnation by substituting the language of the discipline as opposed to the substance of the discipline as the main research area. New applications of refined tools (either in terms of building theoretical systems or of generating empirical estimations) defines the fast track in the profession more than solving a problem in the economy. Whereas the neoclassical project began as an attempt to develop a general theoretical framework which would illuminate the human condition, it has become an intellectual enterprise preoccupied with free-floating abstractions and the techniques developed to aid these flights of mental imagination. In contrast, if the Austrians can come to terms with tension between their aspiration for universal application and the necessity to recognize the contingent and the unique in human affairs if the problem situation of time and ignorance is to be seriously dealt with, then perhaps it is not too late for the original neoclassical project to become a more viable and relevant discipline and fulfill its promise as an engine for inquiry into the social world.

Conclusion

The formal theory of mainstream economics possesses syntactic clarity, but, unfortunately, much of what passes for 'theory' lacks semantic clarity. Theory in the social sciences does not need to reject rigor in argumentative standards to ensure both syntactic and semantic clarity, but the language of mathematics is not designed to deal with issues of semantic meaning. The network externality produced by the substitution of mathematical language for natural language within the economic profession resulted in a simplification of the problem situation analyzed, which in turn transformed the discipline of economics. A lack of relevance to solving real world problems was one of the most obvious consequences, but less obvious results include the progressive elimination from the economic discourse of scholars who possessed a philosophical mind or a historian's penchant and patience. Case study methodology, archival history, as well as more sociological types of knowledge derived from interviews and surveys have been pushed aside as lacking in formal rigor. Ronald Coase prepared his study of the firm by visiting various industrial enterprises, and interviewing company officials from the accounting office to the factory floor, and later in his career his insights on the problems of social cost and difficulties in standard public good theory emerged in detailed case studies and archival history. The modern student of these issues would pursue such real world explorations only as a hobby (or afterthought) not as a vehicle for understanding.

What economics needs today is an anchor in the world. The educational proposal that I would suggest would be a re-evaluation of the history of economic thought (as theory) and economic history (as empirical touchstone) in our curriculum. Both of these courses have been eliminated from most graduate and undergraduate courses of study. But by introducing students to the history of the discipline and the motivating questions of the discipline (on a theoretical and empirical level) it is hoped that something would touch an intellectual cord within the next generation.[22] Formal models as heuristic devices are fine, provided they are constrained by an understandability criterion.[23] Improved statistical techniques are also desired, but again they must be constrained by the goal of achieving a better understanding of the historical situation under investigation. Return graduate students to the library to read the old books and to the archives to sort through the old records, and our knowledge of both the universal and particular will improve.

Austrians can join with the heterodoxy in challenging the methodological premises of the mainstream and the characteristic assumptions of the basic model of text-book neoclassicism. But, the Austrians are part of a neoclassical heritage, and as such their research program is closely wedded to one of instrumental rationality models of human agency, an appreciation of systematic market forces, and a project designed to explain the social processes that emerge as the unintended by-product of the rational choices of individuals. Many of the heterodox criticisms of the analytical project of neoclassicism, therefore, cannot be accepted by Austrians. The problem situation within neoclassical economics is unduly restricted, but individuals do pursue their interests; society cannot choose, only individuals do; markets do tend to clear when left free to their own devices; and wishing it so doesn't make it so in public policy.[24]

So, what is wrong with neoclassical economics? It is the problem situation to which the mainstream restricts its analysis. What is still wrong with Austrian economics? We have failed to fully come to terms with our neoclassical heritage and our heterodox critique. And, perhaps, when contemporary Austrians do come to grips with these currently uncomfortable aspects of their thought, the promise of Hans Mayer (1932, p. 149) that the way to scientific enlightenment in economics is along 'the road on which the great system-builders of the "older" German historical school meet up with the founders of the "Austrian School"' will be fulfilled and a new political economy will be forged that simultaneously satisfies our humanistic desire to *understand* ourselves, our scientific impulse to *know* the underlying forces at work, and our humanitarian *belief* that philosophical understanding and scientific knowledge can be employed in concert with one another to improve the human condition.

Notes

Acknowledgements
I would like to thank Israel Kirzner, Mario Rizzo, William Butos, Dan Klein and Roger Koppl for their comments on an earlier draft. The usual caveat applies. Financial support from the Austrian Economics Program at New York University is gratefully acknowledged.

1. The story of studying for a PhD qualifying exam in industrial organization by visiting the local grocery stores in Chicago was told to me by Mario Rizzo, who studied with Stigler in the early to mid-1970s. Friedman also taught his price theory course at the time with

ample reference to daily affairs reported in the newspaper, and Becker challenged students with reports of seemingly irrational behavior in the daily market (such as lines for Broadway shows or quality restaurants when the line could be eliminated by raising the price) and demanding a rational-agent explanation of the continued existence of these and other practices which on the face of it seem to violate the maxims of economic behavior.

2. The language of 'syntactic' and 'semantic' clarity simply refers to the difference between the grammatical form of a statement as compared with the meaning of a statement. With regard to economic models, this distinction comes from Coddington (1975, p. 159).

3. The Austrian economist, Fritz Machlup (1955, 1967) has often been seen as defending the 'as if' turn in economics in his methodological discussions of verifiability and the critique of behaviorist theories of the firm, such as that offered by Lester. But, Machlup was explicit that the one criterion that separated his position from that of Milton Friedman was the core 'test' of *understandability*. On the importance of this and how the standard literature mischaracterized Machlup's position see Langlois and Koppl (1991). Also see Lavoie (1990) for a re-examination of the Lester/Machlup debate.

4. This is where the Mengerian essentialistic critique of mathematical economics meets the consequentialist critique of a Marshall or (as we will see) Coase. It is precisely because mathematical economics cannot capture the essence of the economic problem individuals confront in the world that its consistent use leads to the elimination from the field of study of the very questions which the real world of economic life demands that we, as a profession, ask.

5. One of the great classical economists, Jean-Baptiste Say, argued that the philosophical/moral dimension of political economy 'does not admit of mathematical estimation' and that 'The forms of algebra are therefore inapplicable to this science, and serve only to introduce unnecessary perplexity' (Say 1821, p. 327, fn.). Even Keynes, no enemy of mathematical analysis, raised his concern of the misuse to which mathematical models could be put in economics. 'Too large a proportion of recent "mathematical" economics are mere concoctions, as imprecise as the initial assumptions they rest on, which allow the author to lose sight of the complexities and interdependencies of the real world in a maze of pretentious and unhelpful symbols' (1936, p. 298). In our own day, one of the main contributors to social choice theory, Amartya Sen (1987), has argued that our discipline has both an engineering component and a moral-philosophic component to it, and that unfortunately the past few decades have witnessed an overemphasis on the engineering side to the exclusion of the moral-philosophical.

6. An important survey of Coase's work is provided by Medema (1994).

7. For an overview of the contemporary Austrian research project see Boettke (ed.) (1994). Also see Rizzo (1995) for a discussion of the changing agenda within Austrian economics due to the focus on the problem situation of time and ignorance.

8. This is why the problem of economic calculation became central to Austrian economics as a positive analytical contribution as opposed to the obvious normative implication of the argument. In a world not only of scarce capital goods, but also heterogenous capital goods that must be joined in combination with other capital goods in order to coordinate production decisions to match with consumer demands the problem of economic calculation can never be treated as a simple imputation (as Schumpeter asserted). Socialism, by denying in principle, the institutions and practices which afforded economic calculation within a private property economy, denied the very possibility of rational economic calculation. As a result, the Austrian claim went, socialist policies would generate results which would be viewed as undesirable from the perspective of those desiring the policies in the first place, and in the extreme, would prove impossible to implement in practice.

9. Hayek, for example, argued that 'rational economic behavior' was a habit of learning inculcated by the institutional environment and prodded by competition rather than a core assumption of analysis. Man, independent of the competitive environment, while purposive, would lean toward laziness and would not be particularly alert to opportunities for gain.

10. See Horwitz (1992) for a contemporary Austrian discussion of the social significance of money beyond its transaction economizing role.

11. Mises claimed that Menger's theory of money was not only 'an irrefutable praxeological

theory of the origin of money' but also that it demonstrated the 'fundamental principles of praxeology and its method of research' (Mises 1949, p. 405).

12. There were, of course, logical flaws in the classical system of price determination which led to the neoclassical revolution in which the Austrians were crucial figures in the 1870s. In addition, the Austrians stressed the subjective nature of choice as much as the marginal nature of decisions in their explanation of economic phenomena. Ricardian analysis (then and now) masks the essence of economic phenomena by focusing on the objective conditions rather than the subjective evaluation of decision makers on the margin.

13. Again note that Austrians do not reject the neoclassical project of rational choice explanations that strive for universality. Israel Kirzner has criticized my depiction of the basic gulf between Austrian economics and neoclassical economics. It is not the problem situation, Kirzner suggests, but the lack of a theory of process that separates the two projects. But, unless the problem situation of the individual is recognized as one entrapped in the flux of time and imperfect knowledge, then I do not see that there would be much of a need for a theory of process. The Walrasian theory of pre-reconciliation of plans flows from the problem situation, just as the Austrian theory of the market process is an implication of the problem situation as postulated by Menger, Mises, Hayek and Kirzner.

14. See, for example, Hayek (1952, pp. 108–9).

15. The fact that this question is also being raised by new institutional economists reflects that in terms of the modern intellectual landscape in economics new institutionalism is the closest analytical ally to Austrian economics, though perhaps not so with regard to methodological concerns (in which case Austrians are more allied with other non-positivistic heterodox writers). For a fascinating discussion of the problems of new institutional economics that parallels many of the points I've raised in this chapter see Furubotn (1994).

16. Of course, as pointed out to me by Mario Rizzo, it cannot be otherwise. One cannot include every empirical detail in a model. But what I want to suggest by the term *selective realism* is that while some parameters of the basic model are adjusted to represent the new problem situation, the basic parameters of the model are left unadjusted so that what results is not really a change in the problem situation but a restricted ability of the agents in the model to cope (because they are precluded by assumption from possessing the ability to cope).

17. Hans Mayer (1932) provides a detailed critique of functional theories of price in contrast with genetic-causal theories of price. Mayer's essay demonstrates the extent to which many of the same critical themes that modern Austrian economics raises against the neoclassical mainstream were evident from the beginning of the Austrian tradition. On the importance of genetic-causal theories in economics see Cowan and Rizzo (1995).

18. The distinction between appreciative theory and formal theory in economics can be found in Nelson and Winter (1982, pp. 46–7). Karen Vaughn (1994) has persuasively argued that such a limited view of Austrian economics as that of a footnote to standard neoclassical analysis cannot be seriously entertained by Austrian economists. While I have stressed that Austrian economics must be understood as a variant of the neoclassical project, I completely endorse Vaughn's claim. The point I am seeking to stress is that Austrian economics is an alternative conception of the entire neoclassical project and as such promises a more general theory of economic processes (perhaps with standard theory found in the footnotes of such a reconstructed neoclassical economics).

19. I want to make it clear that I am not suggesting that Austrian economics lies somewhere between the neoclassical mainstream and heterodox critics and that this middle-ground position somehow privileges Austrian theory. My point is to locate the Austrians on a different spectrum, one that begins with a shared understanding of the problem situation with the heterodox critics (a problem situation of social embeddedness, imperfect knowledge, the passage of time, the error-prone nature of human decisions, etc.), yet strives to establish a general theory of universal applicability out of that problem situation using a basic model of instrumental rationality. Austrians, like general equilibrium theorists, are deductive theorists committed to deriving principles of economics through exercises in

logic, but the basic core assumptions within the deductions are given to them by the problem situation of the heterodoxy.

20. Alan Coddington summed up the general position I am holding out for the Austrians nicely in his discussion of Shackle's contributions to economics. 'If this account is sound, it leads to the seemingly paradoxical (but in fact straightforward) idea that carefully imprecise concepts can give a more *accurate* expression of the economic world than precise ones. On these grounds, the kind of precision aimed at by the axiomatisers can be seen to be quite artificial in that to increase the precision of formalisms in no way contributes to a clarification of the mode of correspondence between the formalism and the economic world it is supposed to represent; and it is on the robustness of this correspondence that understanding (as opposed to the manipulation of symbols) ultimately rests' (Coddington 1975, pp. 158–9, emphasis in original).

21. I have sought to sort out the issues of positive and normative analysis in Austrian economics in the wake of the postmodernist critique of objective knowledge, see Boettke (1995).

22. Kenneth Boulding, in classic contra-Whig fashion, argued that the key issue is the evolutionary potential of a system of ideas. To the extent that ideas still possess evolutionary potential, it is part of our extended present. The Whigish notion that all that was good in the ancients must already be contained in the moderns fails to appreciate the evolutionary potential of debates and ideas found in the distant past for solving current problems in the discipline today. See Boulding (1971).

23. As I alluded to in the discussion of Machlup's methodology, it has been argued that this criterion was the dividing line between Machlup's and Friedman's position on the scientific testability of economic propositions. Machlup inherited the test from the founders of the Austrian school. To Wieser, for example, economics was applied common sense; any layman knows the substance of the theory of value from his own experience – lay people just haven't studied the matter theoretically. 'If this be true, how else shall we better prove our scientific statements than by appealing to the recollections which every one must have of his own economic actions and behavior?' (Wieser, 1893, p. 5). This has been the Austrian appeal to intuition as a source of knowledge in economics (not to the private intuitions of the analyst, but to the intersubjective intuition of our shared social space). We have access to information that is denied the physical sciences, and a major error is committed if we deny ourselves this knowledge.

24. This doesn't mean that economic liberalism necessarily flows from economic science and therefore one cannot be an economic scientist and deviate from laissez-faire. It does mean, however, that economics as a tool of critical appraisal does place certain parameters on various utopias, and is capable of informing us on the costs and benefits of various institutional arrangements. Economics, for example, cannot determine whether profits are deserved or not, but it can yield insights into the consequences for the patterns of exchange and production of the different answers to that question.

References

Becker, Gary S. (1976), *The Economic Approach to Human Behavior*, Chicago: University of Chicago Press.

Boettke, Peter J. (1995), 'Why Are There No Austrian Socialists?', *Journal of the History of Economic Thought*, **17** (Spring), 35–56.

Boettke, Peter J. (ed.) (1994), *The Elgar Companion to Austrian Economics*, Aldershot, UK: Edward Elgar.

Böhm-Bawerk, Eugen (1891), 'The Historical vs. the Deductive Method in Political Economy', *Annals of the American Academy of Political and Social Science*, Vol. 1; reprinted in Israel M. Kirzner (ed.), *Classics in Austrian Economics*, 3 volumes, London: William Pickering, 1994, Vol. 1, 109–29.

Boulding, Kenneth (1948), 'Samuelson's *Foundations*: The Role of Mathematics in Economics', *Journal of Political Economy*, **56** (June), 187–99.

Boulding, Kenneth (1971), 'After Samuelson, Who Needs Adam Smith?', *History of Political Economy*, **1** (Fall), 225–37.

Coase, Ronald H. (1988), *The Firm, the Market, and the Law*, Chicago: University of Chicago Press.

Coddington, Alan (1975), 'Creaking Semaphore and Beyond: A Consideration of Shackle's "Epistemics and Economics"', *British Journal of the Philosophy of Science*, **26**, 151–63.

Cowan, Robin and Rizzo, Mario J. (1995), 'The Genetic-Causal Tradition and Modern Economic Theory', unpublished manuscript, Department of Economics, New York University.

Furubotn, Eirik G. (1994), 'Future Development of the New Institutional Economics: Extension of the Neoclassical Model or New Construct?', *Jena Lectures*, Max-Planck-Institute for Research into Economic Systems.

Galbraith, John K. (1958), *The Affluent Society*, Boston: Houghton Mifflin.

Hayek, Friedrich A. (1944), *The Road to Serfdom*, Chicago: University of Chicago Press.

Hayek, Friedrich A. (1952), *The Counter-Revolution of Science*, Indianapolis: Liberty Press, 1979.

Horwitz, Steve (1992), 'Monetary Exchange as an Extra-Linguistic Social Communication Process', *Review of Social Economy*, reprinted in David L. Prychitko (ed.), *Individuals, Institutions, Interpretations*, Aldershot, UK: Avebury, 1995, 154–75.

Keynes, John Maynard (1936), *The General Theory of Employment, Interest, and Money*, New York: Harcourt Brace Jovanovich, 1964.

Klamer, Arjo and Colander, David (1990), *The Making of An Economist*, Boulder, CO: Westview Publishing.

Krueger, Anne O. et al. (1991), 'Report of the Commission on Graduate Education in Economics', *Journal of Economic Literature*, **29** (3), 1035–53.

Langlois, Richard N. and Koppl, Roger (1991), 'Fritz Machlup and Marginalism: A Reevaluation', *Methodus*, **3** (2), 86–102.

Lavoie, Don (1990), 'Hermeneutics, Subjectivity, and the Lester/Machlup Debate', in Warren Samuels (ed.), *Economics as Discourse*, Boston: Kluwer Academic Publishers, 167–84.

Machlup, Fritz (1955), 'The Problem of Verification in Economics', *Southern Economic Journal*, reprinted in Fritz Machlup, *Methodology of Economics and the Other Social Sciences*, New York: Academic Press, 1978, 137–57.

Machlup, Fritz (1967), 'Theories of the Firm: Marginalist, Behavioral, Managerial', *American Economic Review*, reprinted in Fritz Machlup, *Methodology of Economics and the Other Social Sciences*, New York: Academic Press, 1978, 391–423.

Machovec, Frank M. (1995), *Perfect Competition and the Transformation of Economics*, New York: Routledge.

Mayer, Hans (1932), 'The Cognitive Value of Functional Theories of Price', translated and reprinted in Israel M. Kirzner (ed.), *Classics in Austrian Economics*, 3 volumes, London: William Pickering, 1994, 55–168.

McCloskey, Donald N. (1995), 'He's Smart. And He's a Nice Guy, Too', *Eastern Economic Journal*, **21** (1), 109–12.

Medema, Steven G. (1994), *Ronald Coase*, New York: St. Martin's Press.

Menger, Carl (1883), *Investigations into the Methods of the Social Sciences with Special Reference to Economics*, New York: New York University Press, 1985.

Mises, Ludwig (1949), *Human Action: A Treatise on Economics*, Chicago: Henry Regnery, 1966.

Morgenstern, Oskar (1964), 'Pareto Optimum and Economic Organization', reprinted in Andrew Schotter (ed.), *Selected Economic Writings of Oskar Morgenstern*, New York: New York University Press, 1976, 253–66.

Nelson, Richard R. and Winter, Sidney G. (1982), *An Evolutionary Theory of Economic Change*, Cambridge: Harvard University Press.

Pigou, A.C. (ed.) (1925), *Memorials of Alfred Marshall*, New York: Augustus M. Kelley, 1966.

Rizzo, Mario J. (1995), 'Time and Ignorance: After Ten Years', C.V. Starr Center for Applied Economics, New York University, RR#95–24.

Samuels, Warren J. (1989), 'Determinate solutions and valuational process', *Journal of Post Keynesian Economics*, **11** (4), 531–46.

Samuelson, Paul (1947), *Foundations of Economic Analysis*, Cambridge: Harvard University Press.

Say, Jean-Baptiste (1821), *A Treatise on Political Economy*, New York: Augustus M. Kelley, 1971.
Sen, Amartya (1987), *On Ethics and Economics*, Oxford: Basil Blackwell.
Shackle, G.L.S. (1972), *Epistemics and Economics*, New Brunswick: Transaction Publishers, 1992.
Simmel, Georg (1908), 'How is Society Possible?', in Donald N. Levine (ed.), *Georg Simmel on Individuality and Social Forms*, Chicago: University of Chicago Press, 1971.
Stiglitz, Joseph (1994), *Whither Socialism?*, Cambridge: MIT Press.
Thomsen, Esteban (1992), *Prices and Knowledge*, New York: Routledge.
Vaughn, Karen I. (1994), *Austrian Economics in America*, New York: Cambridge University Press.
Wieser, Friedrich (1893), *Natural Value*, New York: Augustus M. Kelley, 1971.

3 Geo-economics

Kris Feder

Foundations of geo-economics

Geo-economics is a developing paradigm of political economy. Its roots lie in the classical tradition, from Locke and Smith to Mill and George; its branches reach nearly every subdiscipline of modern economics. This paradigm informs a research program of profound significance, and yields crucial insights regarding the foremost issues of political economy. The present chapter briefly reviews the main theoretical arguments of the school.

Geo-economic thought is characterized, not by any unorthodox methodology or special behavioral assumptions, but by two basic ideas, one normative premise and one positive theorem. The former is the conviction that, while the products of individual human effort are rightfully private property, the land and natural resources of the Earth should be treated as the common heritage of all. The latter is a practical proposal for achieving rough equality of access to natural opportunities with remarkable economic efficiency. A relatively simple fiscal device is said to yield staggering efficiency gains, a more equal distribution of wealth, and enhanced politico-economic stability. It is only because of ill-designed public institutions that society appears to confront a dismal trade-off between fairness and freedom – 'equity versus efficiency'. Geo-economics reveals the ultimate goals of socialism and capitalism to be potentially compatible and mutually reinforcing.

The 'geo' in geo-economics has a double meaning: it refers to land, in the classical sense – to the matter and forces of nature which constitute the raw material of all production. Geo-economics emphasizes the neglected role of the earthly foundation of the economy. 'Geo' also alludes to the nineteenth-century American political economist Henry George, whose philosophy underlies much of the geo-economic approach to political economy.

The ethical basis of geo-economic thought, the belief that the earth should be treated as the common property of all, is ancient wisdom – canonized by John Locke in terms of universal rights to life, liberty, and 'estate', that is, land. Justice requires that individuals have rights to property in themselves and in what their peaceful efforts (working, thinking, saving, and planning) produce, as well as the right of association and exchange. However, in order to work and produce, individuals must have access to materials. Although many resources are themselves produced, all production ultimately requires not only human labor, but also land. Economic land includes all natural (nonproduced) resources, such as soil, water, minerals, fuels, clean air, and electromagnetic spectrum; site location with respect to other natural and artificial resources; and space itself – standing-room.

Henry George drew two conclusions. First, most involuntary taxes violate the principle of self-ownership. Second, because land is not produced by individuals, its rent cannot rightfully be claimed by individuals. Moreover, George argued, when land is scarce, individual ownership of land-products interferes with individual rights to labor-products, including the rights of future generations. Therefore, absolute private property in the gifts of nature is unjust. Land rent should be shared, through the agency of representative government.

What is new with George is the discovery of a way to fulfill Locke's famous proviso in his chapter 'Of Property': that individuals may rightfully take and use land as private property only so long as 'there is enough and as good' left in common for others (1947 [1690], p. 134). The basis of geo-economics is the recognition that in a freely competitive monetary economy, there is a practical way to share natural resource rents equitably and efficiently. Moreover, failure to do so obstructs the operation of land markets.

Obviously, land should not be treated as unowned commons with unlimited public access; this is a path to tragedy (Hardin, 1968). Exclusive rights of use are frequently unsurpassed for assuring efficient resource allocation. Nor should land that is now under private ownership be geographically divided up and redistributed, as perhaps it can be in the simplest agrarian society. Yet society is not compelled to alienate land to absolute individual ownership. George's solution was 'to make land common property' (1879, p. 326) by using the government's taxing power to collect the rent of land, leaving titles to the *use* of land in private possession. Rent would then be distributed fairly among citizens through government provision of public goods, elimination of distortionary taxes, and perhaps direct cash dividends. Both the production and the distribution of wealth, George believed, would thereby be improved.

> ... to take for public purposes the increasing values that attach to land with social growth ... [is] the only means by which it is possible in an advanced civilization to combine the security of possession that is necessary to improvement with the equality of natural opportunity that is the most important of all natural rights. (1879, p. 434)

In short, geo-economics proceeds from the notion that the distinction between individual and common property forms a rational basis for distinguishing the domain of public activity from that of the private. George put it plainly:

The value of land expresses in exact and tangible form the right of the community to land held by an individual; and rent expresses the exact amount which the individual should pay to the community to satisfy the equal rights of all other members of the community. (George, 1879, p. 344)

Taxes and excess burden

The only efficiency argument for taxing rent mentioned regularly in textbooks is the argument that such a tax has no distortionary substitution effect, and therefore no excess burden. The textbooks usually botch the case, relying on the supposition of a vertical market supply curve of land. Some even note – correctly – that the market supply of land services is less than perfectly inelastic, but wrongly conclude that a tax on land rent is not efficient after all (Feder, 1993, pp. 69–72).

The reason why the market supply of land is not perfectly inelastic is that there generally exist nonmarket 'reservation' uses of land, just as there are for labor effort. When an increase in the demand for land raises rent, a larger quantity of land services may be supplied to the market, *ceteris paribus*. It is true, however, that the total amount (in acres) of land existing in a taxing jurisdiction is fixed and unresponsive to price signals. This puts a determinate upper limit on the quantity supplied as price rises, and is likely to mean that supply is highly, though not perfectly, inelastic. Those who argue that land supply is elastic because more land can be produced in response to price incentives commit one or both of two errors: first, they restrict the definition of economic land so that it refers to dry surface land, a distinction more relevant to geology than to economics. Second, they fail to distinguish between nonproduced resources and produced capital.

The Georgist tax is not a tax on the market supply of a productive factor. Rent is not income; it is the opportunity cost of land occupancy (Gaffney, 1972). It measures, not the net revenue from land as it is actually used, but the annual amount which others in the market would be willing to pay for its use. A landowner cannot influence the rent by varying the nature, intensity or timing of land use. The tax base is geographically fixed by the boundaries of the taxing jurisdiction; unlike capital, land cannot be moved, or be allowed to depreciate and be rebuilt elsewhere, even in the long run.

No change in behavior allows the landowner to avoid a tax which collects a fixed proportion of the market-determined rent; 'the man who wished to hold land without using it would have to pay very nearly what it would be worth to any one who wanted to use it' (George, 1879, p. 437). It follows that the burden cannot be shifted to tenants, consumers, or even future buyers of land. The owner must pay the charge which buys exclusive possession – or, sell the land at a price which is discounted by the capitalized present value of future taxes. Thus, public collection of land rent induces no decrease in the market supply of land, no increase in land users' willingness to pay for the marginal unit, and no change in either the equilibrium quantity or the demand price of land. It has no production-inhibiting substitution effects, and zero excess burden of taxation.

The efficiency of a tax on rent is shared by few or no other significant tax bases. To the extent that taxes on production and exchange suppress economic activity, replacing them with a land rent tax will stimulate it. George was a supply side economist: 'Today taxation operates upon energy, and industry, and skill, and thrift, like a fine upon those qualities' (1879, p. 434).

Land allocation and land speculation

A lesser-known argument for the efficiency of rent taxation, one of great practical significance, observes that capital markets are inherently imperfect, since they rely on estimates of future values which cannot be known with certainty. Producers acquire access to capital on unequal terms; depending on their economic power and collateral, they face different discount rates. Consequently, an investor who discounts future returns at a low rate can sometimes offer a higher price for land than can an investor who borrows at a higher rate, even when the latter can employ the land more productively. The allocative inefficiency is greatest for land which is appreciating in value (Gaffney, 1973).

A tax on rent or land value improves the efficiency of land allocation by reducing dependence on imperfect capital markets. Since it is capitalized into lower land prices, the tax substitutes an annual payment for a lump-sum purchase price of equal present value. This bypasses interest rate differentials to neutralize the distorting effect of credit discrimination. The result is a decrease in tenancy, a wider distribution of land ownership, and a continuing market pressure for land, especially appreciating land at the fringes of growing cities, to be transferred to the most productive users (George, 1879, p. 436–8; Gaffney, 1973).

Henry George identified land speculation as a destructive and destabilizing force in progressive economies. Speculation, or holding land not for use but for a future rise in price, was a fundamental cause of both microeconomic and macroeconomic disturbances – of inefficiencies in land allocation and of cyclical fluctuations in aggregate output. George argued that sufficiently high taxation of land values would demolish the incentive to speculate in land. Opponents have argued that speculation serves the socially useful function of preventing premature investment of fixed capital on land whose optimal use is changing over time. Geo-economists respond that LVT is neutral with regard to socially optimal speculation: efficient development timing (and intensity) enables the investor to maximize the present value of after-tax net return, since annual net return equals gross return minus the fixed amount of tax.

However, inefficient forms of land speculation also do occur. One general reason is the imperfection of credit markets already discussed. Other reasons for hoarding land involve asymmetric information, political manipulation, adaptive expectations, gambling, problems of land assembly, monopolization of non-reproducible resources and unique locations, simple inertia, and above all, the transactions costs of leasing, lending, and the hiring of managerial labor (Gaffney, 1961; Cleveland, 1994; Feder, 1993, pp. 228–30). Land taxation increases the penalty for at least some forms of inefficient speculation, even if investor discount rates are uniform. The tax is capitalized in land value, which leaves total holding costs – interest plus taxes – unchanged. But the higher is the tax rate, the smaller is the capital gain for which those constant holding costs are incurred (Brown, 1927; Feder, 1993, p. 236). More broadly, by substituting an explicit recurring charge for the (frequently implicit) interest cost of land purchase, 'incentive taxation' alerts landowners to the value of their land claims, encouraging them either to put their land to its most highly valued use or to yield it to others who will (Gaffney, 1973).

George held that land speculation, supported by an 'elastic' or accommodating banking system, was a major underlying cause of industrial depressions. His detractors have sometimes claimed that what George observed were merely regional land booms caused by unique circumstances (gold discoveries and extension of railroads). Be that as it may, recent events in Japan and the United States (the S&L crisis) are consistent with George's analysis (Hudson, 1995a). Michael Hudson has recently shown the importance of macroeconomic and monetary theory for the renewal of classical and Georgist economics (Hudson, 1995b; see also Harrison, 1983).

Public collection of rent, George believed, would remove this fundamental source of instability. Tax reform would initially cause land values to fall as speculators desert the land market. In the long run, however, the resulting increase in production 'would lead to an increase in the value of land – a new surplus which society might take for general purposes' (George, 1879, p. 432). The distribution of wealth would become less unequal, as rents are diverted from private to public uses, while 'wages would rise to the fair earnings of labor' (George, 1879, p. 436).

Wealth and portfolio effects of land value taxation
Henry George emphasized a fundamental distinction between 'value from obligation' and 'value from production'. The former, which includes land titles and monopoly privileges, does not constitute wealth from a social viewpoint, since in the aggregate each such credit is balanced by a debit. George believed that when ownership of these assets substitutes for ownership of produced wealth, the economy suffers (George, 1879, p. 434; see also Hudson, 1995a). The existence of private property in land diverts private

savings away from investment in capital. Conversely, taxing either rent or land values reduces the private equity and increases the public equity in land. Substitution of produced real capital for land in investor portfolios promotes long-run economic growth, raising the employment and wages of labor.

It is noteworthy that wealth effects may shift a part, perhaps a significant part, of the burden of the tax to owners of capital, since by diminishing returns, an increase in capital may decrease the marginal productivity of capital relative to that of fixed land (Dwyer, 1982, p. 369; Skouras, 1977; Feldstein, 1977). (This argument ignores the impact of private and public capital formation on land values in the aggregate. The total impact depends also upon how the revenues are spent.)

Since land and other assets are not necessarily equally risky investments, a tax may be shifted through portfolio effects as well, by reducing the ratio of land to capital in private portfolios. If land and capital are not perfect substitutes, investors try to buy land and sell capital in order to return to their desired asset ratios. In the short run this drives land prices up and the prices of existing capital down (Feldstein, 1977, p. 354–8).

Tax shifting through income, wealth, and portfolio effects does not compromise the efficiency of the Georgist tax program. It reflects no tax 'wedge' sending distorted price signals to market participants. Instead, by rerouting savings toward productive investment, the tax promotes development efficiently and even-handedly, without recourse to government controls, subsidies, or price manipulation.

Recycling rent to support public services

Henry George did not miss the fact that urban land values were overtaking agricultural land values in relative importance. While decrying the maldistribution of soil, minerals, and other natural resources, he focussed special attention on the rents arising from the provision of utilities and other government services, and from the spatial externalities associated with the actions of private citizens. The most productive uses of any individual site depend not only on its physical characteristics, but also on its location with respect to other sites near and far, and to the improvements and activities thereon.

Many of the benefits provided 'free' by local governments at taxpayer expense are not really free to users *per se*. They are sold to users by the owners of the lands served. To buy or lease a site for commerce or housing is to purchase scarce access to a certain mix of benefits, since competitive site rents reflect the demand for access to roads, schools, police and fire protection, utilities, and other public services. When land is privately owned, the benefits of collectively-produced goods are largely forfeited to well-situated individual landowners.

The unintended externalities generated by private activity are also a source of land value. Ideally, perhaps, everyone would pay for the specific external costs he imposed on others, and would be compensated for the external benefits he bestowed (Vickrey, 1970). But unless Coasian private bargaining can be accomplished with low transaction costs, the difficulties of measurement and enforcement greatly limit the extent to which the ideal can be realized in practice. A tax on land rent, if it excludes the imputed rent of unowned commons, cannot by itself induce efficient production of externalities. What it can do is to make their distribution more efficient. When access to spatial externalities is rival and scarce, the market price of access is measured in site rents.

Geo-economists argue that, insofar as the various externalities impinging on any site cannot with any accuracy be assigned to specific persons or activities, the rents they yield are best treated as common property, along with the rents intentionally generated by the activities of governments. A tax on site rent intercepts all such publicly-created gains, making them available to finance the services which yielded them. Each individual effectively pays society for the use of positive externalities which are accessible only from particular lands. Symmetrically, the landowner is compensated by a reduction in his assessment for any loss in land value caused by negative externalities. Moreover, private cooperatives and communities such as residential associations can, and sometimes do, finance their activities by assessments on land values (Foldvary, 1994).

Since site values are generated by the productive activities of government and society, geo-economists often say that what they propose is not a tax proper, but a user charge (Rybeck, 1983). If the natural resources of the earth are considered to be common property, then a tax on the rents of scarce natural resources is a user charge, too, always assuming that the revenue is returned to the community through the agency of democratic government. As Henry George expressed it:

> The tax upon land values falls upon those who receive from society a peculiar and valuable benefit, and upon them in proportion to the benefit they receive. It is the taking by the community, for the use of the community, of the value that is the creation of the community. It is the application of the common property to common uses. (1879, p. 421)

George argued that as material progress goes on, the increase of specialization and exchange (and population growth) means that individuals become more economically interdependent. As a result, the legitimate sphere of collective action enlarges, and the responsibilities of government grow over time. One result of increasing interdependence, however, is that the productive activities of governments and individuals raise land values, increasing the base of a tax on rent (1879, p. 436). If local government efficiently provides the public services which citizens want, then under full rent taxation, those services are self-financing. Distortionary taxation of production, exchange, or income is unnecessary.

George thought that land rent would always be adequate to finance worthwhile public expenditures. Indeed, the so-called 'Henry George Theorem' in urban economics indicates that, under certain rather general conditions of mobility and competition, a tax on land rent is necessary for full efficiency. Moreover, the rents generated by the optimal level of public expenditure, supplemented for congestible public goods by efficient marginal-cost user fees, are precisely sufficient to finance the optimal expenditure (Stiglitz, 1974; Vickrey, 1974; Arnott and Stiglitz, 1979; Mieszkowski and Zodrow, 1989). The head taxes which supplement rent taxes in versions of the theorem which involve publicly-provided private or congestible goods are, under the assumptions of these models, also equivalent to user charges.

Taxes levied on land to support the services which give land its value are not only efficient; they are equitable under the benefit principle of taxation, and they are widely perceived as reasonable and fair by citizens who understand them. Consider a recent letter, never printed, to the editor of *The New York Times*. It regards a proposed plan to create an improvement district which would tax local property owners to finance expenditures on Central Park:

> As a property owner just off Central Park, I heartily support Commissioner Stern's proposal to finance Central Park maintenance with a 'tax' on adjacent property owners .... The rehabilitation of Central Park in the last ten years has probably added over $100,000 to the value of my property. It is only fair that I pay a bit of this back for the benefit I have received. And it is very much in my own self-interest that Central Park continue to be well-maintained, so much so that I will gladly pay my share of the cost – provided that other benefitted property owners pay their share as well. (Haines, 1995)

Geo-economics and the environment
Geo-economic principles of public finance offer ready support for the goals of environmental preservation and ecosystem health.

First, the artificial environments of urban areas are said to enjoy significant benefits from the substitution of a land value tax for other taxes. With the tax bias against improvements removed, structures are built better, yet replaced sooner. Valuable urban land is used more intensively, providing more indoor space per person, reversing urban sprawl, and decreasing transportation costs, especially for public transit. Reduced dependence on the automobile means less traffic congestion, less pollution, and fewer accidents.

As Mason Gaffney has emphasized, high density downtown means low density elsewhere. With speculation and sprawl curbed, good farmland at the fringes of urban areas would be preserved, as would the wildlands beyond (Gaffney, 1994). Also, Georgist tax reform makes it easier for local governments to acquire land for public uses. High land taxes are capitalized into low land prices. Moreover, 'open space' and other public reserves will pay for themselves by the resulting increases in surrounding land values and, therefore, tax revenues (Dwyer, 1981, p. 225).

Taxation of the rent of natural resources induces their fair and efficient use. For depletable resources, geo-economic principles call for a severance tax 'equal to the discounted value of the most remote future liquidation receipt' (Gaffney, 1964–5, p. 556). In conjunction with an annual tax on the value remaining in the ground, such a charge is neutral with respect to the optimal rate of extraction (Gaffney, 1967, p. 557).

The growing scarcity and degradation of environmental resources has prompted a recent trend toward public oversight and regulation of formerly unowned resources, particularly of nonexclusive, depletable 'common property' such as the atmosphere and oceans. Effluent taxes charged to polluters are assessments for the rent of environmental resources. (Congestion tolls for roadways and other public spaces are also rent charges.) Many environmental economists agree that well-designed pollution fees can achieve cost-effective and even-handed pollution control. This is a compelling argument for preferring them as a source of public revenue. Add the normative judgment that the public has the right to collect the rents of environmental resources, and it becomes a Georgist argument.

Many environmentalists assert common rights in the atmosphere, waters, and wildlife (by way of regulation and conservation) but fall short of challenging private property in solid surface land, except for parks and reserves where sensitive and valuable ecosystems are set aside for preservation. However, geo-economics emphasizes that even land which is more or less solid and immobile, even ordinary residential and commercial land, has qualities characterized by nonexclusion. The advantages of any particular site are largely determined by the activities occurring on neighboring lands – by the markets, the public services, the pollution, and the crime in the vicinity. In this respect, land, air, and sea differ only in degree, not in kind. Georgists and environmentalists are natural allies.

Rent-seeking and public choice

Democratic government as we know it offers individuals and interest groups myriad opportunities for using public institutions to obtain private advantages for which the social costs exceed the social benefits. The situation is so serious that some public choice analysts fear the demise of the system (Mitchell and Simmons, 1994). Rent-seeking, unproductive activity in pursuit of profit, runs rampant in the sphere of collective action – unless surpluses are distributed automatically in unchallengeable ways.

Whenever some of the costs of government activities are borne by people other than those who benefit, collective decisions tend to be inefficient. Geo-economists argue that if the benefit principle of taxation, and specifically the collection of land rent for public revenue, were constitutionally established, then citizens would tend to pay, in land costs, the marginal social costs of the services from which they benefit. Special interests would be unable to pass the costs of their programs onto unwitting taxpayers. Only government services for which expected total net benefits are positive would be likely to receive effective public support (Gaffney, 1989).

A Georgist system of public finance promises to improve incentives on the supply side, as well as the demand side, of the political market. At least one writer has argued, for example, that relying on rent for revenue would induce budget-maximizing bureaucrats to find and adopt socially optimal policies, since these tend to maximize aggregate land values (the publicly-created surplus) within the taxing jurisdiction (Dwyer, 1981, p. 236).

In a federal system of government with mobile people and capital, competition among local governments and interjurisdictional externalities engenders further inefficiencies and inequities. The problems of tax competition and fiscal zoning are well known. For a single example, cities which attempt to finance the increasing costs of municipal services by raising business taxes, building taxes and wage taxes often find that they have merely chased their economic base out of town, deepening urban poverty and raising the per-capita cost of public services still higher. In general, when the marginal private net benefit of migration diverges from the marginal social net benefit, the geographic distribution of people and capital will be inefficient.

Nicolaus Tideman has outlined a geo-economic approach to intergovernmental cooperation that promotes optimal public and private decision making in a federal system. Ideally, for both equity and efficiency, 'the value that land would have in the absence of local development' should be shared nationally or globally, while 'the addition to rental value that comes from the growth of communities and the provision of public services ... should be regarded as the income of the locality, which the locality may collect and spend as it sees fit' (Tideman, 1994, p. 8; note, 'Citizens should not be able to oblige localities to spend money on them by moving from one place to another', p. 9).

Land tenure and the distribution of wealth

Many familiar taxes are justified by appeal to the ability-to-pay principle of tax equity, not the benefit principle with which Georgists defend site value taxation. Yet a more equitable distribution of wealth was even more important to Henry George than was economic efficiency. His proposal would lay the foundation by guaranteeing everyone entitlement to an equal share in natural opportunities, and the right to use or exchange whatever his peaceful labor produces. In contrast, our present system yields private property in land to individuals unequally, then attempts to moderate the resulting social conflict by *re*distributing incomes after the fact. Unfortunately, widespread tax shifting means that redistributive measures are grossly inefficient and are of uncertain incidence.

Worse, theory and evidence suggest that these transfers are largely self-defeating in the long run. Since people work for after-tax income, forcible redistribution induces pre-tax (and pre-subsidy) incomes to adjust to a new, more unequal, equilibrium, returning after-tax incomes toward the initial distribution (Holcombe, 1988, pp. 283–4).

Assertion of common rights resolves the question of initial entitlements to land, which at present are based on the original chaos of first-come first-served, mutilated beyond recognition by might-makes-right. It also provides for a fair distribution of the increments and decrements of land values in particular places at particular times, pooling for the whole community the gains and losses of opportunities which are outside of individuals' control. This is of utmost importance because the durability and immobility of land makes it peculiarly subject to large windfall gains and losses. Not surprisingly, land wealth tends to be distributed more unequally than income.

Implemented worldwide, Georgist principles suggest a just and rational basis for solving territorial disputes. Tideman writes that the territorial claim of a commonwealth ought to be 'justified by a correspondence between the fraction of the world's population making the claim and the fraction of the world's land (in terms of rental value) being claimed' (1991, p. 109).

Revenue potential of land taxation
George's contemporary adversaries feared that the revenue from a single tax on land rent would be so great that it would foster unnecessary and dangerous growth of government. Today, we are more likely to hear that land rent accounts for a small and declining share of national income. Can the 'single tax' on rent yield revenue sufficient for the needs of government? The Henry George Theorem suggests that it can, if governments efficiently provide the services people want.

Empirically, the share of land in national income is far greater than is generally recognized, especially when 'capital' gains are taken into account (Hudson, 1995b; Gaffney, 1970).

Moreover, making resource rents the primary source of government revenue should cause rents to rise. An elementary implication of economic theory is that ordinary taxes are in large part shifted backward to durable, immobile land – so their removal would raise land values dramatically. Rents may actually rise by more than the amount of the tax shift, since the taxes being reduced will have imposed an excess burden by penalizing productive activity.

On the other side of the budget, the costs of government are expected to fall in a Georgist system of public finance. First, Henry George argued that the machinery of tax collection would be simplified. He was probably correct, even before computerized mapping of land values. It is in most respects easier to assess land than buildings. And unlike income, land cannot be hidden from the tax collector. On the other hand, the far-reaching externalities of pollution and the complex implications of zoning and other land use regulations today have added new theoretical and administrative challenges.

Second, geo-economists argue, bureaucratic incentives would tend to be better aligned with the public interest. Regionally, a more compact and rational pattern of land use would cut the costs of providing municipal and other local government services. Nationally, by guaranteeing everyone a share in the income from common property, by raising real wages and employment, and by reducing income and other taxes, the system would, in theory, reduce the cost of social insurance programs. More broadly, to establish a just political constitution, one which guarantees both private property in produced wealth and equality of access to natural opportunities, promises ultimately to diminish social conflicts ranging from petty theft to world war, thereby shrinking the economic costs of police, courts, and standing armies.

Equity and efficiency

Economists often lament a painful policy 'trade-off' between efficiency and distributive equity. They point out that redistributive policies such as progressive income taxes and public assistance dampen productive incentives, while policies intended to promote growth, such as tax breaks for savings and capital gains, lead to wider inequality.

Geo-economists suspect that correct interpretation of economic principles reveals the goals of efficiency and equity to be fundamentally harmonious. Efficient and stable operation of an economy cannot be sustained if principles of fairness and individual liberty are ignored. The use of rent for public revenue is one key to reconciling the apparent conflict. Otherwise, inequality in land ownership, once established, tends to produce further inequality, ultimately leading to stagnation and decline. A society without economic as well as civil justice is plagued by systemic inefficiencies, rooted in ill-managed conflict. Ultimately, growing inequality arising from institutional maladjustments can, and does, bring whole civilizations down. 'In justice', wrote Henry George, 'is the highest and truest expediency' (1879, p. 367; see also Hudson, 1994).

Capitalism and socialism

In the aftermath of stunning political changes worldwide, socialism is widely perceived to have failed. Yet the Western economic system appears to be failing too. The policies of welfare capitalism, which attempt to ease poverty by forcible redistribution, have done more to hinder the operation of the market than to assure equality of opportunity. They have yielded neither efficiency in the production of wealth, nor equity in its distribution. Keynesians sought to treat the symptoms of systemic failure by manipulating government taxes and expenditure, once presumed to be justifiable only on the basis of the net benefits of the services financed. Keynesian policy, however, did not end the cycle of inflation and unemployment; instead, it left us with uncontrolled government deficits. Our complex, bureaucratic, limping 'mixed economy' is a set of debilitating 'trade-offs' and failed compromises.

Consider a socialist system in which both land and capital are state-owned. Since real capital is produced by the primary factors of labor and land, the productive efforts of individuals must be at least partly owned or controlled by the state, too. Insofar as this severs the natural link between productive effort and reward, moral suasion enforced by police power substitutes for market incentives. A vast bureaucracy is needed to operate the economic system. Rents are largely dissipated in the inefficiency of the controlled economy; those that remain are easily seized for private uses by the public officials who control the distribution of resources and goods.

In a typical capitalist system, the primary factors of production, land and labor, are for the most part privately owned, as are their products and services, including capital. There is voluntary market exchange of goods and factors. However, production and income are subjected to involuntary taxation to support public expenditure. Increasingly, the social instability caused by the inequities of the system necessitates transfers to the poor financed from taxes on the rich – or realistically, the middle class. The problems of chronic unemployment and disruptive business cycles seem intractable. There are social tensions: the rich resent and evade the ever-growing burden of taxation, though, to a point, they submit to it to stave off discontent and rebellion. The stigma and economic trap of welfare dependency deepens poverty, crime and anti-social behavior.

For natural resources not easily subjected to private property, such as the atmosphere and oceans, the old principle of might-makes-right is usually applied. Until very recently, polluters have generally not been expected to compensate society for the environmental resources they deplete. Today, ecological necessity has begun to force the public sector to reclaim control of environmental resources, but indignant polluters demand compensation for the public encroachment upon their accustomed privileges.

Government protects the privileges of rent-takers while installing social programs to keep the system afloat. Government debt grows until debt service itself consumes a hefty share of the spiraling deficit. Conservative governments promise to shrink the welfare state and balance the budget – but faced with social and political realities, they cannot, not as long as unearned incomes from private ownership of natural and public resources are sacrosanct. The very taxes and transfers used to keep the economic system afloat slowly drag it down. Rent surpluses are diminished as a result of economic inefficiency.

Socialism and capitalism both engender a perpetual struggle of individual rights versus common rights. They are not opposites; they share a blindness to the primacy of the basic relationship of humankind to nature. With welfare capitalism, they meet in the middle – a false compromise. As Fred Harrison has argued, the redistributive institutions of welfare capitalism are mere scaffolding erected to prop a flawed structure (Gaffney and Harrison, 1994, p. 179). In the United States, deepening debt impels the federal government to pass off responsibility for provision of public services to states, counties, and cities, themselves in deepening crisis. The alarm bells sound louder as the last remaining global frontiers – sites of cheap resources and spills for surplus labor – are closed. Ethnic rivalry simmers as workers collude to protect their jobs from fierce competition.

Henry George wrote that the 'capitalist' ideal of individual liberty and property and the 'socialist' vision of equality and community are both satisfied by the public collection of resource rents for public uses. Government defends individual property rights to the products of labor, administers nonexclusive public resources used in common, and collects the public revenue from land rent for public uses. Once it is accepted that land rightfully belongs to everyone, there is a clear rationale for a fiscal structure which guarantees every citizen a minimum real income that represents, not public charity, but the individual's share of common property. At the same time, the reward of individual productive effort would be undisturbed by burdensome taxation.

Private and public action

Many governments perversely tax productive enterprise while leaving nonproduced resource rents in private hands. As a result, a centrifugal force seems to yield an ever-widening distribution of wealth, compelling governments, whether liberal or conservative, Democrat or Republican, to tax the winners ever more to provide life support for the losers. Progressive (?) taxes and subsidies sustain yet cripple capitalist systems today.

Geo-economics makes a point of discerning which sorts of things are rightfully individual property, and which common. It is concerned with how, in practice, both private and public rights can be assured. It seeks to identify an efficient, equitable, and sustainable system for adjudicating the competing claims of individual, society, and ecosystem. Georgists propose a dramatic reorientation of public finance – the substitution of user charges, pre-eminently land and natural resource rents, for confiscatory taxes. The rent of land is considered to be a natural fund for the support of government.

To summarize the position: the market value of a parcel of land reflects both its endowment of natural resources and its mix of social resources, that is, all the opportunities afforded by its location with respect to the people, land, capital, and human activities in the surrounding region. In the geo-economic model of public finance, land rent is regarded as the common property of all people – many would say, all living beings – in all generations. Government is an institution democratically established to administer the common property and to provide public goods.

When rent is turned to common purposes, say Georgists, it will be easier to establish policies which respect individual property in the products of productive effort. Confiscatory taxes can be greatly reduced, both because public investment will be self-financing through site rents, and because, with natural resource revenues shared fairly, welfare state mechanisms to moderate the extremes of wealth and poverty will tend to wither away. Further, geo-economics suggests a rule for resolving territorial disputes peacefully, as well as a way to align personal and national motives with the larger goal of preserving natural resources, environments and ecosystems for future generations.

Public collection of economic rent does not compromise the efficiency of market resource allocation. In fact, it generates incentives which tend to correct certain types of market failures. Substituting a rent charge in place of distortionary taxes on production and exchange, so that everyone pays the social opportunity costs of the territory he occupies and of the community resources he depletes, promotes stable and sustainable development whose benefits are universally shared.

Political economy for the twenty-first century
Georgist principles, while not new, carry renewed urgency in our times. Intriguingly, anyone familiar with the philosophy of Henry George can see ideas like his cropping up in public debate. The failure of Communist regimes has re-opened fundamental questions of political philosophy, including that of land tenure rights. In the United States, supply-siders have warned for years of the depressing effect of taxes and subsidies on the economy. Local governments, desperate for infrastructure and urban renewal, are beginning to reevaluate the hated property tax, especially now that the federal government has been abdicating some of its responsibilities to the states. Cities in Pennsylvania and elsewhere have begun reform of the local property tax on real

estate, gradually raising the tax rate on land while lowering the rate on improvements. They get private markets to generate urban renewal, as it should be.

Environmental issues have come to the forefront of public attention. In the past, George's critics pointed to rising relative wages and falling materials prices as evidence that land is no longer an important factor of production. Yet the apparent gains in the efficiency of materials use have come at the cost of drastic increases in the volume and toxicity of wastes spilled into air and water. Resource depletion and pollution impress upon us the realization that economic land is scarce and valuable. The public increasingly demands that polluters assume responsibility for fouling the air, water, and soil; economists support emissions charges to achieve cost-effective control. There are calls to correct the underpricing of our national forests, water supplies, and other government-managed resources; to raise logging, grazing, and drilling fees on federal lands to market levels – or higher, to reflect the environmental costs of these activities. There are demands for international agreements to allow fair, efficient, and sustainable use of the remaining global commons – the oceans, atmosphere, and electromagnetic spectrum. Development econo- mists are beginning to admit that the problems of population and world poverty cannot be solved without radical reform of land tenure systems.

Thus, many of the tenets and policy conclusions of geo-economics are widely shared by social scientists and other thinking citizens. Public opinion seems in many respects to be bending in George's direction – the recent political backlash in the United States notwithstanding. Most discussants, how- ever, appeal to the standard efficiency/equity 'trade-off', now in the guise of a supposed conflict between economics and environment. Few are aware that Georgists claim to offer a theory and an ethical basis for integrating diverse issues of public policy (Noyes, 1991; Andelson, 1991; Gaffney, 1994). Power- ful interests produce and maintain the conceptual rigidity of the prevailing neoclassical economics (or 'anti-classical', Hudson, 1995a), which nearly man- ages to obscure the fact that human life revolves around the earth just as surely as the earth revolves around the sun (Gaffney and Harrison, 1994).

Paradigm or panacea? The research agenda of geo-economics

> Georgist policy has been shown as a means to revive dying cities, and in the process to reconcile equity and efficiency, to reconcile supply side economics with taxation, and to reconcile capital formation with taxation of the rich. It can be seen as a means of harmonizing collectivism and individualism, in the most constructive possible ways. (Gaffney, 1989, p. 15)

Perhaps it is not too surprising that George's tax exclusively on rent is often dismissed contemptuously as a 'panacea', a bogus cure-all obviously too simple-minded to accomplish the wondrous results claimed for it. Geo-economists respond, however, that their principles represent rather a paradigm of politico-economic organization which compares favorably to the reigning paradigms of 'capitalism' and 'socialism' (Noyes, 1991; Harrison, 1994). The Geo-Economic Society, founded in 1994, is a professional association of economists dedicated to empirical and theoretical research guided by the geo-economic paradigm.

A panacea is a pat answer to all questions, a prescription to treat all ills. A paradigm, by contrast, is a pattern, model or ideal, a conceptual framework which yields an approach to solving certain kinds of problems. A good paradigm inspires and organizes a richly productive research agenda. Its basic principles should be simple, few, and evident; but its applications should be many and varied.

The celebrated single tax, perhaps unfortunately, is not a panacea. What geo-economics provides are useful principles for sorting out some of the toughest problems society must face. Without doubt, many questions remain unanswered – many, I suspect, still unasked. Some important geo-economic research questions are implicit in the foregoing discussion. Here are a few more:

There is the basic issue of whether rent or land value is the proper tax base. There is a complex of problems concerning the distinctions among the factors of productions, and in particular, the definition and measurement of rent. Empirically, how large is rent, and how large can it potentially become under an ideal system of public finance? What is the distribution of rent and land gains under existing political regimes?

In microeconomics, the difficulties of valuing environmental and natural resources and charging for their use are immense. There are complex interactions among taxes, and between taxes and regulations, particularly zoning and other land use controls. The practical implications of the insight formalized by urban economists in the Henry George Theorem need to be worked out, as do the consequences for intergovernmental relations in a federal system. How does Georgist policy affect population density? What are its implications for the structure of territorial government? What additional policy instruments can be fashioned to achieve Georgist objectives?

There is a variety of questions related to the theory of public choice. Most obviously, what is the proper disposition of the revenue once rents are collected? I have hinted at some further implications for incentives of citizens and public servants in the public arena. Fundamental issues are raised regarding the nature of government and of collective action in general.

Macroeconomic issues include: would revenue flows be stable? Would variations in rents and, therefore, revenues be pro-cyclical or countercyclical? Study of the macroeconomic (as well as microeconomic) effects of speculation in all its forms has barely begun. Can geo-economic policy dampen business cycles? Raise wages and employment? How does the proposed system of public finance influence, and respond to, fluctuations in prices, interest rates, and monetary policy? Uncertainty and error? Migration and international capital flows?

Every reform, however warranted, catches some people by surprise and imposes at least transitional losses on a few. Who gains and who loses in the short run in a move toward a Georgist regime, and can the losers be compensated? How can the transition be accomplished with a minimum of disruption? Every reform must also face the perennial problem of how to survive attempts by individuals and interest groups to exploit or alter the system for private advantage at public expense. What constitutional rules or other devices are available to ensure that tax assessments are fair and revenues well-spent? What further changes should ensue?

This list is merely suggestive. The geo-economic paradigm of political economy supplies many more worthwhile research projects than there are economists presently interested in pursuing them.

References

Andelson, Robert V. (ed.) (1991), *Commons Without Tragedy: The Social Ecology of Land Tenure*, Savage, Maryland: Barnes and Noble.

Arnott, Richard J. and Stiglitz, Joseph E. (1979), 'Aggregate Land Rents, Expenditure on Public Goods, and Optimal City Size', *Quarterly Journal of Economics*, **43** (4), 471–500.

Boulding, Kenneth E. (1982), 'A Second Look at *Progress and Poverty*', in Richard W. Lindholm and Arthur D. Lynn, Jr. (eds), *Land Value Taxation: The 'Progress and Poverty' Centenary*, Madison: University of Wisconsin Press, 5–18.

Brown, Harry Gunnison (1927), 'Land Speculation and Land Value Taxation', *Journal of Political Economy*, **35**, 390–402.

Cleveland, Mary M. (1994), 'Land Taxes and Market Failure – Was Henry George Right?' Paper prepared as Visiting Scholar, Department of Agricultural and Resource Economics, University of California at Berkeley, 18 July 1994.

Dwyer, Terence Michael (1981), 'A History of the Theory of Land Value Taxation', PhD dissertation, Harvard University.

Dwyer, Terence Michael (1982), 'Henry George's Thought in Relation to Modern Economics', *American Journal of Economics and Sociology*, **41** (4), 363–73.

Feder, Kris (1993), *Issues in the Theory of Land Value Taxation*, PhD dissertation, Temple University.

Feder, Kris (1994), 'Public Finance and the Co-operative Society', in Michael Hudson, G.J. Miller, and Kris Feder, *A Philosophy for a Fair Society*, London: Shepheard-Walwyn, 123–62.

Feldstein, Martin S. (1977), 'The Surprising Incidence of a Tax on Pure Rent: A New Answer to an Old Question', *Journal of Political Economy*, **85**, 349–60.

Foldvary, Fred (1994), *Public Goods and Private Communities: The Market Provision of Social Services*, Aldershot, UK: Edward Elgar.

Gaffney, Mason (1961), 'The Unwieldy Time-Dimension of Space', *American Journal of Economics and Sociology*, **20** (5), 465–81.

Gaffney, Mason (1962), 'Land and Rent in Welfare Economics', in Joseph Ackerman *et al.* (eds), *Land Economics Research*, Baltimore: Johns Hopkins Press.

Gaffney, Mason (1964), 'Property Taxes and the Frequency of Urban Renewal', *Proceedings of the National Tax Association*, **57**, 272–85.

Gaffney, Mason (1964–5), 'Soil Depletion and Land Rent', *Natural Resources Journal*, **4**, 537–57.

Gaffney, Mason (1970), 'Adequacy of Land as a Tax Base', in Daniel Holland (ed.) (1970), *The Assessment of Land Value*, Milwaukee: University of Wisconsin Press, 157–212.

Gaffney, Mason (1972), 'Land Rent, Taxation, and Public Policy: The Sources, Nature, and Functions of Urban Land Rent', *American Journal of Economics and Sociology*, **31**, 241–57.

Gaffney, Mason (1973), 'Tax Reform to Release Land', in Marion Clawson (ed.), *Modernizing Urban Land Policy*, Baltimore: Johns Hopkins Press, 115–51.

Gaffney, Mason (1989), 'The Role of Ground Rent in Urban Decay and Revival', *Distinguished Papers* N 89F–1 (November), in *The Henry George Lecture*, October 1988, Jamaica, NY: Business Research Institute, St. John's University.

Gaffney, Mason (1994), 'An Economic Look at Land Use Planning: The Environmental Perspective', address sponsored by the Community, Regional, and Environmental Studies Program of Bard College, 24 October 1994.

Gaffney, Mason (1994b), 'Neo-classical Economics as a Stratagem against Henry George', in Mason Gaffney and Fred Harrison, *The Corruption of Economics*, London: Shepheard-Walwyn, 29–163.

George, Henry (1879, 1971), *Progress and Poverty*, New York: Robert Schalkenbach Foundation.

Haines, Thomas H. (1995), personal communication, unpublished letter to *New York Times*, January 22.

Hardin, Garrett (1968), 'The Tragedy of the Commons', *Science*, **162**, 1243–8.

Harrison, Fred (1983), *The Power in the Land: An Inquiry into Unemployment, the Profits Crisis and Land Speculation*, London: Shepheard-Walwyn Publishers.

Harrison, Fred (1994), 'The Georgist Paradigm', in Mason Gaffney and Fred Harrison, *The Corruption of Economics*, London: Shepheard-Walwyn, 165–235.

Holcombe, Randall G. (1988), *Public Sector Economics*, Belmont, CA: Wadsworth.

Hudson, Michael (1994), 'Land Monopolization, Fiscal Crises and Clean Slate "Jubilee" Proclamations in Antiquity', in Michael Hudson, G.J. Miller and Kris Feder, *A Philosophy for a Fair Society*, London: Shepheard-Walwyn, 81–121.

Hudson, Michael (1995a), 'What's Wrong with Economics: A Classical View', paper presented at a conference of the Eastern Economic Association, 18 March 1995.

Hudson, Michael (1995b), 'How Rent Gets Buried in the National Income Accounts', paper presented at the Council of Georgist Organizations Annual Meeting, Evanston, Illinois, 30 June 1995.

Lindholm, Richard W. and Lynn, Arthur D., Jr. (eds) (1982), *Land Value Taxation: The 'Progress and Poverty' Centenary*, Madison: University of Wisconsin Press.

Lissner, Will, and Lissner, Dorothy Burnham (eds) (1991), *George and the Scholars*, New York: Robert Schalkenbach Foundation.

Locke, John (1947, [1690]), *Two Treatises of Government*, New York: Hafner Press.

Mieszkowski, Peter M., and Zodrow, George R. (1989), 'Taxation and the Tiebout Model: The Differential Effects of Head Taxes, Taxes on Land Rents, and Property Taxes', *Journal of Economic Literature*, **27**, 1098–1146.

Mitchell, William C. and Simmons, Randy T. (1994), *Beyond Politics: Markets, Welfare, and the Failure of Bureaucracy*, Boulder, Colorado: Westview Press.

Noyes, Richard (ed.) (1991), *Now the Synthesis: Capitalism, Socialism, and the New Social Contract*, New York: Holmes & Meier.

Rybeck, Walter (1983), 'The Property Tax as a Super User Charge', in C. Lowell Harriss (ed.) (1983), *The Property Tax and Local Finance*, N.Y.: Robert Schalkenbach Foundation, 133–47.

Skouras, Athanassios (1977), *Land and Its Taxation in Recent Economic Theory*, Athens, Greece: Papazissis.

Skouras, Athanassios (1980), 'Land and Its Taxation as Issues in Economic Theory: What is the Reason for Their Eclipse?' *American Journal of Economics and Sociology*, **39** (4), 373–82.

Stiglitz, Joseph E. (1974), 'The Theory of Local Public Goods', in Martin S. Feldstein and R. Inman (eds) (1974), *The Economics of Public Services*, London: Macmillan, 274–333.

Tideman, T. Nicolaus (1991), 'Commons and Commonwealths: A New Framework for the Justification of Territorial Claims', in Robert V. Andelson (ed.), *Commons Without Tragedy: The Social Ecology of Land Tenure*, Savage, Maryland: Barnes and Noble, 109–29.

Tideman, T. Nicolaus (1994), 'Revenue Sharing Under Land Value Taxation', manuscript.

Vickrey, William (1970), 'Defining Land Value for Taxation Purposes', in Daniel Holland (ed.), *The Assessment of Land Value*, Milwaukee: University of Wisconsin Press, 25–36.

Vickrey, William S. (1977), 'The City as a Firm', in Martin S. Feldstein and R. Inman (eds) (1974), *The Economics of Public Services*, London: Macmillan, 334–43.

4   The Virginia school of political economy

Charles K. Rowley and Michelle A. Vachris

Introduction

In a *de facto* sense (Tollison, 1992), the Center for Study of Public Choice
has been located at three universities since its inception in 1957 as the
Thomas Jefferson Center for Studies in Political Economy at the University
of Virginia. This Center was established by James M. Buchanan and G.
Warren Nutter with its name designed to signal a break with the narrow
preoccupations of neoclassical economics and a return to the classical economists' emphasis on the study of political economy. There followed a decade
of scintillating success in which major scholarly reputations were forged, the
discipline of public choice was established and a sequence of outstanding
graduate students made their way into the academy.

It was at the Thomas Jefferson Center that James Buchanan and Gordon
Tullock wrote *The Calculus of Consent* (1962), that Warren Nutter formed a
profound skepticism about the performance of the Soviet economy and angered
left-leaning neoclassical economists by rejecting self-serving statistics emanating from the Soviet Empire, and that Ronald Coase formulated his famous
theorem concerning the problem of social cost. Indeed, the basic scholarship
that would earn two Nobel Prizes in Economic Science was carried out at the
Thomas Jefferson Center during this exceptionally productive decade. The
journal that would help to launch and consolidate the new discipline of Public
Choice (initially entitled *Non-Market Decision Making*) also saw the light of
day in 1966 under the brilliant, unorthodox editorship of Gordon Tullock.

As Adam Smith (1776) had noted, however, '[t]here is a great deal of Ruin
in a Nation'. Without question, there was a great deal of ruin in Mr. Jefferson's
University during the middle years of the twentieth century as a fashionably
left-leaning, singularly unimaginative bureaucracy sought to strike down its
most original and enterprising program of research.

Concern had been first registered in 1960 when the Ford Foundation had
refused to provide a grant to the Thomas Jefferson Center ostensibly because
it objected to a statement in the Center's brochure to the effect that the
scholars involved wished to preserve a social order based on individual
liberty (Breit, 1986, p. 8). Kermit Gordon, the officer in charge of grants in
the field of economics, stated that the foundation could not consider making
any grants to support work at Virginia until the Department of Economics
became as balanced politically as those at Harvard and Yale!

Concern intensified in 1963 when Warren Nutter took a semester's leave of absence to serve as an advisor in the Barry Goldwater presidential campaign. A secret self-study report on the Department of Economics was written in 1963 by a Virginia faculty committee for examination by an external accreditation group. The Department was not consulted during the compilation of the report, nor was it informed of its contents. Only in 1974 did the report inadvertently surface with such witch-hunting contents as: (1) 'Additions should be made to the staff of full professorial members of different "modern" outlook'; and (2) 'Care should be taken in making or renewing non-tenure appointments, as well as those of higher rank, to avoid recruitment from the Chicago School' (Breit, 1986, p. 9).

There then followed a sequence of administrative actions designed to destroy the new research program. In 1964, the University refused to counter-offer to retain Ronald Coase following an offer from the University of Chicago. In 1966, the University refused to counter-offer to retain Andrew Whinston following an offer from Purdue University. In 1967, following a refusal to promote him from associate to full professor on three occasions, Gordon Tullock left for Rice University, to be followed in 1968 by James Buchanan who departed for the University of California, Los Angeles. In 1969, Warren Nutter took a leave of absence to serve as assistant secretary of defense for international security affairs. The Thomas Jefferson Center, effectively, was dead.

The Virginia school, however, was very much alive. In 1968, Gordon Tullock moved to Virginia Polytechnic Institute in Blacksburg and was joined there in 1969 by James Buchanan. Together with Charles Goetz, they established the Center for Study of Public Choice, and the Virginia school reemerged unscathed and fortified as it regrouped in the foothills of the Appalachian Mountains to carry the baton of the public choice research program on a second, decisive, fifteen-year lap (Goetz, 1991).

Between 1968 and 1983, when the Center moved once again, down from the mountains to George Mason University by the City of Fairfax, the public choice message was internationalized and refined into a format that even entrenched neoclassical economists no longer could ignore. Once in Fairfax, public choice would focus its attention on big government with a vengeance from its strategically important location just fifteen miles west of the Potomac River.

The Virginia school?
The research program identified with the Thomas Jefferson Center and the Center for Study of Public Choice has exerted a profound impact on modern economics, political science and philosophy. Nonetheless, Mancur Olson has named the program the *Virginia School of Political Economy* (Mueller, 1985).

The question here to be addressed is whether Olson was justified in making this assertion, whether, indeed, it is legitimate to speak of a *Virginia school* within the field of public choice.

Noting that the appellation 'school' is used only sparingly in economics, Dennis Mueller (1985) identified three or four such schools of thought, namely the Chicago school, the Austrian school, the Cambridge (England) school and (arguably) the Marxist school. He identified three characteristics that such schools share.

The first characteristic is a distinctive methodology. Chicago clearly qualifies with a methodology of positive economics (Friedman, 1962), now the orthodox methodology. Chicagoans deploy the rational man assumption 'to the point where man is not only capable of behaving consistently when making choices, but possesses powers bordering on clairvoyance' (Mueller, 1985, p. 2). Austrian economics qualifies with a methodology that is sharply antipathetic toward some of the fundamental methodological presumptions of neoclassical economics, notably the latter's reliance on equilibrium conditions, on risk rather than uncertainty (in the sense of Frank Knight) and on objectivism rather than subjectivism in its analysis of individual choice. The Cambridge school is more amorphous, critical of neoclassical economics from a mixed Keynesian and Marxist perspective and more distrustful of market outcomes than neoclassical economics. The Marxist school is (was) methodologically unique with its adoption of the dialectic approach, its concepts of surplus value and alienation and its substitution of class for the individual as a building block of analysis.

The second characteristic of a school is a distinctive *Weltanschauung*, or world view: a systematic body of ideas especially about life or culture (Mueller, 1985, p. 3). In Mueller's judgment, the work of the major figures in the development of each of the schools of thought was imbued with a clear *Weltanschauung*, notably with respect to the questions asked. Each school of thought has focussed its attention upon a set of interrelated questions that distinguish it from the other schools of thought.

Those who have been attracted to each school have been drawn by a belief that the questions asked by members of their school are the most important of the day. No reader of the writings of Adam Smith, Ludwig von Mises, John Maynard Keynes or Karl Marx can deny that these scholars were astute observers of human behavior, who asked unusual questions about individual behavior and the operation of economic institutions. In so doing, they each generated research programs that justly earned the title of a school of thought.

The third, less tangible, characteristic of a school, according to Mueller, is excitement for new ideas usually associated with a central location, where scholars can interact and enthuse each other through regular interaction. The importance of the existence of a center cannot be overemphasized. Three of the four schools identified by Mueller are named after places; the body of research to which reference is made in each instance cannot be associated with the name of a single person, but rather is the product of numerous scholars working together over time at the place which gives the work its name. For such a location to achieve the name of a school, the work emanating from it must share not only methodological and ideological cohesiveness but also that extra degree of enthusiasm 'which makes members of the school excited about their own work and infects others with similar excitement' (Mueller, 1985, p. 6).

The importance of location is underlined by reference to the Marxian school. Marx was not associated with a university, or with any other scholarly location. When he died, no single place existed where Marxists studied and taught. In consequence, Marxism failed to evolve as an intellectual field. Instead, the issues that it addresses (the immiseration of the working class, imperialism etc.) remain the same today as in the 19th century despite the massive changes that have occurred in the industrialized nations.

In what sense is it legitimate to speak of a Virginia school of political economy? Is there a methodology and an ideology that is sufficiently identifiable that we can designate those who espouse them as members of a distinct school of thought? Do members of that research program have the same enthusiasm for their scholarship as members of other schools? If the Virginia school exists, is its research program progressive or degenerate at the present time? These are fundamental questions that do not give rise to simple answers.

As will be outlined in subsequent sections, the methodology of the Virginian approach to public choice, in its positive dimensions, is not dissimilar to that of the Chicago school, though it is less extremely market-orientated in its auxiliary conditions. It places much greater emphasis on institutions than does Chicago and focuses much more specifically on the prospect of political market failure. Unlike Chicago, Virginian scholars vigorously deploy an ideology (or normative approach) which tends to castigate the normal processes of politics as leading to political market failure while acknowledging that constitutional processes may resolve institutional failure and provide for efficient outcomes.

The Virginia research program is unique in public choice in its combination of the analysis of political failure with the potential for good of suitably devised political institutions. The Virginia research program is also highly distinct in its vigorous reintegration of the disciplines of economics and public choice by its unrelenting application of the self-interest axiom across all aspects of political economy (Mitchell, 1988).

The third characteristic of the Virginia research program, that sets it aside from other scholarship in public choice, is the existence of the Center for Study of Public Choice, which has played a powerful role in generating intellectual excitement and enthusiasm not only among resident scholars but also among a diverse set of visiting scholars and resident graduate students (Tollison, 1991, 1992). The Center has been a magnet for all those who have become influenced by the widening reach of Virginian political economy, not least because the influential journal, *Public Choice* has always been published from that location. Without the Center and the journal it is doubtful that the Virginia research program could have justified the appellation of the Virginia school, despite the heroic pioneering contributions of its creators, James M. Buchanan and Gordon Tullock.

The Center, of course, no longer is at its 'cock-crowing and morning star'. With the loss of Gordon Tullock in 1987, it suffered a major setback from which it has not fully recovered. With its relocation in Fairfax in 1983, the diffuse temptations of the big city have eroded the intellectual cohesiveness and locational proximity of its resident scholars. The well-earned award of the Nobel Prize in Economic Science to James M. Buchanan in 1986, though a remarkable recognition of the contributions made by the Virginia school, has proved to be a mixed blessing, bringing insider status to a program that thrived best in an outsider role.

Inevitably, some of the initial excitement and enthusiasm has dissipated as normal science has come increasingly to dominate paradigm shift. In this sense, the Center is a victim of its own success. Yet, the Center remains a Mecca for the growing list of scholars – even those who do not fully share its ideology – who have been exposed to the public choice approach. The Virginia school now has transcended its locational origins. It is a worldwide phenomenon.

The Chicago challenge to the Virginia school

In December 1989, Donald Wittman published a controversial article in The *Journal of Political Economy* that purported to explain why democracies produce efficient results. The argument was theoretical, general and unqualified. Countries that embrace democracy are rewarded by the maximization of wealth.

Wittman argues that political and economic markets both work well. He purports to show that democratic political markets are organized to promote wealth-maximizing outcomes, that these markets are highly competitive and that political entrepreneurs are rewarded for efficient behavior. He suggests that many of the arguments claiming that economic markets are efficient apply equally well to democratic political markets and, conversely, that economic models of political market failure are often no more valid than the analogous arguments for economic market failure. In the light of this paper, Wittman suggests that the burden of proof should be on those who argue that democratic political markets are inefficient.

In arguing that democratic political markets tend toward efficiency, Wittman does not imply that political markets are generally superior to economic markets. Rather, he implies that democratic governments will allocate to economic markets those tasks in which the economic market is most efficient. He does not claim that democratic political markets are just. They merely aggregate, equally or unequally, the preferences of the participants in the political process. He does not claim that individuals are uninterested in power or that they desire efficiency for its own sake. Rather, he claims that the pursuit of self-interest leads to efficient results. He does not claim that democratic political markets are devoid of error. Rather, he suggests that economists should focus on normal and not on pathological behavior in political markets and should look for efficiency explanations for abnormal behavior, much as they do when analyzing economic markets.

It is not our intention to dispute Wittman's proposition that unregulated economic markets are efficient. Indeed, we strongly concur with his judgement that arguments levelled against economic markets – monopoly, externalities, public goods, asymmetric information, transaction costs and the like – are much exaggerated in the welfare economics literature (Rowley and Peacock, 1975). However, we take serious issue with his contention that political markets behave in ways closely similar to economic markets. Problems that are insignificant for economic markets, in our contention, are highly significant for democratic political markets for reasons that are inescapably associated with the institutional characteristics of such markets.

Basic concepts

Wittman's article is extremely general in nature offering arguments concerning global efficiency presumed to be relevant to democracies of whatever kind. For the most part, such arguments have not been welcomed in mainstream neoclassical economics which rewards a much narrower and more circumspect approach. In this section, therefore, we subject a number of the concepts that he uses to a critical review.

(a)   Democracy

Does it matter for efficiency whether a democracy is based on the principle of universal suffrage, allowing the propertyless access to the electoral register, or whether it is based on a property qualification? Does it matter whether a democracy consists of a direct assembly or a representative system of government? Does it matter whether the legislature is uni- or multi-cameral, whether the vote mechanism is simple or supra-majority, whether the system of government is parliamentary or based on a separation of powers, whether government is endowed with limited or unlimited powers, whether or not it is federal or confederate in nature? These questions are neither posed nor answered in Wittman's article.

By inference, such institutional differences are deemed to be irrelevant. All that matters is the absence of autocracy. In this respect, Wittman's view corresponds with a more general Chicago view that institutions are less decisive than competition in securing economic efficiency. We shall argue forcefully that such is not the case with respect to political markets.

(b) Efficiency

In essence, the potential compensation principle is the concept of efficiency utilized by Wittman in his evaluation of democratic markets, albeit with an important particularizing assumption. For Wittman, expected wealth is the only (or at least the largely most important) argument in each individual's utility function. A wealth-maximizing system thus is utility maximizing in the sense of his social welfare ethic.

In the absence of coercion, fraud, externalities and other well-articulated sources of market failure, private exchange is widely viewed as moving individuals from Pareto inferior to Pareto superior positions, since no rational individual would trade to lower his own utility. It is a much more open question, however, whether political markets, in which exchanges between majorities and minorities are often involuntary, embrace that rationality assumption. If they fail to do so, then Wittman's proposition – that all redistribution, whether voluntary or involuntary, promotes aggregate wealth maximization – must be viewed as remarkable. Is that a good model of United Kingdom experience over the period 1945–1979 or the Indian experience of 1948 to the present?

Because our view of political markets is less Panglossian than that of Wittman, we find it necessary to retreat from the global concept of economic efficiency and to review the proposition that political markets conform to other more circumspect notions of efficiency, notably, *technical efficiency* (Becker, 1983) or *political efficiency* (Stigler, 1992).

Gary Becker's (1983) theory of competition among pressure groups for political influence arguably supports the notion that political markets promote wealth redistribution in a technically efficient manner. In his model, political equilibrium depends on the efficiency of each group in producing pressure, the effect of additional pressure on their influence, the number of persons in different groups, and the deadweight cost of taxes and subsidies. An increase in deadweight costs discourages pressure by subsidized groups and encourages pressure by taxpayers. Competition among pressure groups serves to minimize the deadweight social welfare cost of politically-engineered transfer programs. We advance an alternative hypothesis that such transfer processes tend to be technically inefficient for reasons ignored or underestimated by Becker.

George Stigler (1992), defining political efficiency tautologically as the attainment of goals adopted by society through its government, suggests that democratic political markets are politically efficient. Stigler hypothesized that every durable social institution or practice is efficient, or it would not persist. In essence, this hypothesis simply applies his renowned economic market survivor principle to political markets. New and experimental institutions or practices will rise to challenge existing systems. Often the new challenges will prove to be inefficient or even counter-productive; but occasionally they will succeed in replacing the older system. Tested institutions and practices found wanting will not survive in a world of rational people. We take issue with this hypothesis and argue that democratic political markets are not necessarily politically efficient.

The concept of political market failure

The new welfare economics that emerged during the early 1950s (Arrow, 1951; Samuelson, 1954, 1955) focussed attention upon the ubiquity of economic market failure and made the case for efficiency-improving interventions by omniscient, impartial and benevolent government. By offering a powerful, internally consistent rationale for government intervention, the new welfare economics forced even the most market-oriented of Western economists onto the defensive.

The extent of the retreat can be readily gleaned from Milton Friedman's classic book, *Capitalism and Freedom* (1962), in which the author finds it necessary to counter market failure arguments by advocating essentially interventionist solutions to alleged problems of market failure (e.g. vouchers for education). It can also be gleaned from the fact that the two leading advocates of free market economics, Ludwig von Mises and Friedrich von Hayek, were both marginalized by the economics profession.

Within such an unpromising environment, it was left to a tiny group of scholars at the University of Virginia, led by James M. Buchanan and Gordon Tullock (1962), to expose the errors of the new welfare economics and to turn against government itself the market failure arguments that had been so skillfully levelled against economic markets. In so doing, they launched a public choice research program, now of some thirty years maturity, that essentially has levelled the playing field in the comparative analysis of economic and political markets (Mitchell, 1988, 1989; Goetz, 1991; Tollison, 1989). It is our intention to draw upon the theoretical results of this public choice program to sketch out a set of political market failure propositions that stand in stark contrast to Wittman's efficiency proposition.

Some problems of competition

Wittman relies heavily in his analysis on the efficiency-augmenting competitive qualities of political markets. This begs two questions, namely, whether democratic political markets are necessarily competitive, and if so, whether competition in political markets is necessarily efficiency-augmenting.

Let us focus on the case of parliamentary democracy, the example utilized by Anthony Downs in his 1957 book. Downs assumed the existence of two competing spatially mobile political parties, each seeking to maximize votes, as the basis for his derivation of the famous median voter theorem. But Downs ignored the possibility that the two parties might collude in order to secure greater discretionary power, preferring to explain observed convergence in policy space as the consequence of unremitting competition. Since the incentives to collude are clear (ignoring unresolvable differences in ideology among the representatives) Wittman's casual reliance on the existence of two or more parties as evidence of competition is clearly suspect.

The concept of party competition, as it is developed in the literature of political science, is directed to the closeness of the outcome of elections (Stigler, 1972). A country is viewed as having a competitive party structure when victory in the legislature is won by even the less successful party in a substantial share of elections, when the average share of votes of the losing party is not much less than fifty per cent and when the parties do not exhibit long runs of electoral success or failure. It is commonly asserted that the more competitive the parties, in this sense, the more responsive the political system will be to the desires of the majority.

As Stigler (1972) has demonstrated, such assertions must be viewed with caution. Even assuming spatial mobility, and the median voter outcome, suppose that the two parties behave like Cournot oligopolists in competing for the emoluments of office. In such circumstances, the emoluments of the party functionaries are larger than is necessary to attract them from alternative occupations (technical inefficiency), falling between the monopolistic and the competitive levels. Any conspiracy between the parties would raise the level of emoluments available for distribution across the entire legislature conceivably to the monopoly level (accentuating technical inefficiency).

As Stigler (1972) noted, the analogy between economic and political competition cannot be carried far before a fundamental difference is encountered: political products are usually, whereas economic products are rarely, if ever, mutually exclusive. If a country has a specific social security system with a tax rate of 6 per cent, it cannot simultaneously have a different social security system with a different tax rate. In contrast, the provision of one size and type of automobile does not preclude the simultaneous provision of other sizes and types.

In consequence of such exclusivity (or indivisibility), political processes almost necessarily are coercive in the sense that many voters may prefer other policies. The voters who support a losing party may receive nothing in return: no representative in the government, even no representative in the legislature. This reality has given rise to the all-or-nothing concept of political competition which, in turn, easily blends into the notion of the state as monopoly firm (Auster and Silver, 1979), leading to economic inefficiency.

Let us respond to the question whether competition in political markets is necessarily efficiency-augmenting, focussing specifically on the imperfect competition model relevant for political markets. As Stiglitz (1994) has argued with respect to economic markets, there are no simple results for imperfect competition. This is quintessentially the case for political markets, since exit is not a viable option for voters who find themselves attached to a losing political party, and since voice is a far from costless option.

Imperfect competition between political parties may foster technical inefficiency when it takes a destructive form. One broad category of this form is the situation in which one party does better by making the other party do worse (i.e. where it raises its rival's costs). There are many opportunities for such behavior in political markets because of the exclusivity/indivisibility problem. For example, a successful political party may raise its rival's costs by changing electoral registration requirements in a manner designed to obstruct its rival's members, or it may gerrymander voting districts or change campaign funding rules to favor incumbent legislators. By implicitly relying on the perfectly competitive model, Wittman skirts around such realities.

There are other contexts in which political competition does not serve efficiency goals. Resources are often dissipated in the competition for rents (Tullock, 1967), as special interests seek to access public largesse either in the form of direct expenditures or through protection from competition. Although rent-seeking is played down by Chicago economists as part of the normal cost of the business of government (Becker, 1983, 1985; Wittman, 1989), there is growing evidence that such is not the case (Laband and Sophocleus, 1988). If rent-seeking is an endemic feature of political markets, Wittman's assessment that rents will be shifted efficiently across political markets, that the seeking of those rents will involve minimal social cost, and that rent seeking is no more serious in political than in economic markets, is wrong.

The problem of externalities and public goods
In economic markets, Pareto-relevant externalities occur in competitive equilibrium when the marginal conditions of optimal resource allocation are violated. For such an externality to occur, some individuals' utility or produc-

tion functions must include real variables whose values are chosen by others who do not pay or receive compensation for the cost or benefit of this activity. Externalities may take the form of public bads or public goods characterized by jointness in consumption and by non-excludability. If the positive Coase theorem (zero transaction costs) fails to hold, externalities and public goods are often projected as sufficient justification for government intervention. Indeed, they are often cited as prime arguments for the existence of the productive and regulatory state (Baumol and Oates, 1988).

In 1962, Buchanan and Tullock shifted the focus of such analysis by suggesting that externalities and publicness problems were a pervasive feature of the political market place, that government might be the problem and not the solution with regard to this alleged catalyst of market failure. Because the individual is not decisive in a democratic political market, and because public policies tend to be indivisible, choices contrary to the individual's own interest may be registered by any decision rule that falls short of unanimity. For this reason, participation in collective activities on the basis of less than unanimity vote rules carries with it significant expected external costs. Yet, the rule of unanimity carries with it unacceptably high expected decision costs. This insight formed the basis of the famous economic theory of constitutions that attempted to supply a logical foundation of constitutional democracy.

Writing well before the problem of rent-seeking had been identified (Tullock, 1967), Buchanan and Tullock argued that a constitutional democracy based on universal consent was feasible as individuals unanimously selected less than unanimity rules for collective decision making designed to minimize the overall expected external and decision making costs. By thus falling back on meta-level decision making, the authors felt able to conclude that majority or supra-majority rules, evidently in violation of the Pareto principle, nevertheless might be rationalized as Pareto efficient.

Despite this powerful conceptual rationalization, we suggest that it is inappropriate to apply the calculus of consent as a vehicle for dispensing with externalities as a source of political market failure under democratic conditions. In reality, constitutions and constitutional rules are never endorsed unanimously by those eligible to vote. The United States Constitution itself was not endorsed by many delegates who absented themselves from Philadelphia rather than sign the parchment. With the passage of time, new generations of voters are deemed to embrace the Constitution without any real opportunity to demur. Also with the passage of time, the Constitution itself is eroded by judicial neglect and/or malfeasance so that its application bears but a distant relationship to its wording and its original intent.

Once the prospect of rent-seeking is allowed to enter into the calculus of consent, the contractarian solution to externalities is rendered even less realistic (Rowley, 1987). Since the contractarian impulse is driven by potential gains-from-trade, expectations that such gains-from-trade will be dissipated in the post-constitutional political market place inevitably erode *ex ante* incentives to legitimize the state, or at least raise the likelihood that the constitutional contract will legitimize only a severely shackled minimal state. The large unlimited states that are characteristic of almost all modern democracies – states that lie somewhere between state capitalism and the plantation state in the sense of Jasay (1985) – almost certainly are more the consequence of unresolved externalities in political markets than the appropriate response to externalities in economic markets.

The problem of imperfect information

The new welfare economics initially emphasized the importance of perfect (or near perfect) information as a prerequisite for economic market efficiency (Arrow, 1962). This position was eroded by contributions from Chicago (Stigler, 1961; Demsetz, 1969) that warned against the fallacy of the free lunch. If information is scarce, and search costs are positive, efficient markets will economize in the use of information: the marginal cost of search will equal the marginal benefit from search in the efficient solution.

Nevertheless, new welfare economists continue to argue that the first fundamental theorem of welfare economics – asserting the efficiency of competitive economies – is fundamentally flawed by the existence of imperfect information (Stiglitz, 1994). Whenever perfect information is not present, the market is not constrained Pareto efficient; that is, there are interventions by the government that could be unambiguously welfare improving. The essential insight (Greenwald and Stiglitz, 1986) is that when markets are incomplete and information is imperfect, the actions of individuals have externality-like effects on others, which they fail to take into account. In such circumstances, the government can set taxes and subsidies in such a way as to mitigate the effects of adverse selection and moral hazard even if it is not itself fully informed.

This view assigns to government a public interest motivation that public choice categorically has challenged. It also denies Hayek's (1945) insight that information is highly disaggregated across society and cannot be assimilated by any central planning agency. It further ignores the particular problems of imperfect information that manifest themselves in political markets as a consequence of output indivisibility (rational voter ignorance) and nonmarket decision-making (bureaucratic control loss). The government certainly possesses powers (of coercion) that the private sector does not have. There can be no confidence that such powers can or will be used to effect a Pareto improvement.

New welfare economists have also attacked economic markets as being incapable, without government assistance, of dealing with problems posed by the existence of asymmetric information (i.e. an imperfect information environment in which certain individuals are better informed than others). The most famous contribution in this genre is that by Akerlof (1970) suggesting that information asymmetries in the secondhand automobile market (sellers are better informed than buyers on quality) results in a market in which only 'lemons' can be marketed. Bad cars drive out good cars because both sell at the same price which is dragged down to that appropriate for 'lemons'. Although a range of private remedies such as guarantees and brand names are viewed as potential remedies for such market failure, licensing and certification feature high on the author's list of corrective mechanisms.

The problem of information asymmetry is far more serious in political than in economic markets. Once again, the trigger is the indivisibility of political market outputs. It manifests itself most significantly in the form of rational voter ignorance (Downs, 1957). Since the probability of a voter being decisive in any national or state election is minute, the expected net benefit to his vote is very low. The rational voter in consequence has little incentive to invest in political market information. In sharp contrast, special interest groups have much greater incentives to be informed on issues directly relevant to the group since they can influence policy through campaign financing. In consequence, political markets are biased towards policies that provide concentrated benefits to well-organized, small groups and that spread costs widely across less well-organized voters (Tullock, 1993). Information asymmetries are a non-trivial source of political market failure.

The problem of transaction costs

Kenneth Arrow has defined transaction costs as 'the costs of running the economic system' (1969, p. 48), the economic equivalent of friction in physical systems. Only following seminal contributions by Coase (1937, 1960) was the relevance of transaction costs recognized as a crucial component of institutional analysis in economics. It is now the fulcrum of the new institutional economics (Williamson, 1985).

The Coase theorem (1960) sets the scene for our discussion. In the absence of transaction costs, private markets allocate resources efficiently once property rights have been determined. If transaction costs are sufficiently high, however, a role for government conceivably (although not necessarily) may exist. It is precisely on such grounds that new welfare economists argue the case for government intervention as a response to externalities, public goods and informationally imperfect markets (Stiglitz, 1989), a low cost alternative to the economic market-place.

Stiglitz (1989) suggests, for example, that the cost of forming a voluntary organization to deal with a class of market failures may be prohibitive, whereas it would pay the government to direct its attention to the problem.

He further argues that free rider (public good) problems give rise to transaction costs which governmental provision can avoid. Finally, he notes the large costs associated with running markets, many of them arising from imperfect information and from adverse selection. Government, he claims, is the only institution capable of resolving such problems.

In the wake of the public choice research program, Stiglitz (1989) acknowledges that political markets are not free of significant transaction costs. Specifically, problems of imperfect information and incomplete markets are pervasive in the public sector, and the lack of competition within the public sector seriously attenuates incentives. Let us focus attention, however, on the two most serious defects of political markets from the transaction cost perspective, the attenuation of property rights and the tilt towards redistribution and away from gains-from-trade.

The importance of property rights for ensuring good incentives is now widely recognized. Untruncated property rights provide individuals with clearly defined authority to use their resources as they wish, and to transfer their resources to whomsoever they wish, whenever they so choose, either through voluntary exchange or as gifts and bequests. Such rights, to be fully effective, must be enforceable through a well-functioning, non-invadable legal system. In such circumstances, resources tend to move to their highest valued uses, irrespective of their initial assignment (Coase, 1960).

In political markets (notwithstanding Weingast and Moran, 1983), property rights are so poorly defined and severely attenuated as to be devoid of efficiency incentives (Rowley and Vachris, 1993). Legislators and bureaucrats in general have no way to appropriate any increase in a nation's wealth that results from their political activities. They have no way to transfer such poorly defined rights as they hold, and they have no recourse to a system of binding commitments equivalent to the law of contract in economic markets.

Democratic governments confront fundamental problems in making binding commitments (Stiglitz, 1989), since each government is sovereign. In many societies, the government itself establishes the conditions under which individuals can sue it to recover compensation for contract breach. There is no property right impulse in political markets that might serve to minimize transaction costs.

Moreover, any interest of voters in favor of technical efficiency is severely attenuated by the problem of asymmetric information that strengthens the influence of special interest groups and weakens that of the rationally ignorant voter. In conjunction with the absence of property rights, asymmetric information opens up political markets to wealth redistribution battles that are characterized by high rent-seeking and rent-protection costs (Tullock, 1993).

In economic markets, wealth redistribution occurs only on a voluntary basis and is utility-enhancing. In political markets, wealth redistribution takes a coercive form, tantamount to theft, in which decisive groups seize the wealth of less decisive groups for redistribution to themselves or to favored third parties. Wealth redistribution may be transparent as taxes and subsidies, or opaque, as with complex regulations. Public choice predicts that opaque redistribution will be more successful (Crew and Rowley, 1988), although both margins will be mined.

Coercive redistribution is a negative sum game, since it does not create wealth; yet it is costly. It occurs extensively in political markets, and is difficult to constrain. In democratic political markets, redistribution tends to be the primary focus and wealth-creation only a secondary consideration when government expands beyond the minimal state (Rowley, 1993). The Pareto principle, even augmented by potential compensation, is silent with respect to the efficiency implications of coerced wealth transfers.

In terms of wealth maximization criteria, the rent-seeking state clearly is wealth-reducing. Resources dissipated in rent-seeking and rent-protection in political markets are lost to economic markets (Rowley, Tollison, Tullock, 1988). Furthermore, wealth transfers in political markets carry high excess burdens (Crew and Rowley, 1988). To determine whether or not such wealth transfers are politically efficient, we must take account of the institutional structures of political markets.

Efficiency and the median voter theorem

Early contributions by public choice scholars (Downs, 1957) suggested that political market equilibria reflected the preferences of the median voter. If so, the amount of a public good provided would be where

$$V_m = T_m \tag{4.1}$$

where V_m represents the market valuation of the median voter and T_m represents his marginal tax rate.

In general, this condition will not satisfy the conditions for economic efficiency which require that the sum of marginal valuations of the good should equal the sum of marginal taxation:

$$\sum_{i=1}^{n} V_i = \sum_{i=1}^{n} T_i \tag{4.2}$$

Further problems arise when multi-dimensional policies are subjected to a single-dimensional method of control e.g. where there is a fixed relationship between the amount of a public good and the tax incidence. In such circumstances, political market failure is predictable. McKelvey (1976) demonstrated in a model with two candidates, two-dimensional policy vectors and three voters that the trajectory of possible winning platforms can go any-where in policy space and, in particular, can go outside the Pareto-optimal set. In order to restrict outcomes to the Pareto-optimal set, Wittman (1989) is forced to make unrealistic assumptions about probabilistic voting.

Subsequent work in public choice demonstrated the stringency and lack of realism of the conditions necessary for the median voter theorem to hold: (i) the election must be contested only by two political parties; (ii) policies must collapse into one left–right space dimension; (iii) voter preferences must be single-peaked over policy space; (iv) political parties must be able and will-ing to move in policy space; (v) political parties must be well informed of voters' policy preferences; (vi) voters must be well-informed of the policy positions of the political parties; (vii) voters must vote; and (viii) voters must punish governments that deviate from their electoral manifestos.

Once any of these assumptions is relaxed in real political markets, the median voter outcome cannot be relied upon (Rowley, 1984). In some in-stances, the existence of political equilibrium is unlikely. More generally, the uniqueness and stability of equilibrium is called in doubt. With cycles preva-lent, structure-induced equilibrium influenced by agenda control plays an important role in political markets. Even during elections, political parties may be able to break free from the median voter. Between elections govern-ments enjoy significant discretionary power (Romer and Rosenthal, 1978, 1979).

In a representative democracy, society has selected a method of choosing political agents (one man – one vote) that is unlikely to lead to efficient outcomes. First, the right to run the government is not auctioned off to the highest bidder. It is granted in a voting process, the characteristics of which vary from country to country. As McCormick and Tollison (1981) show, not only is the size of the bids from political agents to voters important, but so is the distribution of those bids across the voters. Therefore, the highest bidder will not necessarily win the contract.

Second, voters have no way other than outward migration, successful revolution, or *coup d'état*, to liquidate their ownership rights in the indivis-ible outputs of government. They cannot extract payment from politicians *ex ante* but must wait for settlement, usually in the form of in kind payments, *ex post*. This inability to transfer property rights predictably has significant implications for a principal–agent problem between voters and their repre-sentatives that manifests itself in political market failure (Alchian and Demsetz, 1972).

Third, politicians do not run separately, issue by issue, in electoral compe-tition, but rather bundle policies, thus further forcing voters to exercise indi-visible choices. This bundling presents opportunities for political parties to full-line force their policies, protecting electorally unattractive programs by attaching them to electorally attractive programs. Competition between political parties ameliorates this problem to the extent that either party abandons policies preferred by its candidates and focuses exclusively on policies preferred by its targeted electorate (i.e. abandons ideology).

Fourth, political parties can rely upon voter memory decay to protect them from subsequent electoral damage when they deviate from policy manifestos at an early stage in their incumbency. They may also excuse platform-slippages as efficient responses to unanticipated external shocks. Predictably, they can rely upon rational ignorance to impose relatively light costs on large numbers of voters as a means of funding specific, highly-valued transfer benefits to the few.

For these reasons, the vote motive cannot be relied upon as a consistent control mechanism in political markets. The median voter equilibrium must be viewed as an occasional rather than as a dominant feature of democratic political markets.

Efficiency and the logic of collective action
For a long period, many economists took for granted the notion that groups of individuals with common interests would act collectively to further common interests, much as individuals would do for themselves. They would do so equally in political as in economic markets. Since Olson's (1965) contribution, however, the explicit analysis of the logic of the individual optimization in groups with common interests has led to a radically different view of collective action (Olson, 1987).

If individuals in a group share a common interest, the furtherance of the common interest will automatically benefit each individual in the group, whether or not any particular individual has borne any of the costs of that collective action. Thus, the existence of a common interest need not provide any incentive for individual action in the group interest. Since the benefits of collective action in the interest of the group with a common interest constitute a public good, free-riding incentives erode the incentive to supply pressure. For this reason, many groups that could gain from collective action will not organize to act in their respective common interests.

Although some groups can never act collectively in their common interest, other groups can. There are two conditions, either of which, coupled with effective leadership, is sufficient to make collective action possible: (1) that the number of individuals that must act collectively to further the common interest is sufficiently small; (2) that the group should have access to selective benefits. These selective benefits either punish or reward individuals depending on whether or not they have borne a share of the costs of collective action.

The logic of collective action suggests that individuals with common interests will be differentially successful in achieving their goals through political markets. Small groups and groups that can provide selective benefits to members will do well, even when they are a minority, notwithstanding a majority vote rule. Other groups lose wealth as they fail to organize effectively against rent-seeking pressures. Rational ignorance prevents median voters from penalizing legislatures for indulging minority pressures as long as governments observe the golden rule of dispensing benefits to concentrated groups and dispersing costs widely across the general electorate.

The influence achieved by effective interest groups predictably varies with the institutional characteristics of particular political markets. Where political party influence is weak, as in the United States, and where individual legislators are able to court their respective constituencies without fear of loss of party support, interest group politics predictably will dominate. Legislators will logroll to service politically effective interests located within their districts together with more geographically dispersed interests prepared to finance their campaign expenditures.

In general, interest groups are less influential in predominantly two party parliamentary systems, like the United Kingdom, where single party government is typical and where representatives must maintain party loyalty. In such circumstances, agenda control is largely retained by the executive (the cabinet) and interest groups cannot easily lobby at the district level. The executive typically responds relatively more to national than to local interests, much as the President does in the United States. The vote motive, albeit weakened by rational ignorance, exercises greater influence in such circumstances

However, most parliamentary systems are multiparty in nature, with governments forged from shifting coalitions between minority parties. Many European political systems, based on proportional representation, take this form. With a weak executive branch, interest groups are able to influence policy even from a minority position by threatening the stability of existing coalitions and/or by offering support to alternative coalitions in return for programmatic success.

Where interest groups exert influence, they do not do so in an efficiency enhancing way as Becker (1983, 1985) suggests. They do so on the basis of wealth-dissipating rent-seeking and by focusing attention on redistributive policies. Because they fare better in an opaque environment, they achieve wealth redistribution in a technically inefficient manner, with high excess burdens. To the extent that legislators respond conscientiously to effective interest groups, one might argue that political efficiency is maintained. But it is a peculiar notion of political efficiency, certainly not one that voters would readily endorse.

Efficiency and the economic theory of bureaucracy

Early theories of bureaucracy emphasized the role of civil servants as loyal servants of the government, conscientiously carrying out the policies of their political masters (Weber, 1947). Early challenges to this model stemmed from Parkinson (1957), Tullock (1965) and Downs (1967) each of whom explored the behavior of bureaucrats from the perspective of the rational choice perspective. In 1971, Niskanen subjected bureaucracy to a comprehensive critique which encompassed both its internal organization and its external environment.

On the assumption that senior bureaucrats seek to maximize budget size, Niskanen (1971) demonstrated that bureaus would seek and predictably would obtain outputs significantly in excess of those justified by economic or political efficiency. Demand-constrained bureaus would supply such outputs in a technically inefficient manner. Budget-constrained bureaus would achieve technical efficiency. In 1975, Niskanen acknowledged that senior bureaucrats, under certain institutional conditions, might pursue maximum budget discretion, rather than maximum budget size, in so doing curtailing output. Even so, high demand legislatures would ensure that bureau outputs exceeded economically efficient levels. Information asymmetry would ensure that bureaus secured excessively large budgets which would be dissipated in technically inefficient ways. In Niskanen's model, the bureaus systematically outmaneuver the politicians in bilateral bargaining over budgets.

More recently, there has been an attempt to resuscitate Weberian views on bureaucratic behavior. Weingast and Moran (1983) recast the relationship between politicians and senior bureaucrats into a principal–agent format and suggest that any potential principal–agent problem is ameliorated by the incentive-cost structure established by the US Congress. Even with respect to the United States, we are skeptical of this judgement (Rowley and Vachris, 1993).

Economic markets ameliorate potential principal–agent problems through a proprietary setting in which individuals bear the consequences of their actions directly in terms of changes in their net worth. The political setting in contrast, is a nonproprietary environment in which individuals do not bear the full economic consequences of their decisions. Behavioral differences in the two settings reflect these significant differences in institutional constraints. Even within the complex structure of US oversight and appropriations committees, there is no equivalent to the capital market to revise the value of political portfolios in well-functioning and deviant bureaus. In such circumstances, agency problems will emerge and will not easily be removed.

In parliamentary systems, where elaborate oversight mechanisms typically do not exist, Niskanen's bilateral bargaining model is much more likely to prevail. Herein lies a potent source of political market failure of which even rationally ignorant voters are now only too well aware.

Conclusions

Wittman (1989) sketched out in very general outline a Panglossian theory of democratic political markets. In this paper, we have sketched out a radically different general outline which defines a far less optimistic perspective on such markets. Both outlines are drawn from public choice scholarship, Wittman's primarily Chicagoan in emphasis and ours primarily Virginian. In our view, the Virginia school of political economy has a much better grasp of the nature of political markets and a superior ideological approach to the issue of resolving political market failure than any of the competing research programs, the most notable of which is Chicago political economy.

Note

Charles Rowley is grateful to The Lynde and Harry Bradley Foundation for supporting this research. The sections of the paper addressing the issue whether or not democracy is efficient draw upon our paper published in the Fall 1995 issue of *The Journal of Public Finance and Public Choice*.

References

Akerlof, G.A. (1970), 'The Market for "Lemons": Quality Uncertainty and the Market Mechanism', *Quarterly Journal of Economics*, **84** (August), 488–500.

Alchian, A. and Demsetz, H. (1972), 'Production, Information Costs and Economic Organization', *American Economic Review*, **68** (December), 777–95.

Arrow, K.J. (1951), *Social Choice and Individual Values*, New York: Wiley.

Arrow, K.J. (1962), 'Economic welfare and the allocation of resources for invention', in *The Rate and Direction of Inventive Activity*, Princeton: Princeton University Press, 609–25.

Arrow, K.J. (1969), 'The organization of economic activity', in *The Analysis and Evaluation of Public Expenditure: The PPB System*, Vol. 1, Joint Economic Committee, 91st Congress, 1st Session, Washington, DC: US Government Printing Office, 59–73.

Auster, R.D. and Silver, M. (1979), *The State as a Firm*, Boston: Martinus Nijhoff Publishing.

Baumol, W.J. and Oates, W.E. (1988), *The Theory of Environmental Policy*, Cambridge: Cambridge University Press.

Becker, G.S. (1983), 'A Theory of Competition Among Pressure Groups for Political Influence', *Quarterly Journal of Economics*, **63**, 371–400.

Becker, G.S. (1985), 'Public Policies, Pressure Groups and Dead Weight Costs', *Journal of Public Economics*, **28** (December), 329–47.

Breit, W. (1986), *Creating the 'Virginia School': Charlottesville as an Academic Environment in the 1960's*, Fairfax: Center for Study of Public Choice.

Buchanan, J.M. and Tullock, G. (1962), *The Calculus of Consent*, Ann Arbor: University of Michigan Press.

Coase, R. (1937), 'The Nature of the Firm', *Economica*, **4**, 386–405.

Coase, R. (1960), 'On the problem of social cost', *Journal of Law and Economics*, **3**, 1–44.

Crew, M.A and Rowley, C.K. (1988), 'Toward a Public Choice Theory of Monopoly Regulation', *Public Choice*, **57** (1), 49–68.

Demsetz, H. (1969), 'Information and Efficiency: Another Viewpoint', *Journal of Law and Economics*, **XII** (1), 1–23.

Downs, A. (1957), *An Economic Theory of Democracy*, New York: Harper and Row.

Downs, A. (1967), *Inside Bureaucracy*, Boston: Little Brown and Company.

Friedman, M. (1962), *Capitalism and Freedom*, Chicago: University of Chicago Press.

Goetz, C.J. (1991), *Uncommon Common Sense vs Conventional Wisdom: The Virginia School of Economics*, Fairfax: Center for Study of Public Choice.

Greenwald, B. and Stiglitz, J.E. (1986), 'Externalities in economies with imperfect information and incomplete markets', *Quarterly Journal of Economics*, **101**, 229–64.
Hayek, F.A. (1945), 'The Use of Knowledge in Society', *American Economic Review*, **35**, 519–30.
Jasay, A. de (1985), *The State*, Oxford: Basil Blackwell.
Laband, D.W. and Sophocleus, J.P. (1988), 'The Social Cost of Rent-Seeking: First Estimates', *Public Choice*, **58**, 269–75.
McCormick, R.E. and Tollison, R.D. (1981), *Politicians, Legislation and the Economy*, Boston: Martinus Nijhoff.
McKelvey, R.D. (1976), 'Intransitivities in Multi-dimensional Voting Models and Some Implications for Agenda Control', *Journal of Economic Theory*, **12**.
Mitchell, W.C. (1988), 'Virginia, Rochester and Bloomington: Twenty Five Years of Public Choice', *Public Choice*, **56** (February), 101–20.
Mitchell, W.C. (1989), 'Chicago Political Economy: A Public Choice Perspective', *Public Choice*, **63** (December), 283–92.
Mueller, D. (1985), *The 'Virginia School' and Public Choice*, Fairfax: Center for Study of Public Choice
Niskanen, W.A. (1971), *Bureaucracy and Representative Government*, Aldine-Atherton.
Niskanen, W.A. (1975), 'Bureaucrats and Politicians', *Journal of Law and Economics*, **18** (December), 617–44.
Olson, M. (1965), *The Logic of Collective Action*, Cambridge: Harvard University Press.
Olson, M. (1987), 'Collective Action' in J. Eatwell, M. Milgate and P. Newman (eds), *The New Palgrave: A Dictionary of Economics*, Vol. 1, New York: Macmillan and Stockton Press, 474–7.
Parkinson, C.N. (1957), *Parkinson's Law and Other Studies in Administration*, New York: Ballantine Books.
Romer, T. and Rosenthal, H. (1978), 'Political Resource Allocation, Controlled Agendas and the Status Quo', *Public Choice*, **33** (4), 27–43.
Romer, T. and Rosenthal, H. (1979), 'The Elusive Median Voter', *Journal of Public Economics*, **12**, 143–70.
Rowley, C.K. (1984), 'The Relevance of the Median Voter Theorem', *Journal of Institutional and Theoretical Economics*, (March), 104–35.
Rowley, C.K. (1987), 'Rent Seeking in Constitutional Perspective', in C.K. Rowley, R.D. Tollison and G. Tullock (eds), *The Political Economy of Rent-Seeking*, Boston: Kluwer Academic Publishing, 447–64.
Rowley, C.K. and Peacock, A.T. (1975), *Welfare Economics: A Liberal Restatement*, Oxford: Martin Robertson.
Rowley, C.K. (1993), *Liberty and the State*, Shaftesbury Papers 4, Aldershot: Edward Elgar.
Rowley, C.K., Tollison, R.D. and Tullock, G. (1988), *The Political Economy of Rent-Seeking*, Boston: Kluwer Academic Publishers.
Rowley, C.K. and Vachris, M. (1993), 'Snake Oil Economics versus Public Choice', in C.K. Rowley (ed.), *Public Choice Theory*, Volume III, Aldershot: Edward Elgar, 573–84.
Samuelson, P.A. (1954), 'The Pure Theory of Public Expenditure', *The Review of Economics and Statistics*, **36** (4), 387–9.
Samuelson, P.A. (1955), 'Diagrammatic Exposition of a Theory of Public Expenditure', *The Review of Economics and Statistics*, **37** (4), 350–56.
Stigler, G.J. (1961), 'The Economics of Information', *Journal of Political Economy*, **LXIX** (3).
Stigler, G.J. (1972), 'Economic Competition and Political Competition, *Public Choice*, **XIII** (Fall), 91–106.
Stigler, G.J. (1992), 'Law or Economics', *Journal of Law and Economics*, **XXXV** (2), 455–68.
Stiglitz, J.E. (1989), *The Economic Role of the State*, Oxford: Basil Blackwell.
Stiglitz, J.E. (1994), *Whither Socialism*, MIT Press.
Tollison, R.D. (1989), 'Chicago Political Economy', *Public Choice*, **63** (3), 293–8.
Tollison, R.D. (1991), *Graduate Students in Virginia Political Economy 1957–1991*, Fairfax: Center for Study of Public Choice.

Tollison, R.D. (1992), *Visitors to the Center for Study of Public Choice 1957–1992*, Fairfax: Center for Study of Public Choice.

Tullock, G. (1967), 'The Welfare Costs of Tariffs, Monopolies and Theft', *Western Economic Journal*, **5**, 224–32.

Tullock, G. (1965), *The Politics of Bureaucracy*, New York: University Press of America.

Tullock, G. (1993), *Rent Seeking*, The Shaftesbury Papers 2, Aldershot: Edward Elgar.

Weber, M. (1947), *The Theory of Social and Economic Organization*, New York: The Free Press.

Weingast, B.R and Moran, M.J. (1983), 'Bureaucratic Discretion or Congressional Control?' Regulatory Policy Making by the Federal Trade Commission, *Journal of Political Economy*, **91**, 765–800.

Williamson, O.E. (1985), *The Economics of Capitalism*, New York: Macmillan.

Wittman, D. (1989), 'Why Democracies Produce Efficient Results', *Journal of Political Economy*, **97** (6), 1395–1424.

Yeager, L. (1988), *Ethics in the History and Doctrine of the Virginia School*, Fairfax: Center for Study of Public Choice.

5 The institutional approach to political economy

Charles J. Whalen

Adam Smith saw political economy as a broad study of the many forces contributing to national wealth. Over the years, however, academics have narrowed 'political economy' to 'economics' – a discipline in which the mainstream confines its analyses to issues involving market allocation under conditions of scarcity. In contrast, institutionalists seek to retain a more expansive scope of analysis. Their approach yields theories and policy views that are often markedly different from those offered by neoclassical economics. The present chapter describes and discusses the institutional (or evolutionary) approach to political economy.[1]

Origins and development

The name 'institutional economics' is said to have been coined by Walton Hamilton in 1919. But the tradition's roots can be traced to at least the 19th century, when three influences contributed most significantly to the birth of institutionalism: the German 'historical school', American 'pragmatism' and Thorstein Veblen's writings on the preconceptions of economic science. After a brief explanation of these influences, six leading institutionalists are discussed.[2]

Influences

In the 1870s, Richard T. Ely and other American scholars were introduced to the historical school of political economy while studying in Germany. That school emphasized the interrelated and dynamic nature of reality; a need to ground theories in data obtained through empirical investigations; and attention to human institutions, social reform, and state economic-development activities. When the Americans returned home, many incorporated such views into their own writing and teaching. They were determined, writes Paul McNulty (1980, p. 131), to put new marrow into what they called the 'dry bones' of 'the old political economy' dominant in both England and the United States.

Another early influence on institutionalism was the creation of an American philosophical perspective called pragmatism. This perspective, outlined first by Charles Peirce and later by William James and John Dewey, views

notions of absolute truth and teleology with skepticism. Instead, it emphasizes the element of uncertainty in human understanding. It also stresses the
practical consequences of belief; pragmatists treat scientific investigation as
an important step in the process of resolving practical problems, not merely
as an intellectual exercise. Pragmatism provides institutionalism with both an
epistemological foundation and a social philosophy.[3]

Veblen (1857–1929) was a student of both Ely and Peirce. His turn-of-the-
century articles on economics revealed the discipline's methodological foundations. They also presented the case for what he called an 'evolutionary'
science. In these works one finds many of the ingredients needed to establish
an institutionalist approach to economics (see Veblen, 1919). Veblen's ideas
are further developed in volumes including the following: *The Theory of the
Leisure Class* (in which the phrase 'conspicuous consumption' first appears);
The Theory of Business Enterprise; and *Absentee Ownership and Business
Enterprise in Recent Times* (Veblen, 1967, 1904, and 1923).

Commons, Mitchell and Ayres
Central figures in the early development of institutionalism included John R.
Commons, Wesley Mitchell and Clarence Ayres.[4] Like Veblen, Commons
(1862–1945) was a student of Ely. In fact, Ely interested Commons in the
labor field and later secured a post for him at the University of Wisconsin – a
home base from which Commons launched a variety of industrial relations
explorations and economic reform efforts (including those involving protective labor legislation, public-utility regulation, and price stabilization).
Commons was also the first to write a book that attempted to explain institutionalist thinking (see Commons, 1934).

Commons's students did not grasp his theoretical formulations in the field
of economics – formulations that sought both to give collective action 'its
due place' in economic theory and to develop a 'volitional' alternative to the
mechanistic theories of economic orthodoxy (Commons, 1934, p. 5; 1924,
p. vii).[5] They understood clearly, however, that institutionalism should help
resolve practical problems. As a result, while Commons's conceptual works
have usually been ignored, most of his students and followers have remained
united by an atheoretical notion of 'economics in action' (Witte, 1954, p. 132).
As one Commons biographer wrote in reference to these institutionalists,
'The emphasis on public policy and practical economic problems [is] enough
for them' (Harter, 1962, p. 206).[6]

Another early leader in the institutionalist movement was Mitchell (1874–
1948). A student of Veblen – with a special interest in Veblen's distinction
between 'industrial' and 'pecuniary' employments – Mitchell emphasized the
role played by money in a capitalist economy.[7] In fact, he always intended to
write a detailed and explicitly institutionalist treatise on what he called the

'money economy'. After some initial writing on this topic, however, Mitchell believed the project required additional research into business cycles. Although for many years he viewed the work on cycles as 'a special aspect' of his larger vision of a money economy, Mitchell gave the business cycle the bulk of his attention for the rest of his career (Dillard, 1987, pp. 1629–30).[8]

Despite failing to complete a book on the money economy, Mitchell contributed to institutionalist thinking in many ways: by writing essays on economic theory and the need for a historically-grounded science of human behavior (institutionalism) rather than an ahistorical science of price tendencies (economic orthodoxy) (Mitchell, 1937); by producing applied work on economic fluctuations (Mitchell, 1913); by creating the National Bureau of Economic Research (NBER) and establishing it as the premier US center for empirical investigation and statistical measurement in economics; and by developing a popular course on the history of economic thought (Mitchell, 1949). Over time, however, his concentration on economic statistics became so great that the NBER lost its institutionalist orientation. Today, in fact, that organization is controlled by neoclassical researchers – and Mitchell is known best not for interpreting facts but for collecting them.

Clarence Ayres (1891–1972) was introduced to the ideas of both Dewey and Veblen through studies in philosophy and economics at the University of Chicago. His interest in institutionalism grew as a result of working at Amherst College with Walton Hamilton (one of Veblen's students), and in the wake of discussions with Herbert Davenport (another student of Veblen) and Morris Copeland (an institutionalist influenced by Mitchell). His major attempt to explain and apply institutionalism – to the field of economic development – is found in *The Theory of Economic Progress*, a volume published while he served on the faculty at The University of Texas (Ayres, 1944).[9]

Unlike Commons and Mitchell, Ayres succeeded in transmitting a conceptual framework to subsequent generations of students. Many of today's leading institutionalists have studied with either Ayres or his students. In Austin, meanwhile, faculty members kept the Ayres tradition alive until the mid 1980s.[10]

Myrdal, Gruchy and Galbraith

Among more recent institutionalists, prominent contributors include Gunnar Myrdal, John Kenneth Galbraith and Allan G. Gruchy.[11] Myrdal (1898–1987) began his career in Sweden as a conventional monetary economist. While hints of his movement toward institutionalism are glimpsed in pioneering work on economic dynamics, Myrdal's conversion to institutional economics resulted primarily from his heavy involvement in policy matters at home and abroad. Myrdal served, for example, as a member of the Swedish parliament; as his nation's minister of trade and commerce; and, in the wake of World

War II, as executive secretary of the United Nations Economic Commission for Europe. He also conducted landmark studies on both race relations in America and the problems of developing nations (Myrdal, 1944, 1968). His efforts, which earned him the Nobel prize in 1974, led him to conclude that real-world problems require a holistic approach which looks beyond the conventional boundaries of economic science (Myrdal, 1973, 1978).

Gruchy (1906–90) founded two professional organizations designed to provide institutionalists with an opportunity to share and develop their ideas – the Association for Evolutionary Economics (sponsor of the *Journal of Economic Issues*) and the Association for Institutional Thought (sponsor of annual meetings held in conjunction with the Western Social Sciences Association). His scholarly contributions were in two areas – institutionalist thought and national economic policy. His work on economic thought led to three volumes that traced institutionalism from Veblen to the contributors of the late 1980s (Gruchy, 1947, 1972, 1987). His research on national economic policy stressed the need for policy guidance extending beyond Keynesian aggregate-demand management – and the value of lessons found in the experience of nations such as Norway and Sweden (Gruchy, 1977, 1984). As Dudley Dillard wrote shortly after Gruchy's death, both areas of research 'were intimately related in Allan's thinking' (Dillard, 1990, p. 668).

Galbraith (1908–) is perhaps the most prolific and widely-read economist of this century. Since publishing an article entitled 'Monopoly Power and Price Rigidities' in 1936 (Galbraith, 1936), he has focused much of his attention on pricing behavior, corporate power, and their implications for not only inflation and unemployment but also national wealth and human welfare.[12] Galbraith has also drawn special attention to the *cultural* sources and dimensions of economic activity. This is evident from the very title of *The Culture of Contentment* (Galbraith, 1992), but it is also clear from *A Short History of Financial Euphoria*, in which he examines the 'crowd psychology' that engenders recurrent episodes of speculative 'insanity' in financial markets (Galbraith, 1993).

Preconceptions
Many critics have argued that institutionalists share only a rejection of economic orthodoxy. But what unites institutionalists is a common methodological foundation – a shared set of philosophical preconceptions. These preconceptions can be grouped into the following four categories: a conception of society; an image of the economic process; an approach to values; and a philosophy of science.[13]

Society and the economy

The institutionalist conception of society is holistic in nature. In other words, social reality is viewed as a unified whole. Thus, institutionalist analyses – unlike those of the neoclassicals and traditional Marxists – cannot begin with the world neatly divided into 'economic' and 'noneconomic' realms. As Charles Wilber and Robert Harrison write, 'institutionalism's holistic theories are rooted in the belief that the social whole is not only greater than the sum of its parts but that the parts are so related that their functioning is conditioned by their interrelations' (Wilber and Harrison, 1978, p. 73).

Institutionalists also view society from a 'processual' perspective. This means they view social systems as dynamic, ever-developing entities, and are keenly aware of the fact that all social activity occurs in both historical time and an environment of uncertainty regarding the future. Their view contrasts sharply with the neoclassical emphasis on an 'equilibrium' state of rest.[14]

While most economists define economics as a study of the price mechanism and market transactions, institutionalists adopt a broader view. To evolutionary political economists, economics is a science of 'social provisioning' – one that must allow room for explorations of not only resource allocation but also the nature of both production and want creation.[15] According to this definition, markets represent only one type of human institution involved in provisioning. Institutionalists recognize that other institutions – including the state, the family, indeed culture in its totality – are also significant.[16]

Another difference between institutionalists and most other economists is that the former view economic systems as having no inherent tendency toward either self-regulation or self-destruction. Rather, evolutionary political economists see economic 'order' as a creation of the parties within a particular social system. As Gruchy writes, 'Actual economic systems exhibit cultural coherence, rather than the equilibrating forces of a mechanistic system' (Gruchy, 1987, p. 4).[17] For this reason, institutions and social processes considered to be noneconomic 'frictions' by neoclassicism are very often elements that warrant a prominent place in institutionalist analyses.[18]

Values and science

Institutionalists consider the concept of value to be multifaceted. For example, depending on the problem, institutionalists might focus on use values, exchange values, individual values, or social values. In contrast, neoclasssicals and Marxists take a narrow view of value – their approaches emphasize market prices and labor exertion (rooted in the 'labor theory of value'), respectively.

Evolutionary political economists recognize that both their own judgments and those of public officials are important elements in public-policy analysis. The neoclassical suggestion that economics can be value free is dismissed in favor of the position of Joan Robinson (1970, p. 122): 'An economist's attempt to be purely objective must necessarily be either self-deception or a device to deceive others. A candid writer will make his preconceptions clear and allow the reader to discount them if he does not accept them'.[19] Moreover, although institutionalists see much validity in the public-choice perspective on politicians, they also recognize its limitations and maintain that the state can also play a *creative* role in the economy by helping to expand individual liberty and shape community preferences and social institutions.[20]

The institutionalist philosophy of science, meanwhile, rests on a belief that economics should contribute to an understanding of actual processes of social provisioning. Institutionalists strive for theories with realistic assumptions, logical consistency and testable predictions, but they reject the neoclassical treatment of prediction as the preeminent goal of science. They also emphasize the importance of re-evaluating theories regularly, and the need for theories that help resolve real-world problems.[21]

Review
Institutionalists are united by a shared belief system – one that is holistic, processual, non-teleological and pragmatic. It is also problem-oriented and explicitly value-laden. This belief system provides a methodological foundation for institutionalist analyses. Examples of such analyses are considered in the next section.

Applications

Methods, tools and general theories
The institutionalist methodology has been applied to a wide range of topics throughout the 20th century. In the course of their work, institutionalists have produced and employed a number of research methods, tools of analysis and theories. One method employed since the days of Veblen is that which presents a detailed description of economic behavior and/or institutional change. This work is often considered 'preliminary' in nature, a preamble to more 'serious' future scholarship. But it can *also* be work of considerable value. To neglect such research – as today's mainstream economists do often – is to increase significantly the risk that certain new features of the economy are overlooked (Lind, 1993, p. 9; Whalen, 1996a). Further, as Wassily Leontief reminds us, 'To keep the ... engine of our economy in good working order we must ... be acquainted with the details of its actual design' (Leontief, 1971, p. 7). Descriptive accounts can also be valuable if they provide new interpretations of familiar phenomena and processes.

While institutionalists from Veblen to Galbraith have made considerable contributions to political economy through description, others – such as

Mitchell, Copeland, and Gerhard Colm – have been pioneers in the development and use of statistics and quantitative data.[22] Although most advanced statistical methods are currently developed by mainstream economists, institutionalists continue to engage in quantitative research.[23] Still other institutionalists, many with intellectual roots to Commons, have pioneered use of more 'qualitative' methods – including participant observation, comparative case studies, interviews and surveys.[24] These methods are used only rarely by neoclassical economists.[25]

Turning from research methods to tools of analysis, Veblen is again a prominent figure. Indeed, perhaps the most distinctive tool used by evolutionary political economists is the 'Veblenian dichotomy'. This device recognizes that human activities contain some elements that are 'instrumental' – involving actual causal sequences and relations – and others that are merely 'ceremonial' (see Waller, 1982). The dichotomy figures prominently in the work of Ayres and his followers, but it also appears in Mitchell's work in the form of his distinction between making goods and making money, and in Commons's writings as part of his analysis of transactions.

The Veblenian dichotomy is well-suited for use in general economic theories – theories not confined to time and place. Two theories of this sort that incorporate the dichotomy are Wendell Gordon's theory of economic development and Commons's theory of economic transactions. Gordon's theory of 'economic progress' involves the dynamic interaction of technology (instrumental), institutions (ceremonial), natural resources, and human biology (Gordon, 1980). Commons, meanwhile, viewed *transactions* – exchanges of ownership rights (not necessarily involving money) – as the fundamental units of economic life. His general theory of transactions interprets economic activity by giving equal weight to five interrelated factors that explain such exchanges: working rules (institutions), productivity (technology), scarcity, power and expectations (Commons, 1950). This framework incorporates insights from not only Veblen but also economic orthodoxy, Marxism and Austrian economists, respectively.[26]

Theories of a particular time and place
After World War II, institutionalists devoted much attention to the structure of business institutions in the United States. Two important contributions here are Robert Averitt's *The Dual Economy* and John Kenneth Galbraith's *Economics and the Public Purpose* (Averitt, 1968; Galbraith, 1973). Instead of the competitive industrial system posited by neoclassical economists, both volumes described an economy with two very different types of firms. A few hundred large firms were described as being at this economy's 'center'. These corporations were guided by highly-trained technical experts and managers; had extensive resources and production capabilities (usually in key

industries such as manufacturing, communications and finance); wielded a significant amount of economic power; and often coordinated activities with each other. On the economy's 'periphery', meanwhile, Averitt and Galbraith found literally millions of small, highly-competitive firms.

By adopting a dual-economy perspective and exploring the operations and interactions of the center and periphery, Averitt, Galbraith and other institutionalists (such as Eichner, 1976) sought a reconstruction of microeconomic theory as both an end in itself and as a more realistic foundation for macroeconomics. Much attention given to their 'new economics of microstructure' centered on the mark-up pricing behavior of the economy's powerful 'megacorps'.[27] But the institutionalists argued that even business activity in the periphery departed significantly from what is described in neoclassical analyses – primarily because corporate life in the periphery was conditioned by behavior in the center economy (see Galbraith, 1973). Attention to the problem of stagflation, a problem receiving much attention in the 1970s, offers an opportunity to both illustrate this last point and present an example of an institutionalist theory that focuses on a particular social problem.

Because neoclassicals (including monetarists *and* Keynesians) saw inflation and recession as inversely related, they had great difficulty explaining the stagflation phenomenon. The problem becomes entirely comprehensible, however, from a dual-economy perspective. The key is to understand what happens when traditional anti-inflation policies are implemented. According to institutionalists, center firms respond to such policies by reducing output and employment, not prices. In fact, some of these enterprises will even *raise* prices in an effort to stabilize revenues and profits (see Wachtel and Adelsheim, 1976) – a step that could cause public officials to intensify their anti-inflation activities. Firms in the periphery, meanwhile, cannot insulate themselves from the effects of state action. As a result, inflation fighting has a more profound and damaging impact on small firms than neoclassical economics would anticipate (Galbraith, 1973).

Since institutionalism recognizes the dynamic nature of economic life, institutionalists are continually re-evaluating and modifying their analyses of the dual economy (and the structure of the US economy in general) – especially in light of economic globalization and rapid technological developments (see Galbraith, 1989; Gruchy, 1987, chapter 5; Munkirs, 1985; Harrison, 1994; Harrison and Bluestone, 1988). But their processual perspective has also caused institutionalists to go beyond documenting change and to develop theories of *how* economic systems change over time. One example is their analysis of business cycles.

While neoclassicism asserts that capitalist systems are stable, institutionalism maintains that such economies – at least as structured in the major industrialized nations of the 20th century – are inherently prone to macroeconomic fluctuations. In particular, institutionalists argue that robust business earnings raise expectations about future earnings and cause bank loans and corporate-investment levels to increase. But while these loans and investment expenditures raise stock prices, employment and output levels (that is, they trigger a boom), they also produce fragile financial structures and push up production costs. Thus, the system eventually cannot support the accumulated debt. As a result, profits fall, bankruptcies occur; and loans, investment, employment and production levels are all reduced. In short, the result is a recession or depression that ends only when business expectations improve and investment levels once again begin to rise, due to either government intervention or a purely psychological change on the part of corporate managers.[28]

While a complete business cycle might involve five or ten years, other institutionalist theories of economic change involve a much longer time horizon. Commons's theory of capitalist development, for example, traces capitalism's history from the industrial revolution to a 20th-Century era he called 'banker capitalism' – a period of multinational corporations and huge investment institutions. Among the insights contained in this theory are the following: (a) that the ultimate conflict in capitalism is between the interests of consumers and producers; and (b) that economic conflicts often lead to political and legislative battles (Commons, 1934).

Recent findings

A number of recent books have examined contemporary economic life from an institutionalist perspective. Among the most valuable are the following: William Dugger's (1989) *Corporate Hegemony*; Juliet Schor's (1991) *The Overworked American*; and Wallace Peterson's (1994) *The Silent Depression*.

Corporate Hegemony describes how the corporation is coming to dominate every aspect of life in Western industrial societies. *The Overworked American* documents – and provides a non-neoclassical explanation of – a decline in US leisure both at work and in the home. *The Silent Depression* analyzes a downward trend in American wages, family income and productivity growth that began in the early 1970s and continues into the mid 1990s.

One new volume that adds a collection of essays – by Dugger, Frederic Lee, L. Randall Wray, Ray Marshall, Barry Bluestone, Lester Thurow, Brent McClintock, Alice Amsden and others – to the institutionalist literature is *Political Economy for the 21st Century* (Whalen, 1996b). Some of its contributors explore perennial matters – such as the nature of resources, wants, and production/reproduction – while others orient their chapters toward problems that have developed only in the past few decades. A few of that book's findings are discussed here for the purpose of rounding out the present discussion of institutionalist applications.

According to Dugger, institutionalism offers a theory in which resources are not 'given' as in neoclassical economics. Instead, resources are 'functions of technological change, evolving property rights, and changing cultural norms'.[29] Similarly, he explains that *wants* are endogenous. He writes:

> Individual utility is not the causal factor in want creation and want satisfaction. The causal factors are external to the subjective preferences of the individual consumer because those preferences are learned, not inherent. Only such basics as hunger and thirst are inherent. A desire for potato chips and beer is learned.

To fill in the details of how advertising and salesmanship 'teach us what we want', Dugger says we must turn to Galbraith's theory of 'revised sequence'. According to this theory, our conventional notion of consumer sovereignty must be reconsidered in light of the fact that producers often create markets for products rather than create products in response to pre-existing consumer needs. Dugger adds that another institutionalist theory with insight into the want process is Veblen's theory of conspicuous consumption, a theory that emphasizes the struggle for invidious distinction that arises in pecuniary culture.

The production/reproduction process, meanwhile, is conceived by Dugger as one involving a wide range of social relations. Economic orthodoxy focuses only on production decisions within business enterprises ('the theory of the firm'); institutionalism considers additional factors including ownership of the means of production, workplace organization, the family, the state, and gender relations. While most mainstream economists view such matters as outside the scope of economics, Dugger stresses that institutionalists offers historically-grounded theories of each.[30]

Lee's focus is on corporate pricing. He emphasizes that price setting is a *social* process. That is, pricing is influenced by 'command' (the state) and 'custom' as well as competition. Lee's finding that product markets are 'social' markets dovetails with those of Wray and Marshall, who demonstrate that money and labor markets are also social markets.

Marshall also looks at recent global trends and stresses that there is ultimately only one path that will allow us to enhance US prosperity while competing in global markets – a path which requires that we compete on the basis of productivity, (product and process) innovation and product quality. Similar themes are developed by Barry Bluestone and Lester Thurow. Bluestone explores the structural roots of recent problems in US economic growth and distribution. These roots include a shift from manufacturing to services; a 'deunionization' of the workforce; an explosion of global trade and transnational capital mobility; a chronic US trade deficit; and increased immigration. Bluestone's conclusion is that structural problems require structural policies – especially in the realms of labor markets, manufacturing and trade. Thurow adds that the static, neoclassical theory of 'comparative advantage' is obsolete in the present era of 'brain-power' industries (such as microelectronics and biotechnology) – an era in which national advantage is determined primarily by strategic public- and private-sector decisions, not natural resources and tangible capital endowments.

Finally, both Brent McClintock and Alice Amsden offer contributions to institutionalist discussions of the international realm. McClintock provides evidence of the trend toward international trade and production; explains that this trend has generated significant economic and social dislocations in the United States; and argues that adapting to such developments will require both national adjustment policies (for workers and declining industries) and greater supranational governance. Amsden explains that the future success of newly-industrializing nations will depend heavily on their ability to learn from other countries and modify aspects of their own economic structure accordingly. The role of the state must be given special attention in this process of 'country model transfer' – analysts cannot be blinded by a doctrinal belief in laissez-faire; and they must look beyond the mere *existence* of government and focus instead on the *nature* of its activities.

Conclusion: challenges
The institutional approach to political economy cannot appeal to everyone. Many will always prefer the comfortable grooves and narrow scope of standard theory. Neoclassicism lends itself to mathematicization – a valuable objective in a discipline where formalism has often been not a secondary feature but 'a central programmatic aim' (Ingrao and Israel, 1990, p. 1). It also offers an optimistic view of economic activity (a world requiring little deviation from laissez-faire), and stands ready with a clear standard for use in evaluating that activity ('efficiency'). In contrast, institutionalism offers a far less tidy and comforting perspective. For example, institutionalism demands a constant re-examination of theories in light of real-world changes; insists that society drives the market, not the reverse; believes there are no neatly-defined 'economic' problems, just 'problems' (and, as Myrdal (1973, p. 142) stressed, 'they are all complex'); promises only a 'managed' – and temporary – economic equilibrium; reveals that efficiency is not only undermined by economic change but exists as just one possible measure of social well-being; stresses that state action can serve to both restrain and expand individual liberty; and recognizes that more government activity does not ensure an improved economy (what is important is the *nature*, not the level, of such activity).[31]

Nevertheless, institutionalists believe that their philosophical outlook (presented above) reflects reality more accurately than does the one found at the root of conventional theory. Institutionalist political economy does indeed raise new questions about theory and policy. But these questions, especially regarding the appropriate nature of public action in particular sectors and selected markets, are essential – how we answer them will influence the future shape of local, national and international economic life.

As institutionalism prepares for a second century, three challenges seem most in need of its attention. One is the development of theory. Veblen long ago stressed that evolutionary economics must offer a body of theory – theories that relate to our modern economy (Veblen, 1919, p. 58). Unfortunately, many contemporary institutionalists have been sidetracked by work on methodology and the history of economic thought.

Perhaps evolutionary political economists get sidetracked because numerous economics departments discourage – and sometimes even display hostility toward – institutionalist scholarship outside these two realms. But another part of the explanation may be that many institutionalists retreat into such work because they find life beyond conventional theory somewhat intimidating (especially when the challenges of a broad framework and time-consuming research methods collide with the heavy classroom responsibilities and limited resources found at colleges and universities most likely to employ such scholars). There is certainly a place for investigations into methodology and history of thought, but there is also – to paraphrase Veblen – a vast economic landscape in need of theoretical formulation. If institutionalism is to remain a viable academic tradition during the next century, and if it is to have more than an occasional and passing influence on public policy, institutionalists must find a way to devote more attention to theory construction and refinement in the years ahead.

A second challenge facing institutionalists is the need to build bridges to other non-neoclassical schools of economic thought. Institutionalists and Austrians have differing views on individualism and the role of the state, but they also agree on the importance of expectations and on the need for analyses that treat economic activity as a process in time. Institutionalists have even more in common with those in other heterodox traditions, including Marxism, Post Keynesianism, and the French 'regulation' school – especially in light of the recent emphasis on structural economic change that exists in the literature of each of these camps. The present is, therefore, a perfect time for institutionalists to interact with political economists of all varieties in an effort to synthesize their work wherever possible. This 'bridge building' will not only enrich individual traditions but it will also strengthen heterodoxy in relation to the neoclassical mainstream.

One relatively new area of inquiry that deserves the attention of institutionalists is feminist theory. Institutionalist preconceptions can serve as a useful methodological foundation for feminist analyses of androcentrism and patriarchy. Existing feminist scholarship, meanwhile, can alert institutionalists to issues that they should have been exploring for years. Two recent volumes – edited by Ferber and Nelson (1993) and Peterson and Brown (1994) – suggest that valuable collaborations across disciplines are possible in this realm.

A third challenge for institutionalism is that it must articulate a policy agenda capable of addressing the economic concerns of ordinary citizens. Institutionalists offered policies to stabilize the economy in the early decades of this century. They also pioneered work on incomes policies in the 1960s and early 1970s. In recent years, however, their agenda has often been unclear.

Since it is unlikely that the current laissez-faire path will provide a secure foundation for future prosperity and rising living standards, institutionalists must be prepared to offer a new strategy for dealing with contemporary problems.[32] This strategy must be able to evolve with changing conditions, but it must also be coherent. It should also give attention to issues of political control. Is it true, as William Greider (1992) and others suggest, that the interests of most Americans are not represented effectively in Washington? And if so, is there any type of political reform that can offer an improvement? An institutionalist agenda for the coming decade will need to address not only on the substance of policy but also the policy-making and electoral processes and the structure of government institutions.

The institutional approach to political economy has made important contributions to US economic thought and policy during the past century. Yet there is much work still to be done, especially since the present is an era of rapid technological, institutional and social change. The work will not be easy – but the most valuable human endeavors never are.

Notes

1. The following provided helpful comments on an early draft of this chapter: Charles Clark, Janet Knoedler, Brent McClintock, Rick Tilman, and Linda Whalen.
2. Hamilton (1919) distinguishes 'institutional economics' from the 'value economics' of the neoclassical mainstream. He explains that while the latter focuses on prices and market values produced under competitive conditions, institutionalism casts a broader net and examines the various institutional structures and processes that explain the nature and extent of real-world economic order and human well-being. Institutionalism is sometimes called 'evolutionary' economics, a term that derives from Veblen (1919, pp. 56–81).
3. For a recent discussion of the influence of Peirce and other pragmatists upon the development of institutionalism, see Liebhafsky (1993).
4. In addition to Commons, Mitchell and Ayres, other important early institutionalists include Robert Hoxie, Walton Hamilton, Rexford Tugwell and Morris Copeland.
5. For evidence that students did not understand Commons's economic theorizing, see Commons (1934, p. 1) and Witte (1954, p. 132). It should be noted, however, that his theorizing on labor matters was much easier to follow. See, for example, Commons (1909); see also Kaufman (1993) for a discussion of Common's contributions to the interdisciplinary field of 'industrial relations'.
6. For evidence of a recent resurgence of interest in Commons's theoretical contributions to economics, see Ramstad (1986); Rutherford (1983); and Whalen (1993).
7. For Veblen's distinction between 'industrial and pecuniary employments', see his chapter

with that title in Veblen (1919). In addition, it should be noted that Dewey was also one of Mitchell's professors.

8. Mitchell chose to accept a post at Columbia University in 1913 so he could move to New York and observe at first hand the financial center of the money economy (Dillard, 1987, p. 1630).

9. For a sketch of Ayres's career and discussion of his scholarship, see Breit and Culbertson (1976).

10. In the mid 1980s, The University of Texas did not replace a number of retiring institutionalists and instead sought to orient the department and its graduate program in a more conventional (neoclassical) direction.

11. A longer list of more recent institutionalists would include many others, including Robert Averitt, Dudley Dillard, William Dugger, Alfred Eichner, K. William Kapp, Ray Marshall, Anne Mayhew, John Munkirs and Wallace Peterson.

12. For an important trilogy by Galbraith, see *The Affluent Society*; *The New Industrial State*; and *Economics and the Public Purpose* (Galbraith, 1958, 1967, and 1973).

13. In this section I draw on earlier attempts to outline the methodology of institutionalism. See, for example, my chapter in Dugger and Waller (1992).

14. For a valuable recent discussion of the importance of considering time in economics, see North (1994).

15. 'Want creation' is important to institutionalists because they do not consider investigations into how individual or group objectives are determined (and modified) as studies that are outside the scope of economics. In addition, evolutionary political economists recognize that producers, workers and consumers are largely cultural products. An institutionalist interpretation of economic behavior must therefore inquire into the various cultural influences shaping that behavior.

16. Institutionalists also stress the importance of technology, both as a body of ideas that shapes social provisioning and as a process that contributes to the dynamic nature of society by providing an ever-changing knowledge base; see Gordon (1980) and Gruchy (1972).

17. As Yngve Ramstad (1985, p. 509) writes, evolutionary political economists maintain that 'institutional adjustment provides the balancing wheel of an economy'.

18. Some economists drawing attention to institutions in recent years are part of a movement known as the 'new institutional economics'. This group applies neoclassical concepts to explain institutional arrangements as 'efficient' outcomes of profit seeking and utility maximization. For more on the 'old' versus the 'new' institutionalism, see Dugger (1990).

19. For more on the role of valuations in economic analysis, see Myrdal (1968, chapter 1; 1983).

20. In contrast to the traditional neoclassical and Marxist views of the state – perspectives that see a corrective and protective entity, respectively – institutionalists look at the state as a creative agent (see Dugger and Waller, 1992).

21. For more on institutionalism's epistemology and pragmatic social philosophy, see Hill and Troub (1995).

22. For a discussion of Colm's work on national budgets, see Gruchy (1972); for Copeland's work on 'flow of funds' accounting, see Copeland (1952).

23. For examples or discussions of institutionalist research with a quantitative orientation, see Radzicki and Seville (1993); Hayden and Stephenson (1992); Peach and Nowotny (1992); Lower (1990); Seccareccia (1988); Eichner (1987); Hickerson (1983); and Bush (1983).

24. The word *qualitative* is in quotes in the text in recognition of the fact that such methods do not necessarily defy quantification.

25. For a classic study employing qualitative methods in the institutionalist tradition, see Doeringer and Piore (1971). While mainstream economics has narrowed the meaning of 'empirical' research to include only analyses using econometrics and other quantitative techniques, this work by Doeringer and Piore reflects the fact that institutionalism has retained the broader definition of that term – namely, work based on observation.

26. The expectational element in Commons's theory also anticipates a key ingredient in today's Post Keynesian economics.

27. The term 'megacorps' comes from Eichner (1976); the notion of a 'new economics of microstructure' is Averitt's (1968, p. 200). Much of the work on mark-up pricing and related aspects of the aforementioned research on microeconomics can be traced to the studies of corporate behavior and administered pricing undertaken by Adolf Berle and Gardiner Means. See Berle and Means (1933) and Samuels and Medema (1990).

28. As indicated early in this chapter, Mitchell was a major institutionalist contributor in the realm of business cycles (see also Veblen, 1904). For more recent institutionalist discussions of cycles, see Dillard (1987), Peterson (1987) and Minsky (1986a). In addition to stressing the endogenous nature of cycles, this literature has drawn attention to an underlying long-term trend toward increasing financial fragility (see, for example, Minsky, 1986b). One final point: we should not be surprised that this topic serves as an important bridge between the institutionalist and Post Keynesian traditions. Keynes and the early institutionalists were well aware of their common interest in, and similar approach to, industrial fluctuations.

29. All passages quoted in the remainder of this section are located in Whalen (1996b).

30. For example, see Dugger and Waller (1992) on the state; and Peterson and Brown (1994) on gender relations.

31. A recognition of the importance of the nature rather than just the level of economic activity is one reason why institutional political economists are interested in looking at the composition of government expenditures and in capital-budgeting proposals that draw a distinction between public consumption and public investment.

32. Robert Kuttner recently stated that the sentiment of most Americans could be expressed as follows: 'If the economy is doing so good, why am I feeling so bad?' Since institutionalists have always understood there is no inherent link between serviceability to the community and business gains, these political economists should be uniquely positioned to fashion an agenda that responds to the concerns of contemporary Americans.

References

Averitt, Robert T. (1968), *The Dual Economy*, New York: W.W. Norton.

Ayres, Clarence (1944), *The Theory of Economic Progress*, Chapel Hill: University of North Carolina Press.

Berle, Adolf and Means, Gardiner (1933), *The Modern Corporation and Private Property*, New York: Macmillan.

Breit, William and Culbertson, William (1976), *Science and Ceremony*, Austin: University of Texas Press.

Bush, Paul (1983), 'An Exploration of the Structural Characteristics of a Veblen–Ayres–Foster Defined Institutional Domain', *Journal of Economic Issues*, **18** (March), 35–66.

Commons, John R. (1909), 'American Shoemakers, 1648–1895', *Quarterly Journal of Economics*, **24** (November), 39–84.

Commons, John R. (1924), *Legal Foundations of Capitalism*, New York: Macmillan.

Commons, John R. (1934), *Institutional Economics*, New York: Macmillan.

Commons, John R. (1950), *The Economics of Collective Action*, New York: Macmillan.

Copeland, Morris (1952), *A Study of Moneyflows in the United States*, New York: National Bureau of Economic Research.

Dillard, Dudley (1987), 'Money as an Institution of Capitalism', *Journal of Economic Issues*, **21** (December), 1623–48.

Dillard, Dudley (1990), 'Allan G. Gruchy, 1906–1990: A Scholar's Life', *Journal of Economic Issues*, **24** (September), 663–72.

Doeringer, Peter and Piore, Michael (1971), *Internal Labor Markets and Manpower Analysis*, Lexington, MA: Heath.

Dugger, William (1989), *Corporate Hegemony*, Westport, CT: Greenwood Press.

Dugger, William (1990), 'The New Institutionalism: New But Not Institutionalist', *Journal of Economic Issues*, **24** (June), 423–32.

Dugger, William and Waller, William (eds) (1992), *The Stratified State*, Armonk, NY: M.E. Sharpe.

Eichner, Alfred (1976), *The Megacorp and Oligopoly*, New York: Cambridge University Press.

Eichner, Alfred (1987), 'Prices and Pricing', *Journal of Economic Issues*, **21** (December), 1555–85.

Ferber, Marianne and Nelson, Julie (eds), (1993) *Beyond Economic Man*, Chicago: University of Chicago Press.

Galbraith, John Kenneth (1936), 'Monopoly Power and Price Rigidities', *Quarterly Journal of Economics*, **51** (May), 456–75.

Galbraith, John Kenneth (1973), *Economics and the Public Purpose*, Boston: Houghton Mifflin.

Galbraith, John Kenneth (1992), *The Culture of Contentment*, Boston: Houghton Mifflin.

Galbraith, John Kenneth (1993), *A Short History of Financial Euphoria*, New York: Viking Penguin.

Galbraith, James Kenneth (1989), 'Trade and the Planning System', in Samuel Bowles, Richard Edwards and William Shepherd (eds), *Unconventional Wisdom*, Boston: Houghton Mifflin.

Gordon, Wendell (1980), *Institutional Economics: The Changing System*, Austin: University of Texas Press.

Greider, William (1992), *Who Will Tell the People*, New York: Simon and Schuster.

Gruchy, Allan (1947), *Modern Economic Thought*, New York: Prentice-Hall.

Gruchy, Allan (1972), *Contemporary Economic Thought*, Clifton, NJ: Augustus Kelley.

Gruchy, Allan (1977), *Comparative Economic Systems*, Boston: Houghton Mifflin.

Gruchy, Allan (1984), 'Uncertainty, Indicative Planning, and Industrial Policy', *Journal of Economic Issues*, **18** (March), 159–80.

Gruchy, Allan (1987), *The Reconstruction of Economics*, Westport, CT: Greenwood Press.

Hamilton, Walton (1919), 'The Institutional Approach to Economic Theory', *American Economic Review*, **9** (Supplement), 309–18.

Harrison, Bennett (1994), *Lean and Mean*, New York: Basic Books.

Harrison, Bennett and Bluestone, Berry (1988), *The Great U-Turn*, New York: Basic Books.

Harter, Lafayette (1962), *John R. Commons*, Corvallis: Oregon State University Press.

Hayden, F. Gregory and Stephenson, Kurt (1992), 'Overlap of Organizations: Corporate Transorganization and Veblen's Thesis on Higher Education', *Journal of Economic Issues*, **26** (March), 53–86.

Hickerson, Stephen (1983), 'Planning for Institutional Change in a Complex Environment', *Journal of Economic Issues*, **18** (September), 631–65.

Hill, Lewis and Troub, Roger (1995), 'Pragmatism as a Normative Theory of Social Value and Economic Ethics', in Charles Clark (ed.), *Institutional Economics and the Theory of Social Value*, Norwell, MA: Kluwer Academic Publishers.

Ingrao, Bruna and Israel, Giorgio (1990), *The Invisible Hand*, Cambridge: MIT Press.

Kaufman, Bruce E. (1993), *The Origins and Evolution of the Field of Industrial Relations in the United States*, Ithaca, NY: ILR Press.

Leontief, Wassily (1971), 'Theoretical Assumptions and Nonobserved Facts', *American Economic Review*, **61** (March), 1–7.

Liebhafsky, E. E. (1993), 'The Influence of Charles Sanders Peirce on Institutional Economics', *Journal of Economic Issues*, **28** (September), 741–54.

Lind, Hans (1993), 'The Myth of Institutionalist Method', *Journal of Economic Issues*, **27** (March), 1–17.

Lower, Milton (1990), 'A Type-of-Product System of National Accounts', *Journal of Economic Issues*, **24** (June), 371–80.

McNulty, Paul (1980), *The Origins and Development of Labor Economics*, Cambridge: MIT Press.

Minsky, Hyman (1986a), 'The Evolution of Financial Institutions and the Performance of the Economy', *Journal of Economic Issues*, **20** (June), 345–53.

Minsky, Hyman (1986b), *Stabilizing an Unstable Economy*, New Haven: Yale University Press.

Mitchell, Wesley (1913), *Business Cycles*, Berkeley: University of California Press.

Mitchell, Wesley (1937), *The Backward Art of Spending Money and Other Essays*, New York: McGraw-Hill.

Mitchell, Wesley (1949), *Types of Economic Theory*, 2 vols, New York: Augustus Kelley.

Munkirs, John R. (1985), *The Transformation of American Capitalism*, Armonk, NY: M.E. Sharpe.

Myrdal, Gunnar (1944), *An American Dilemma*, New York: Harper and Row.

Myrdal, Gunnar (1968), *Asian Drama*, New York: Pantheon.

Myrdal, Gunnar (1973), *Against the Stream*, New York: Pantheon.

Myrdal, Gunnar (1978), 'Institutional Economics', *Journal of Economic Issues*, 12 (December), 771–83.

Myrdal, Gunnar (1983 [1969]), *Objectivity in Social Research*, Middletown, CT: Wesleyan University Press.

North, Douglass (1994), 'Economic Performance Through Time', *American Economic Review*, 84 (June), 359–69.

Peach, James and Nowotny, Kenneth (1992), 'Sharecropping Chicago Style', *Journal of Economic Issues*, 26 (June), 365–72.

Peterson, Janice and Brown, Doug (1994), *The Economic Status of Women Under Capitalism*, Aldershot, UK: Edward Elgar.

Peterson, Wallace (1987), 'Macroeconomic Theory and Policy in an Institutionalist Perspective', *Journal of Economic Issues*, 21 (December), 1587–622.

Peterson, Wallace (1994), *The Silent Depression*, New York: W. W. Norton.

Radzicki, Michael and Seville, Donald (1993), 'An Institutional Dynamics Model of Sterling, Massachusetts', *Journal of Economic Issues*, 28 (June), 481–92.

Ramstad, Yngve (1985), 'Comments on Adams and Brock Paper', *Journal of Economic Issues*, 19 (June), 507–11.

Ramstad, Yngve (1986), 'A Pragmatist's Quest for Holistic Knowledge: The Scientific Methodology of John R. Commons', *Journal of Economic Issues*, 20 (December), 1067–106.

Robinson, Joan (1970), *Freedom and Necessity*, New York: Pantheon.

Rutherford, Malcolm (1983), 'John R. Commons's Institutional Economics', *Journal of Economic Issues*, 17 (September), 721–44.

Samuels, Warren and Medema, Stephen (1990), *Gardiner C. Means: Institutionalist and Post Keynesian*, Armonk, NY: M.E. Sharpe.

Schor, Juliet (1991), *The Overworked American*, New York: Basic Books.

Seccareccia, Mario (1988), 'Systemic Viability and Credit Crunches', *Journal of Economic Issues*, 22 (March), 49–78.

Veblen, Thorstein (1904), *The Theory of Business Enterprise*, New York: Charles Scribner's Sons.

Veblen, Thorstein (1919), *The Place of Science in Modern Civilisation and Other Essays*, New York: Viking Press.

Veblen, Thorstein (1923), *Absentee Ownership and Business Enterprise*, New York: B.W. Heubsch.

Veblen, Thorstein (1967 [1899]), *The Theory of the Leisure Class*, New York: Viking Press.

Wachtel, Howard and Adelsheim, Peter (1976), *The Inflationary Impact of Unemployment*, Washington, DC: US Government Printing Office.

Waller, William (1982), 'The Evolution of the Veblenian Dichotomy', *Journal of Economic Issues*, 16 (September), 757–71.

Whalen, Charles J. (1993), 'Saving Capitalism by Making It Good', *Journal of Economic Issues*, 27 (December), 1155–79.

Whalen, Charles J. (1996a), 'A Note on 'The Myth of Institutionalist Method'', *Journal of Economic Issues*, 28 (September).

Whalen, Charles J. (ed.) (1996b), *Political Economy for the 21st Century*, Armonk, NY: M.E. Sharpe.

Wilber, Charles and Harrison, Robert (1978), 'The Methodological Basis of Institutional Economics', *Journal of Economic Issues*, 12 (March), 61–89.

Witte, Edwin (1954), 'Institutional Economics as Seen by an Institutional Economist', *Southern Economic Journal*, 21 (October), 131–40.

6 Feminist economics: let me count the ways

Ulla Grapard

Introduction

The invitation to join a dialogue among different schools of thought in economics demands that the emerging field of *feminist economics* identifies itself in relation to other methodological approaches and defines the boundaries around its intellectual territory.

For me, this is slightly problematic because it presumes the existence of a relatively fixed core of shared assumptions and methodological practices that unites 'us' and sets us apart from 'them'. One reason for my reluctance to create insiders and outsiders in this manner is the fact that feminism in general is characterized by a multitude of voices which express a broad diversity of assumptions about human behaviors, about western scientific practices, and about interpretations of economic and political realities. At the moment, feminist economics is not so much a separate school of thought, as it is a way of reacting to the prevailing paradigms within the economics discipline. In that role, we critically examine existing schools of thought and point out that there is a fundamental problem with all claims to knowledge and methodologies that systematically and persistently ignore, or downplay, issues of gender.

Consequently, the analyses and policy prescriptions proposed by feminist economics are likely to broaden and change economic inquiry to include such issues. As more scholarship in this vein is produced, a clearer image of the research agenda of feminists economics will undoubtedly emerge. Feminist economics recruits its sympathizers from the existing political and methodological continuum in the profession as well as from practitioners outside the field and outside the academy. Among the adherents engaged with the community of feminist economics there are, for example, neoclassical, institutionalist, and radical feminist economists; there are scholars in other disciplines interested in feminist economics; and there are activists and practitioners positioned outside the academy.

If I am nevertheless to single out what distinguishes feminist economics from other schools of thought, I find it useful to look to three different areas of concerns: (1) questions about human nature; (2) the assumptions and methodologies of western science; and (3) definitions of the proper domain of economic inquiry. While other schools of thought have often criticized the mainstream, neoclassical paradigm in these specific areas, none have systematically emphasized the role gender plays in the economy and in the construction of economic knowledge and methods.

When economists take as axiomatic certain propositions about human nature and rely on behavioral characteristics which are based on 'common knowledge' and that are so 'obvious' or 'self-evident' that they need no further justification, feminists are particularly keen to open up those assumptions to scrutiny. Any foundational proposition in the economics discipline that starts from a naturalized or essentialist position concerning human behavior will therefore be contested by feminist economics. In particular the tendency to focus all inquiry of human behavior on men's behavior and taking male behavior as the human norm will be seen as missing half the picture. The assumptions about human nature which show up as behavioral characteristics of *homo economicus* have thus been shown to be based on a masculine model, a model that in fact is intricately bound up with the repudiation of its oppositional female 'nature'.

When dualistic categories are applied to define what is human as that which is associated with a male human being, those categories are defined in terms of their 'opposites': man is defined by being not woman, rational by being not irrational, objective by being not subjective (Nelson, 1992; Ferber and Nelson, 1993). An analysis of economists' uses of the Robinson Crusoe character makes explicit some of these connections (Grapard, 1995). The economic agent in neoclassical models is created out of nowhere as a Hobbesian mushroom: unencumbered by social ties he need not concern himself with reproductive labor associated with women, children and the elderly.

Feminist economics has benefited greatly from theoretical advances made in other disciplines. New perspectives of interdisciplinary feminist theories allow us to identify more clearly the role played by gender as a category of analysis. These theoretical approaches dispute the notion that the roles men and women perform in any given society are determined by fixed, biological sexual characteristics. Even if we were to agree that the categories male and female are universally found in human societies, the implications in terms of ascribed characteristics and behaviors for the two genders can still vary widely across cultures. What is considered appropriate masculine behavior in one culture may be deemed feminine in another.

While a majority of people may think that the sexual division of labor is natural and that it flows directly from women's ability to bear children, anthropologists have shown that while men and women tend to perform different tasks in different cultures, there is no necessary correlation between the kind of work and the sex of the person across cultures. Our culture's traditional division of labor may well seem consistent with our culture's notions of masculinity and femininity, but that does not tell us what determines what. It is very possible that a hierarchical division of labor is articulated through a gender system thus providing a cachet of naturalness to a social distribution of power over resources. The apparent naturalness, however, should be looked at critically: is not a sufficient reason for adopting an essentialist interpretation that assumes gender roles follow from biology.

When we thus use the word gender rather than sex to talk about a system of masculine and feminine attributes and roles, we are emphasizing the extent to which the categories men and women are socially constructed as part of a larger social system, and not determined by biological invariants. The move away from biological determinism thus allows us to better analyze the changing social, political and economic interests articulated in gendered institutions of our culture. We can look at knowledge creation and assumptions about men and women as specific historical constructs, and we can begin to articulate visions of social change that do not take the categories masculine and feminine as invariate givens.

By opening up some of the fundamental categories through which we think about social issues, feminist economics reveals the extent to which our assumptions, our theories and our policy prescription come out of profoundly gendered world views. This analysis is necessary if we are to understand the mechanisms through which the systematic exclusion of female agency in the conceptual and actual world of economics has taken place.

Concretely, this means that in addition to the theoretical and analytical discussion of the criticisms and changes proposed by feminist economics, the practical arrangement whereby feminist economists have managed to constitute themselves as a group is worth paying attention to. First I will therefore briefly outline the institutional boundaries of the organization created with the expressed purpose of providing a space for the active exploration of feminist economics in the intellectual community, centered in, but not restricted to, the academy. Next, I shall explore how feminist analyses of what has been called the 'gendered lenses' of our culture (Bem, 1993) lead to insights about the economic discipline's assumptions about human nature, the scientific method, the proper domain of economics, and the fundamental categories of economic analysis. In that context I will attempt to document the challenges presented to the 'malestream' profession by the rapidly expanding scholarship coming out of the new field of feminist economics. By necessity, the feminist economic scholarship referred to in this paper will be a small selection of what feminist economists have actually produced. In particular, I want to acknowledge that much valuable feminist work has prepared the way for the current efforts. The choice of considering primarily work closely associated with the establishment of the International Association For Feminist Economics (IAFFE) means unfortunately that a lot of the earlier work goes unmentioned here.

Institutional structures

Since the mid-70s the American Economic Association (AEA) has charged the Committee on the Status of Women in the Economics Profession (CSWEP) with monitoring the position of women in the profession and with undertaking activities to improve that position. CSWEP has been very influential in organizing sessions at the national and regional professional meetings where women economists have had a greater chance for presenting their work. The sessions are of course not restricted to women participants, nor should it be assumed that women economists always work on 'women's issues'. Three times a year CSWEP issues a Newsletter with excellent advice on how women economists can improve their careers; it also documents many of the barriers women face in graduate schools, in the job market and employment generally, and in getting their work published.

Around 1990, a group of mostly women economists decided that although CSWEP was doing an invaluable service to the community of economists interested in the professional advancement of women in economics, there was not much scope in CSWEP's mandate for feminist advocacy that reached beyond the narrow professional interests of mainstream women economists. In the June 1991 CSWEP Newsletter there was a note announcing that a network of feminist economists was being organized by April Aerni of Nazareth College and Jean Shackelford of Bucknell University. At the January 1992 ASSA meetings in New Orleans, a group of founding members decided to form what was to become the International Association For Feminist Economics (IAFFE) as a separate, non-profit member organization of the ASSA. Today, IAFFE has a very active electronic mail network, *Femecon*, and it issues a regular newsletter and bulletins. IAFFE organizes sessions at the national ASSA meetings as well as at the regional meetings, and it holds it own annual summer conferences. In May, 1995, the first issue of the organization's new journal, *Feminist Economics*, was published by Routledge.

I see the institutional structures of IAFFE as providing a forum within which it is possible to talk seriously about feminist economics. IAFFE also defines one set of loose and flexible boundaries within which we can locate the formation of an interpretive community. The following three purposes listed on the organization's promotional pamphlet are particularly relevant to the approach of this paper:

1. to foster dialogue and resource sharing among economists and others from all over the world who take feminist viewpoints
2. to foster evaluations of the underlying constructs of the economics discipline from feminist perspectives
3. to promote interaction among researchers, activists, and policy makers in order to improve scholarship and policy.

These three statements point to aspects that unite feminist economics. Across intellectual and political differences, the commitment to dialogue and to the creation of a community committed to feminist perspectives is important. A close examination of the philosophical and theoretical underpinnings of economic discourse will allow us to identify its gendered nature. The last statement encourages us to bring the consequences of feminist insights into the arena of policy making. These aspects will be further discussed below.

Feminist perspectives

What does it mean to take a feminist point of view? I think it means adopting a perspective that is informed by the understanding that gender – as an organizing principle, as a fundamental way of categorizing – is one of the most important features of our way of thinking and of structuring social relations. Feminist theory from other disciplines has contributed greatly to our realization of how profoundly issues of gender affect what we think and experience. Among the more notable are: philosophy (Bordo, 1987; Harding, 1986, 1993; Longino, 1990, 1993; Minnich, 1990); political science (Elshtain, 1981; Pateman, 1988); history (Scott, 1988; Nicholson, 1986, 1990); psychology (Bem, 1993; Chodorow, 1978; Gilligan, 1982); and the life sciences (Fausto-Sterling, 1992; Haraway, 1988, 1989; Hubbard, 1988; Keller, 1985).

From human nature to economic agent

The assumption that men and women are cultural and social constructs without a given, biologically determined nature is shared by most feminists. Feminist scholarship has shown how earlier medical scientific literature managed to define women solely in terms of their biological role as mothers of the race. Medical and biological scientific assertions thus provided excuses for excluding women from higher education by insisting that young women's reproductive organs would be harmed if the vital flow of blood to women's wombs were to be diverted for use in their brains (Smith-Rosenberg and Rosenberg, 1973). The modern turn to sociobiology can be seen as another attempt to limit our vision of the potential for change, and the empirical foundations for such a view are widely disputed (Bem, 1993; Fausto-Sterling, 1992). If human biological evolution is assumed to prescribe narrowly defined and universal behaviors, we are again in a discourse that sets limits for our imagination and our sense of purpose by insisting that human genes carry unequivocal social messages. If we believe that biology tells us unambiguously what is natural and what is not, the sole reference point for women is again their role as breeders responsible for the continuation of the race. Of course, many scientists do not believe that nature and nurture can be so easily delineated, and some argue that even the categories 'male' and 'female' as representing universally recognized sexed bodies are more ambiguous than we usually think (Fausto-Sterling, 1992). Many economists and sociobiologists, however, seem to enjoy each other's company. They share behavioral assumptions and operate with compatible models of constrained optimization.

England (1993) points out that three basic assumptions of neoclassical economics all flow from a 'separative model' of human nature: (1) that interpersonal utility comparisons are impossible; (2) that tastes are exogenous; and (3) that actors have independent utility functions. Such a separative self is illusory both because all humans begin life in a state of intense dependency, but also because while it may not be from the butcher's benevolence that we expect our dinner, as Adam Smith puts it, most men, in fact, have long expected their dinner from the unremunerated labor of their wives and mothers (Folbre and Hartmann, 1988; Grapard, 1992). Confining the inquiry of economics to the public sphere of the market place makes women's domestic lives and labor invisible and without a measure of economic value. Although feminist economists obviously are not the only ones to contest the view of human nature expressed in the character of *homo economicus* (Gerald Smith's chapter on Humanist Economics does so in this book), they are, however, almost alone in emphasizing that he is a gendered caricature, not just a human caricature. Feminist analysis has pointed to his masculinity even as textbook authors try to fool us by throwing in a liberal dose of the word *she* or by neutering the economic agent.

Feminist perspectives on science
Human nature is not the only concept that has been masculinized in western thought. Feminist philosophers and scientists have increasingly come to question the gendered underpinnings of western scientific practices. In this critical project they are joining a great number of contemporary thinkers from several disciplines who contest the scientific paradigm associated with the Enlightenment's belief in our ability to establish universal and absolute categories of analysis and truth claims based on objective criteria. Kuhn's early work on scientific paradigms (1970) as well as writings by Lakatos (1976), Rorty (1979, 1982) and Lyotard (1984) have been important critical contributions to the current discussion of the scientific method. The discussion of what makes knowledge claims valid in a given scientific field points to the importance of a discipline's first principles and especially to the question of who has the authority and legitimate power to define those principles. The social structures that bind a scholarly community together are thus accorded a practical importance in the recent debates that the positivist creed has long denied.

The feminist community has widely differing opinions about the definition of objectivity. Some feminist empiricists have argued that science is deficient because it has not included women's voices. Including women would make for better science. The stylized facts would stand a better chance of being right, for example, if facts about women and women's lives were confirmed by women's voices. In this view, the search for objectivity isn't futile, but until now the scientific community has not been objective in the sense that it has ignored relevant information by excluding women's experiences and devaluing women's voices (Harding, 1986; Nelson, 1995; Wooley, 1993). Faced with the critique that mainstream economics is a masculinist project, the established discipline can react in several ways. It can dismiss the importance of the critique by saying 'so be it', as Nelson puts it. Or it can try to widen the field to incorporate new dimensions of human behavior in the realization that not to do so would constitute a limitation rather than a strength of economic analysis (Nelson, 1995).

The reconsideration of objectivity that is prompted by the notion that knowledge claims emerge from socially positioned communities in historically specific circumstances forces us to confront new questions. If we move beyond the belief in a universally valid, objective, value-free science, we still need to decide how to distinguish and discriminate among conflicting claims of truth and knowledge. Do we have to abandon all attempts to set up evaluative criteria, or is it possible to recognize that what we call truth will be true to a specific interpretive community, in a specific time and place? (Hubbard, 1981; Haraway, 1988.) The recognition that all knowledge is situated knowledge, and that it depends on a historically constituted community for validation implies that science is in fact social knowledge (Longino, 1990). As such, validation of scientific knowledge claims depends on configurations of economic and political power and on access to institutional set ups which can confer legitimacy and authority (Seiz, 1992; Strassmann, 1993a, 1993b; Strassmann and Polanyi, 1995). This does not mean, however, that anything goes. Saying that the rules are derived in a social context and that standards are maintained by a community with certain interests in the discipline only states the obvious to most researchers.

In economics, McCloskey (1985) is one of the first to have paid attention to the rhetorical practices involved in our discipline's claim to scientific status. McCloskey points out that economists in fact do not practice what they preach: the official rhetoric of economics is wedded to the positivist scientific method, but, in reality, economists argue on much wider grounds when they consider historical precedents, the power of authority, and issues of morality. McCloskey (1994) emphasizes the methodological importance of persuasion, and he discusses the extent to which it marks the efforts of an interpretive community in establishing foundations and boundaries for an intellectual discipline.

Studying Foucault, Derrida and other thinkers associated with the postmodern turn in literary and cultural studies has encouraged a number of economists to pay attention to the rhetoric of the economics discipline and to apply the method of 'deconstruction' to the texts of economics (Amariglio, 1988; Rosetti, 1992; Brown, 1994; see also Chapter 8 in this book). By deconstructing the dichotomies through which western thinking establishes exclusive categories of analysis and hierarchical orderings of opposite pairs, it becomes apparent that most of these opposites in fact are gendered pairs. The masculine characteristics of rationality, intellect, culture, and objectivity are thus contrasted with the feminine characteristics of irrationality, emotions, nature and subjectivity. But precisely because the terms are constructed as opposites, the terms on the masculine side of the equivalencies can not be conceived outside the contrast to its opposite, feminine, concept. For feminist economics this development has been particularly important because it provides the tools with which to unravel and contest the otherwise invisible and hidden gendered structures of disciplinary discourse.

However, a postmodernist approach also forces feminists to examine critically the discourse of their own scholarship (Williams, 1993). If men and women indeed are socially constructed categories, how can we talk about policy measures, for instance, that advance women's interests without acknowledging that the term *women* is not a universal, unambiguous category of analysis? Privileging one perspective on social relations runs the danger of ignoring the extent to which the category *women* is in fact 'unstable' and historically constituted. Depending on class, age, ethnicity, and other characteristics of the speaking subject, the term 'women' can take on a number of possible meanings. The aforementioned demand for a more objective economics that incorporates women's experiences and viewpoints has to confront the issue of which *women*. Is it ever possible to develop a conceptual framework for economics that adequately represents all aspects of gender, race, ethnicity and class? These questions are not easily settled.

The proper domain of economics?

The concrete political and social structures within which *homo economicus* operates are not scrutinized very often by economists. We generally know that the small firms that emerged in England at the time of the Industrial Revolution have served as models for 'the firm' in our model of perfect competition. When it became clear that most exchanges in modern economies did not, in fact, take place in such a competitive environment, economic theories of imperfect competition were developed to explain the implications for output decisions, price formation, profits and consumer surplus. Neoclassical economic theory has not, however, seriously reconsidered the theoretical implications of the gendered structure of the political order that underlies our economic models.

In the field of political science, however, feminist political theorists have shown that the democratic rights of citizens in a liberal democracy in the seventeenth and eighteenth century are in fact defined as *male* rights, and that the separation of civil society into a public and a private sphere rests on an assumption of different male and female natures. The difference invariably relates to women's ability to bear children, and it is used as a natural justification for women's subordination (Elshtain, 1981; Pateman, 1988). Feminist economists have explored how this historical split between the public and the private sphere has influenced economists' view of women and women's roles (Folbre and Hartmann, 1988; Jennings, 1993).

In the history of mainstream economics, we find a strong anti-feminist trend even as a few, such as J.S. Mill, express a concern over the injustice and the consequences of women's lack of political and economic rights (Pujol, 1992). In the Marxist tradition, Engels provides an analysis of the evolution of gender relations and the family that explicitly links property relation to marriage patterns and the sexual division of labor, but he pays little attention to the actual reproductive and caring labor that women perform in the domestic sphere (Engels, 1972). Until fairly recently, women did not have the right to own or dispose of property, and they could not enter into binding contracts or act on their own behalf in a court of law. The distinction between the public and the private sphere meant that women's economic role and the labor undertaken in the private sphere were excluded from consideration by the economics discipline. Since the time of Adam Smith it has thus been the practice to confine economic inquiry to transactions taking place in the market place. In accordance with the views of the social contract theories of Hobbes, Locke and Hume, women are expected to fulfill their 'natural' role as caregiver and nurturer of children in the private sphere. Adam Smith argued that the motives and modes of conduct in the private sphere were entirely separate from what prevailed in the public sphere where men's contractual trade and exchange relationships take place (Folbre and Hartmann, 1988). From Adam Smith to Gary Becker, utility and profit maximizing behavior is assumed to prevail in the public market place while behavior in the household is characterized by altruism and concern for others (England, 1993).

When feminist economics thus wants to foster evaluations of the underlying constructs from a feminist perspective, it means that we need to open up the categories that economists have long 'naturalized' and taken for granted: a division of labor based on the dichotomous view of men's and women's natures and the prescribed public and private activities. The historical tendency to focus exclusively on relations among men in the market place has been accompanied by a complete dismissal of women's productive and reproductive labor in the household.

Economics of the family

Becker's original work on the allocation of time opens up economic analysis to considerations of optimization models with constraints formulated to combine money and time (Becker, 1965). This work has facilitated the development of the economics of the family. The 'New Home Economics', however, presents less of a feminist challenge to neoclassical economics and 'business as usual' than one might have thought possible. While the economics of the family incorporates household activities and provides a three-way choice between market work, household work and leisure, the model ends up being primarily a justification and confirmation of the 'naturalness' of the status quo. For example, in Becker's version (1981), the husband goes to work in the market place while the wife stays at home to raise their children. Based on a standard trade model, the model assumes that women have a comparative advantage in cleaning, cooking and raising children. By naturalizing women's and men's preferences, women's low earnings in the market place are explained as the natural outcome of women's decision to stay at home; and their staying at home is explained as a function of their low opportunity cost! The family maximizes utility, i.e., the *husband* maximizes family utility, since he is altruistic and takes care of everyone. Conflicts are resolved by consensus and by the power of the purse.

In reaction to this 'benevolent dictator' model of a single family utility function, game theoretic approaches to conflicts of interests within the family make it possible to show how decision-making depends on the relative bargaining strengths of the involved parties (Manser and Brown, 1980; McElroy and Horney, 1981; McElroy, 1990; Lundberg and Pollack, 1993). To feminist economists concerned with an explanation or analysis of how bargaining power within a partnership depends on power structures established in the larger economic and political sphere outside the individual household, however, the neoclassical game theoretic approach does not go far enough (McCrate, 1987; Seiz, 1991). Preferences are still not endogenous, and issues of systematic asymmetrical distributions of power cannot be adequately addressed in these models.

Feminist economists do not argue that men and women do not face historically determined different choices and constraints. They argue, however, that choices and constraints are socially constructed in such a way as to systematically turn difference into women's disadvantage. The labor that has traditionally been associated with women's sphere has thus been ignored as productive work and has been defined primarily in terms of emotional relationships ('priceless' labor done for love).

Consequences for policy makers

An evaluation of the intellectual practices of economics leads to a different perspective on the importance of a gendered point of view. If women's activities are made invisible by the categories and taxonomies that economists develop, it would be surprising if the analysis and actual policy prescriptions following from that framework ended up serving the interests of women or the interest of society very well. Feminist economics forces us to confront the issues of systematic biases and the role of gendered power relations because economic analysis and policy prescriptions that are based on terribly flawed assumptions can have unexpected consequences.

I will provide just a couple of examples of the consequences following from conceptual frameworks which ignore issues of gender. In the domestic policy area, it seems clear that the crises we experience in the areas of child care, elder care and health care are reflections of our habit of relying on women's non-paid labor for these services. Economists know that there always is an opportunity cost associated with women's choice to stay home rather than work in the labor force, but as long as many married women stay home or are seen as working for pin-money rather than for economic survival, it is easy to underestimate the value of the contribution to national welfare represented by the reproductive labor going on in the household. However, work performed without pay does not entitle the worker to pension benefits or social security in the worker's own right. Women are thus at a disadvantage in old age whether they stay home or work for traditional low pay in women's jobs, and we find an extremely high number of elderly women living in poverty (Olson, 1990). In Norway, satellite accounts are now being used to integrate unpaid reproductive labor into the calculations of that part of old age pension benefits which is dependent on earned income (Aslaksen and Koren, 1992).

In the field of development economics, the implications of economic experts from the west exporting our culture's gendered lenses and incorporating them into development programs have had serious adverse consequences for women's economic well-being (Elson, 1991). Even after it was pointed out that subsistence agriculture was women's work throughout Sub-Saharan Africa, land rights and cooperative extension projects focused on men (Boserup, 1970). In the case of cattle herding communities in Kenya, development planners' inability to see the relationship between gender, property rights and resource allocation has deprived many women of their livelihood (Kettel, 1992). Projects that encourage men to raise cattle for slaughter may well increase men's cash income. However, it leads to ecologically unsound practices, and it ignores traditional property rights that give women control over milk and milk products. The transfer of economic resources in effect makes it difficult for many women to feed themselves and their children, and without other options, many have ended up in peripheral economic activities in the slums of the cities. Development planning that is based on the assumptions of a western, male-bread-winner model has thus had costly consequences not only for women and children, but also for the traditional industries and trade that rely on women's productive labor.

Conclusion

This paper has attempted to present the concerns and contributions of the emerging field of feminist economics. Because it is a relatively new area within economics, I have chosen to document its focus by looking at the institutional structures that identify its broadly defined interpretive community. Feminist economics spans a wide spectrum of feminist perspectives and draws on feminist insights from other disciplines to critically examine the gendered underpinnings of the established schools of thought within the economics discipline. Much of the work that falls under the rubric of feminist economics points to problematic theoretical concepts in economics that reinforce the status quo and render women and much of their labor invisible. Other work makes it clear that there are very real economic consequences for women's well being following from this neglect. As a result, the formulation of policy measures that explicitly consider gendered power relations and the majority of women's lack of control over economic resources are likely to depend in important ways on the analyses and theoretical reformulations being developed by feminist economics.

References

Amariglio, Jack L. (1988), 'The Body, Economic Discourse, and Power: An Economist's Introduction to Foucault', *History of Political Economy*, **20** (4).

Aslaksen, Iulie and Koren, Charlotte (1992), 'Marriage, Unpaid Household Work, and Social Security Benefits: A Feminist Look at the Norwegian Experience', Paper presented at the First Conference on Feminist Economics, Washington, DC, July 24–6.

Becker, Gary S. (1965), 'A Theory of the Allocation of Time', *Economic Journal*, **75** (299), 493–517.

Becker, Gary S. (1981), *A Treatise on the Family*, Cambridge: Harvard University Press.

Bem, Sandra Lipsitz (1993), *The Lenses of Gender*, New Haven: Yale University Press.

Bordo, Susan (1987), *The Flight to Objectivity: Essays on Cartesianism and Culture*, Albany: State University of New York Press.

Boserup, Ester (1970), *Women's Role in Economic Development*, New York: St. Martin's Press

Brown, Doug (1994), 'Radical Institutionalism and Postmodern Feminist Theory', in Janice Peterson and Doug Brown (eds), *The Economic Status of Women Under Capitalism: Institutional Economics and Feminist Theory*, Aldershot, UK: Edward Elgar.

Chodorow, Nancy (1978), *The Reproduction of Motherhood: Psychoanalysis and the Sociology of Gender*, Berkeley: University of California Press.

Elshtain, Jean Bethke (1981), *Public Man, Private Woman*, Princeton: Princeton University Press.

Elson, Diane (1991), 'Male Bias: An Overview' in Diane Elson (ed.), *Male Bias in the Development Process*, Manchester: Manchester University Press.

Engels, Friedrich (1884, 1972), *The Origin of the Family, Private Property and the State*, Harmondsworth, England: Penguin Books.

England, Paula (1993), 'The Separative Self: Androcentric Bias in Neoclassical Assumptions', in Marianne A. Ferber and Julie A. Nelson (eds), *Beyond Economic Man: Feminist Theory and Economics*, Chicago: University of Chicago Press.

Fausto-Sterling, Anne (1992), *Myths of Gender*, New York: Basic Books.

Ferber, Marianne A. and Nelson, Julie A. (1993), 'The Social Construction of Economics and the Social Construction of Gender', in Marianne A. Ferber and Julie A. Nelson (eds), *Beyond Economic Man: Feminist Theory and Economics*, Chicago: University of Chicago Press.

Folbre, Nancy and Hartmann, Heidi (1988), 'The Rhetoric of Self-interest: Ideology of Gender in Economic Theory' in Arjo Klamer, Donald N. McCloskey and Robert M. Solow (eds), *The Consequences of Economic Rhetoric*, Cambridge: Cambridge University Press.

Gilligan, Carol (1982), *In a Different Voice: Psychological Theory and Women's Development*, Cambridge, MA: Harvard University Press.

Grapard, Ulla (1992), 'Who Can See the Invisible Hand? Or, From the Benevolence of the Butcher's Wife', Paper presented at the First Conference on Feminist Economics, Sponsored by IAFFE, Washington, DC, July 24–26.

Grapard, Ulla (1995), 'Robinson Crusoe: The Quintessential Economic Man?', *Feminist Economics*, **1** (1), 33–52.

Haraway, Donna (1988), 'Situated Knowledge: The Science Question in Feminism and the Privilege of the Partial Perspective', *Feminist Studies*, **14** (3).

Haraway, Donna (1989), *Primate Vision: Gender, Race and Nature in the World of Modern Science*, New York: Routledge.

Harding, Sandra (1986), *The Science Question in Feminism*, Ithaca: Cornell University Press.

Harding, Sandra (1993), 'Rethinking Standpoint Epistemology: What is Strong Objectivity?' in Linda Alcoff and Elizabeth Potter (eds), *Feminist Epistemologies*, New York: Routledge.

Hartmann, Heidi I. (1979), 'The Unhappy Marriage Between Marxism and Feminism: Towards a More Progressive Union', *Capital and Class*, **8**, 1–33.

Hubbard, Ruth (1988), 'Some Thoughts About the Masculinity of the Natural Sciences', in Mary McCanny Gergen (ed.), *Feminist Thought and the Structure of Knowledge*, New York: New York University Press.

Jennings, Ann L. (1993), 'Public or Private? Institutional Economics and Feminism', in Marianne A. Ferber and Julie A. Nelson (eds), *Beyond Economic Man: Feminist Theory and Economics*, Chicago: University of Chicago Press.

Keller, Evelyn Fox (1985), *Reflections on Gender and Science*, New Haven: Yale University Press.

Kettel, Bonnie (1992), 'Gender Distortions and Development Disasters: Women and Milk in African Herding Systems', *NWSA Journal*, **4** (1), 23–41.

Klamer, Arjo, McCloskey, Donald N. and Solow, Robert M. (eds) (1988), *The Consequences of Economic Rhetoric*, Cambridge: Cambridge University Press.

Kuhn, Thomas S. (1970), *The Structure of Scientific Revolutions*, Chicago: University of Chicago Press.

Lakatos, Imre (1976), *Proofs and Refutations: The Logic of Mathematical Discovery*, Cambridge: Cambridge University Press.

Longino, Helen (1990), *Science as Social Knowledge: Values and Objectivity in Scientific Inquiry*, Princeton: Princeton University Press.

Longino, Helen (1993), 'Subjects, Power and Knowledge: Description and Prescription in Feminist Philosophies of Science' in Linda Alcoff and Elizabeth Potter (eds), *Feminist Epistemologies*, New York: Routledge.

Lundberg, Shelly and Pollack, Robert (1993), 'Separate Spheres Bargaining and the Marriage Market', *Journal of Political Economy*, **100** (6), 988–1010.

Lyotard, Jean-Francois (1984), *The Postmodern Condition*, Minneapolis: University of Minnesota Press.

Manser, Marilyn and Brown, Murray (1980), 'Marriage and Household Decisionmaking: A Bargaining Analysis', *International Economic Review*, **21** (1), 31–44.

McCrate, Elaine (1987), 'Trade, Merger and Employment: Economic Theory on Marriage', *Review of Radical Political Economics*, **19** (1), 73–89.

McElroy, Marjorie B. and Horney, Mary Jean (1981), 'Nash-Bargaining Household Decisions: Toward a Generalization of the Theory of Demand', *International Economic Review*, **22** (2), 333–49.

McElroy, Marjorie B. (1990), 'The Empirical Content of Nash-Bargained Household Behavior', *The Journal of Human Resources*, **25** (4), 559–83.

McCloskey, Donald N. (1985), *The Rhetoric of Economics*, Madison: Wisconsin University Press.

McCloskey, Donald N. (1994), *Knowledge and Persuasion in Economics*, Cambridge: Cambridge University Press.

Minnich, Elizabeth Kamarck (1990), *Transforming Knowledge*, Philadelphia: Temple University Press.

Nelson, Julie A. (1992), 'Gender, Metaphor, and the Definition of Economics', *Economics and Philosophy*, **8** (1), 103–25.

Nelson, Julie A. (1993), 'The Study of Choice or the Study of Provisioning? Gender and the Definition of Economics', in Marianne A. Ferber and Julie A. Nelson (eds), *Beyond Economic Man: Feminist Theory and Economics*, Chicago: University of Chicago Press.

Nelson, Julie A. (1995), 'Feminism and Economics', *Journal of Economic Perspectives*, **9** (2), 131–48.

Nicholson, Linda J. (1986), *Gender and History: The Limits of Social Theory in the Age of the Family*, New York: Columbia University Press.

Nicholson, Linda J. (ed.) (1990), *Feminism/Postmodernism*, New York: Routledge.

Olson, Paulette I. (1990), 'Mature Women and the Rewards of Domestic Ideology', *Journal of Economic Issues*, **24** (2).

Pateman, Carole (1988), *The Sexual Contract*, Stanford: Stanford University Press.

Pujol, Michele (1992), *Feminism and Anti-Feminism in Early Economic Thought*, Aldershot, UK: Edward Elgar.

Rorty, Richard (1979), *Philosophy and the Mirror of Nature*, Princeton: Princeton University Press.

Rorty, Richard (1982), *Consequences of Pragmatism*, Minneapolis: University of Minnesota Press.

Rosetti, Jane (1992), 'Deconstruction, Rhetoric, and Economics', in Neil de Marchi (ed.), *Post-Popperian Methodology of Economics: Recovering Practice*, Boston and Dordrecht: Kluwer Academic Publishers.

Scott, Joan W. (1988), *Gender and the Politics of History*, New York: Columbia University Press.

Seiz, Janet A. (1991), 'The Bargaining Approach and Feminist Methodology', *Review of Radical Political Economy*, **23** (1 & 2), 22–9.

Seiz, Janet A. (1992), 'Gender and Economic Research', in Neil de Marchi (ed.), *Post-Popperian Methodology of Economics: Recovering Practice*, Boston and Dordrecht: Kluwer Academic Publishers.

Smith-Rosenberg, Carroll and Rosenberg, Charles (1973), 'The Female Animal: Medical and Biological Views of Woman and Her Role in Nineteenth-Century America', *Journal of American History*, **60** (September), 332–56.

Strassmann, Diana (1993a), 'The Stories of Economics and the Power of the Storyteller', *History of Political Economy*, **25** (1).

Strassmann, Diana (1993b), 'Not a Free Market: The Rhetoric of Disciplinary Authority in Economics', in Marianne A. Ferber and Julie A. Nelson (eds), *Beyond Economic Man: Feminist Theory and Economics*, Chicago: University of Chicago Press, 54–68.

Strassmann, Diana and Polanyi, Livia (1995), 'The Economist as Storyteller: What the Texts Reveal', in Edith Kuiper and Jolande Sap (eds), *Out of the Margin: Feminist Perspectives on Economic Theory*, London: Routledge, 129–50.

Whalen, Charles and Whalen, Linda (1994), 'Institutionalism: A Useful Foundation for Feminist Economics?' in Janice Peterson and Doug Brown (eds), *The Economic Status of Women*

Under Capitalism: Institutional Economics and Feminist Theory, Aldershot, UK: Edward Elgar.

Williams, Rhonda M. (1993), 'Race, Deconstruction, and the Emergent Agenda of Feminist, Economic Theory', in Marianne A. Ferber and Julie A. Nelson (eds), *Beyond Economic Man: Feminist Theory and Economics*, Chicago: University of Chicago Press.

Wooley, Frances R. (1993), 'The Feminist Challenge to Neoclassical Economics', *Cambridge Journal of Economics*, **17**, 485–500.

7   Humanist economics: from *homo economicus* to *homo sapiens*

Gerald Alonzo Smith

In a broad but vacuous sense, all economic theories are 'humanist econom-ics',[1] since all explore the economic systems of human beings,[2] and all necessarily presuppose a definition of what it means to be human. However, an exploration of what it means to be human can either be on center stage or can be pushed into the background. It is possible that economic theorists become so enthralled with a certain intellectual approach that the definition of human nature will be molded to fit the thought processes required by such an approach. This dogmatism inevitably reduces the richness of what it means to be human.

Two visions of humanity

There are two basic and rival visions of human beings which play a decisive role in the formation of any economic theory. According to one vision, *homo sapiens*, it is the nature of humans to strive for that excellence of being which emerges from the deepest and truest part of oneself and which is ultimately, and with difficulty and only partially, recognized by one's reason and will. Some may not recognize this excellence, or even misconceive what this excellence is, and many, if not all, fall short of attaining that excellence of being at which they aim. But all, whatever their degree of recognition, speci-fication, and achievement, are measured by a standard which they discover, first by training and education and then by the very pursuit of that excellence. In brief, humans pursue the good life through a pursuit of reasoned excel-lence.

According to a second image of human beings, *homo economicus*, it is the nature of humans to strive for a particular kind of power, the ability to remake the social and natural world, so far as possible, into conformity with their own desires. The pursuit of this power may be frustrated by failures in judgment or bad luck, but the satisfaction of one's desires, or the maximization of utility, is nonetheless the final goal. In brief, humans pursue the good life through a pursuit of desired goals.[3]

Modern economic theory, while sometimes mentioning in passing the *homo sapiens* view of human nature, has almost always adopted, without question-ing, the *homo economicus* view of human nature as the referent point for their analysis.[4] For the humanist economist a thorough exploration of these two conceptions of human nature is essential.

Spectrum of knowledge

To begin this exploration it is necessary to look at the total picture.[5] Humanity's ultimate challenge is to use the resources of the earth so that as many humans as possible now and in the future maximize the fulfillment of their authentic human selves, whatever this may be. It is helpful to divide up the exploration of this overarching challenge into a spectrum of fields of study. Figure 7.1[6] shows such a spectrum.

Economics is in the middle of this spectrum of knowledge and bridges natural resources and ultimate goals. The humanist economist acknowledges questions within the boundaries of economic theory and also beyond its scope. Human economists acknowledge that for issues such as the availability of natural resources or what constitutes a high-quality human life, the advice of scholars in other fields is invaluable. In turn, these scholars need the advice of economists for aid in analyzing how to allocate material resources to maximize the achievement of fulfilled, high-quality human lives.[7]

Empty world and full world

Serious problems arise for the humanist economist who obtains information from scientists, philosophers and theologians.[8] When economists ask scientists (1) how plentiful are the earth's resources as inputs into the economic system, and (2) how capable is the biosphere of assimilating pollution, they obtain conflicting answers. They can find scientists who view the world's resources as practically unlimited and those who view the world's resources as quite limited. These two conflicting positions have been named (1) the empty-world scenario and (2) the full-world scenario.[9] (See Figure 7.2.)

The humanist economist focuses upon that set of questions which seeks to explore the importance of economic goods and services, since the ultimate goal of an economic system is the fulfillment of human life, and the importance we attach to economic commodities in achieving a high-quality human life will eventually determine how important are the ultimate material resources of the world.[10]

For welfare economics, there are two major implications of these contrasting scenarios about resources. If the empty-world scenario is correct, then because of their plentitude, economic theory can basically ignore natural resources and, consequently, economic growth is certainly possible and will likely continue as a normative goal in macroeconomic theory. If the full-world scenario is correct, then natural resources and their perennial and fragile contribution to the economic process must be somehow directly incorporated into economic theory. A consequence of this approach is that

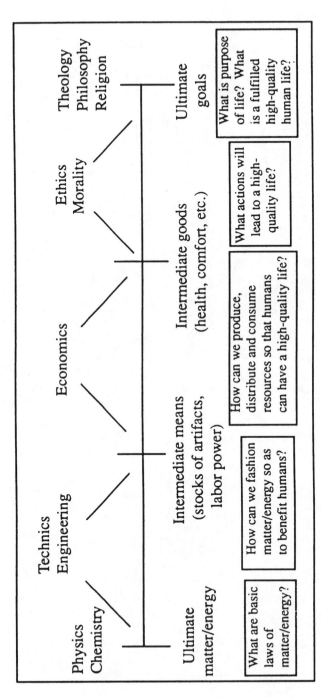

Physics
Chemistry

Technics
Engineering

Economics

Ethics
Morality

Theology
Philosophy
Religion

Ultimate
matter/energy

Intermediate means
(stocks of artifacts,
labor power)

Intermediate goods
(health, comfort, etc.)

Ultimate
goals

What are basic
laws of
matter/energy?

How can we fashion
matter/energy so as
to benefit humans?

How can we produce,
distribute and consume
resources so that humans
can have a high-quality life?

What actions will
lead to a high-
quality life?

What is purpose
of life? What
is a fulfilled
high-quality
human life?

Figure 7.1⁶   A spectrum of knowledge

117

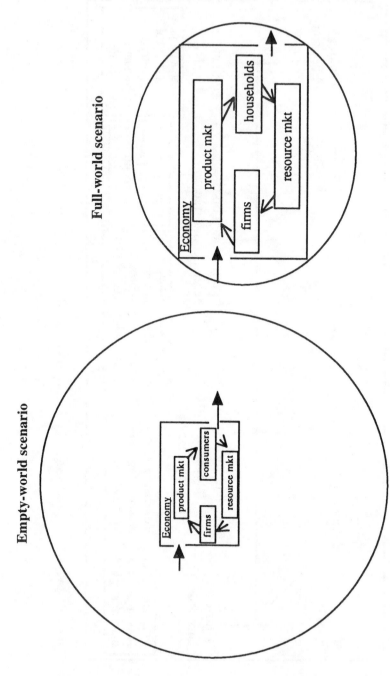

Figure 7.2   The empty- and full-world scenarios

further economic growth may become destructive, and the concept of sustainability rather than economic growth has to become a major, if not *the* major goal, of economic theory. Frugality would have to substitute for profligacy as a desirable item in our economic models. This changing of ultimate goals from growth to sustainability would require major and extended revisions in macroeconomic theory and the corresponding texts, no matter what the school of economics.

Secondly, humanist economists are in a better position to be objective about the question of the plentitude of world's resources than economists of other schools because, in my judgment, of their proposition that economic goods and services produced from such resources are not the ultimate measurement of a high-quality life for *homines sapientes*, as they are for the *homines economici*. This is an important conclusion since if we live on a limited planet, and if human beings are defined as *homines economici* with infinite desires, and the goal of economics is to fulfill as many as possible of these infinite desires, then adherence to an economic theory supporting the never-ending increase in production and consumption of economic goods will inevitably lead to an environmental crisis. A major tenet of the humanist economics creed is that there exists a fundamental harmony between humans and the earth: What is good for the earth must be good for humans, and what is good for humans must be good for the earth.[11]

Humanist versus utilitarian views

Turning to the question of how important are economic goods and services in the achievement of a high-quality human life, it would seem appropriate for economists to seek counsel from philosophers/theologians who take as their topic for study the following ultimate questions: 'What does it mean to be a human person?'; 'What is the purpose of life?'; 'What is a fulfilled life?'; 'What is a high-quality life?' and more specifically, from the ethicists and moral philosophers who study among other questions: 'What is the precise role which economic goods and services play in a high-quality, fulfilled human life?'[12] When one pursues answers to this latter question, one finds a surprising conclusion. The teaching that the fulfillment of human life is to be attained through the satisfaction of desires for economic goods and services is denied by every religion and philosophy known to humankind, except for a shallow variant of Utilitarianism which variant, however, came to rest, in our day, in the theory of contemporary neoclassical economics and in the practice of modern-day 'yuppies'.[13]

Accordingly, I have labeled these two schools of thought on the importance of economic goods and services in a high-quality life as follows: (1) the Aristotelian/religious/humanist view and (2) the utilitarian/yuppie/economist view.

What are the implications for economic theory of these two contrasting schools of thought concerning the importance of economic goods and services to a high-quality human life? First, some general comments are in order.

The utilitarian/yuppie/economics viewpoint would not need to explore further how the economic system leads to a fulfilled human life because of its definition of humans as '*homines economici*' who, as such, are driven by their desires and, by extension, ought to be so driven because there is no known way of evaluating the worth of desires. Thus this school of thought can define as efficient and measure its success by the quantity of desires that it fulfills; or more simply still, as a proxy measurement, by the amount of economic goods and services that people produce and consume; or even more simply by one's income for the individual and by the GDP for the nation. The pursuit of more becomes the goal of economic society. The worst thing that can befall a person or nation is poverty. The role of the primary evaluational adjectives 'good and bad' are replaced by 'more and less'.

Neoclassical economic theory is firmly implanted in the utilitarian/yuppie/economics viewpoint because of two crucial postulates. The first is to treat all effective demand for economic goods and services as equal and given, unquestioned. The second flows from the first and is the decision to choose the maximization of utility as the final goal for an economic system. Since the amount of utility can be measured by the area under the demand curve, and desires are what ultimately determine the shape of this demand curve, it follows that this approach leads directly to the result that desires are the unquestioned and ultimate determinants of value. Though it is called a utility theory of value, it would be more precise to call it a desire theory of value. Since desires are premised as being unlimited, one can never get enough. This is why underlying this school of thought are the two supporting themes of 'More is better' and 'Economic growth is an unquestioned good'. One never finds the word 'enough' in conventional economic literature, nor does one meet the concept of moderation and the related notion of basic limits.[14]

Such economic theory has retreated from the whole discussion of what it means to be a human person. Whatever the cause, the bugle did sound, and the retreat forced all discussion of right and wrong desires and of authentic fulfillment and non-authentic destruction of one's personhood to be moved to the rear and out of sight in economic theory. This retreat was slow, uneven, and also somewhat tentative in the period of classical economics from 1776 to around 1900, but rapid and definitive in the period of neoclassical economics in the twentieth century.

In opposition, humanist economics aligns itself with the position espoused by the major humanistic cultures, philosophies and religions of the world, that economic goods and services are indeed important but only up to a certain point, and that such goods and services are not the final measurement of one's quality of life. Humanist economic theory begins with the traditional definition of the human species as indeed a *homo sapiens* and states that substituting *homo economicus* as a defining attribute of humans is a serious mistake. Translated into English, the *homo sapiens* is a reasoning being who is capable of reflecting upon the world about him- or herself in a reasonable and meaningful manner, who is capable of reflection about one's own nature in a reasonable and meaningful manner, who is capable of reflection about what constitutes authentic fulfillment of this human nature in a reasonable and meaningful manner, and consequently is capable of making reasonable and meaningful and responsible choices leading to one's fulfillment of personhood or excellence of being.[15] By contrast, *homo economicus* is limited to using reason to satisfy as many of one's desires as possible in some sort of mechanistic and calculating manner.

What then would humanist economic analysis involve when it comes to the question of determining the contribution of economic goods and services to a high-quality life? First of all, it neither says nor implies that economic goods and services are unimportant in any absolute sense. When one considers that over two billion people lack sufficient goods to maintain themselves properly, one should not undervalue the efficient production and consumption of goods and services. Nor should one underestimate the efficiency algorithms that neoclassical economics has developed over the past two centuries. Humanistic economics has just as much need for technical and allocative efficiency as does neoclassical economics.

But for the humanist economist, enough of such economic goods and services is enough. After a certain point, the *homo sapiens* realizes that the pursuit of ever more goods and services can become a hindrance rather than an aid in the discovery and pursuit of excellence of personhood. Greed, avarice and addiction to economic goods are to be recognized for what they have always been recognized for by the major religions and humanists: as pathologies rather than accepted as essential components of human nature.[16]

Beyond the pursuit of goods
There is nothing wrong with maximization in itself. The economic nature of allocating given resources for maximum satisfaction cannot possibly be denied, and there is nothing wrong with that economic maximization that wants to produce ever more economic goods and services from fewer resources. What is debatable is whether every one of our desires be considered as final and unquestioned goals in themselves. A similar question is whether we should evaluate our success as individuals and as a nation by the number of desires fulfilled as measured by our personal consumption and GDP. This latter abstraction, derived from the philosophy of utilitarianism, leads us back to *homines economici*, which in turn makes the quantity of economic goods

and services the sole arbiter of what is important in life. In so doing, we do not maximize; nay, we minimize the human person. We maximize production and consumption of things rather than maximize people and their lives. Our economic theory becomes thing-oriented rather than people-oriented.[17] Rather than with the wealth of nations, we should be concerned with the fullness of lives.

A false measurement would not be too harmful, however, if it left only the economics profession in error. But in our times, the economists provide society with the accepted image of economic society, and this image affects the behavior of society.[18] Don Eberle (1995, p. A12) has noted the implications for society in general: 'The 20th century has traded in moral man for economic and psychological man, subjecting him at every turn to either economic inducements or therapeutic treatments. If we are to recover as a society, the 21st century will have to recover a vision of man bearing inherent moral value and moral agency.'[19] The defining aspects of humanity are self-reflection, compassion, commitment to an ideal, and freedom. To take away all four as the concept of *homo economicus* does, is to take away a good share of our humanity.[20]

Major religious and philosophical traditions have emphasized the importance of compassion for those members of the community in need and of sacrifice for the common good in the life of the ordinary human person. These concepts are unable to find any home as such in conventional economic theory, although they sometimes are allowed to exist uneasily in the mind and conscience of the self-interested human being who is at the core of this conventional economics. One almost gets the idea that economists are willing to admit of sacrifice and compassion but consider them as a subtler form of self-interest or as a delusion. Certainly there is some evidence that professional economic training diminishes the importance of sacrifice and compassion in one's own life (see Rhoads, 1985). When one considers the impact of economic theory upon our values, it should come as no surprise that so many Americans vote against paying taxes sufficient to provide important public services. Small wonder that so many public officials think only of their own good and not of the public good.

This lack of compassion, sharing, and sacrifice has another consequence. If a person hopes that the standard of living is to increase in the future, one either has to have faith in technology or one has to have faith in the human spirit and its ability to flourish in an economy that recognizes limits. The *homo economicus* perspective rules out the latter approach for three reasons. First, *homo economicus* does not include compassion as a defining attitude of humanity. Second, *homo economicus* does not ponder about the final goals of life. Third, *homo economicus* desires ever more economic goods and services, so the concept of limits is anathema. It is therefore no accident that conventional economic theorists tend to be optimistic when it comes to technology.[21] Yet, because of addiction to ever more goods and services, there is a basic insecurity.

In contrast, human economists can be and usually are optimistic about the future precisely because of their belief in the compassion, commitment and authentic self-reflection of people, which do not depend on developing powerful technologies and a godlike control of nature. Human economists place their future in the possibility of a virtuous reality rather than in the illusion of virtual reality.

Humanist epistemology

The humanist economist believes that humans should neither be overrated or underrated. In theological terms, modesty will dictate the following conclusions: We are neither god-like men and women who create the world and have total understanding and control of the world that we inhabit, nor are we nullities, accidents of history totally determined by a blind fate.

In epistemological terms, we are aware that we do not know the whole Truth, Truth with a capital 'T'. What we can aspire to know is a reflection of the Truth, truth with a small 't'. The best that human knowledge can aspire to is a reflection of the Truth or some form of correspondence with the Reality that exists (see McCloskey, 1994, pp. 210–12).

Humanist economists are neither absolutists nor relativists. This alone should make us suspicious of that mathematically sophisticated economic analysis which has as a conclusion a whole set of certain and quantifiably exact answers. The only way one can get certain and quantifiable answers when dealing with social problems of humanity is to limit human beings to defined and quantifiable parameters, such as is done with the definition of humans as *homo economicus*. Not surprisingly, as C.S. Lewis (1993) has pointed out, when one aspires to know too much, one ends up by making of one's humanity too little.

The standard education of economists encourages quantifiable measurement and calculation rather than a sense of awe and of one's limits when faced with the basic questions of life. Such an educational approach has the potential to detract more than it adds to the aspiring economist in his/her endeavor to understand the economic system of human society. The mind that pursues predictable regularities can come to feel that such a phenomenon has been explained by these regularities.[22] Conventional economists have a proclivity to ignore the complexity and indeterminateness of reality in favor of the simplicity of the singular. Human economists prefer to confront the complexity and indeterminateness of reality and ignore the simplicity of the singular. Thus not narrow deductive rationality but a balanced rationality and openness to the indeterminate and the irregularities of life is a feature of human economics. It is unwilling to be subjected to the tyranny of quantification and predictability.

Perhaps an even larger and potentially much more significant issue comes into play here if that which Alaisdair MacIntyre has written is true: It is necessary to be striving for the good life, if one wants to write intelligently about the good life.[23] If the humanist economists are to be loyal to the task at hand, they must never forget that they are dealing from first to last with human beings at a certain moment in time with a certain tradition. They must pay due attention to the fact that they themselves are human beings and that the exploration of economics by its very nature is a kind of self-knowledge as well as a certain type of scientific knowledge. Thus humanist economic theory must obey the canons of humanity as well as the logic of science. To state that the purpose of life is to maximize utility by the use of the analytical tools of marginal analysis and quantification, although not totally erroneous, leaves out so much that it tends to make of life a diluted, saccharine, year-long clearance shopping event, a Pepsi-generation taste of life.[24]

The humanist economist recognizes one's limits as well as his/her abilities when dealing with the economic challenges that face humanity. This recognition of limits and sense of awe which turns to poets and artists rather than 'hard' scientists for answers to the basic questions of economics may or may not harm the academic reputation of economists but it will unshackle humanity from the '*homo economicus*' straitjacket that conventional economics would place over the average human being. More than any other reason, this is why it is entitled 'humanist' economics.

Humanist versus conventional economics

Following are eight examples of how humanist economic theory differs from conventional theory.

First, rather than using as a starting point the foundational postulates of neoclassical economic theory, which consist of the necessity of making choices because of limited factors of production and the unlimited desires of the *homo economicus*, the humanist economist would begin with a discussion of the economic goods and services which are needed by the *homo sapiens* in the pursuit of human excellence and authentic self-interest. While it may not be possible to answer these questions in precise detail, it is important to raise the question, how important are economic goods and services to a high-quality life. If such questions are ignored, then they are answered by default. This is a perennial discussion in the sense that as the world evolves and culture develops, so must economic theory adjust. There is no single economic theory adequate for all ages and locations. It is an ongoing narrative. This difference in introductory chapters will reorient the whole economic theory.

Second, humanist economics would have a different definition of economics. Instead of that social science which shows how to make 'efficient' choices when faced with limited resources and unlimited desires,[25] it defines economics as that social science which studies how to make efficient choices using scarce resources so that as many people as possible now and in the future are empowered to pursue excellence.

Third, instead of having as the ultimate goal of the economy the maximization of utility, satisfying as many desires as possible, humanist economic theory has as its overall goal the successful completion of the related dual tasks of making sure that everybody has a sufficiency of economic goods and services and also determining to what extent the economic system makes it possible and contributes to pursue and achieve a fulfilled human life. This clearly is an ambitious task, but one that does believe in the ability of individual humans to be adequate to the task of making such choices. Applied humanist economics deems as efficient and measures as successful the extent to which it accomplishes these dual tasks. In brief, the humanist question is, does the economic system ennoble people to be all that they could and should be?[26]

Fourth, humanist economics, as defined in these pages, would acknowledge the problem of evil in human nature. This is so, because if the pursuit of excellence is a good, then the deliberate pursuit away from excellence has to be labeled as an evil.[27] Conventional economic theory steers even further from the problem of evil than do most modern schools of thought. How could economic theorists explore the problem of evil when beginning by positing that all observed desires are given and therefore the unquestioned basis of its exploration? Ignoring the problem of evil is no solution; it will not help non-excellence become excellence, no matter how much the satisfactions of desires are quantified and maximized. Human economists obviously do not have a complete solution for the problem of evil, but they do acknowledge the problem. This has important consequences for humanist economic theory, not the least of which are that all desires are not equal and, more importantly, that the economic system, along with the political system and other social institutions, has a role to play in combating evil, supporting the search for the good life, and informing action toward that end.

Fifth, the humanist economist believes that since human beings have the ability to a certain degree to distinguish between what is authentic fulfillment and what is not, plus a certain freedom of will to either follow or not follow these authentic desires, what people need is not the satisfaction of the desires they have, but a more authentic set of desires and the support to both pursue and follow these desires. The vital questions are: 'Is it in our best interest to desire more than enough?'; 'Should we encourage such desires?'; 'What are authentic desires?'. The humanist economist appropriately incorporates such questions into economic theory. As a result, a humanist chapter on consumer behavior in microeconomics texts would have to be greatly expanded and would become the key chapter in the text. There would need to be a section on the origin of desires, with possibly a subsection on the role played by persuasive advertising in the formation of our desires. In addition, a discussion would be in order on whether we should pursue happiness through pleasure and satisfaction of desires or through fullness of life and excellence of being.[28]

Sixth, humanist economics questions the total reliance upon the norm of scientific objectivity found in conventional economic theory, leaving out human experience and intuitive information in the process of building up an economic theory. While we need to be careful in using our own experience, the human economist should ask the following question of every (including this one) economic theory: Does it resonate well with my sense of what it means to be a human being?[29]

Seventh is the role that quantification and mathematics plays in these two rival approaches. It is well-known that conventional economic theory, as now taught and practiced in the professional journals, requires that the economist be quite adept in mathematics.[30] The humanist economist may find many uses for quantification and mathematics in his or her analysis, but is nevertheless aware of the limitations of quantification. If it is true that the most important things in life – compassion, the pursuit of truth, commitment to an ideal, the concept of excellence itself – cannot be quantified, then one has to be very careful not to rely excessively upon mathematical techniques. But for the conventional economist, with a *homo economicus* view of human nature, it is a different story. If human nature is a basket of desires, then quantification becomes appropriate. One can measure the desires actually fulfilled by economic goods and services by the area under the demand curve. If all desires are equal and unlimited, more economic goods and services are to be preferred to fewer, and mathematical techniques designed to maximize utility for the consumer and profit for the firm are the criterion by which one can measure one's adeptness and cleverness as an economist. There really is no need for any other evaluative techniques.

Professionals and others
Eighth, since economics, in contrast to the physical sciences, has as its subject matter human society and should have as its goal the achievement of a high-quality life for humans, it is arguable that the ordinary human *qua human* is not so far removed from the expert in economics as he or she is from the expert in physics. As human economists we have to recognize that it is possible for the ordinary person to acquire a significant amount of knowledge about economics from personal human experience, from thoughtfully

observing what goes on around them and then discussing these economic issues with other human beings in a perceptive and disciplined manner. Through the use of common sense, practical, down-to-earth and personal human experiences, the capacity to see analogies, informed intuition, and an inherent potential to recognize and pursue excellence the average non-professionally trained human can come to the possibility of being right. Is it not likely that if all of life is carved up among the professional academic disciplines, leaving no room for being an amateur in such professions, that we all shall be cheated of humanness itself? Thus humanistic economics, while recognizing the many important contributions made by professionally trained economists, refuses to grant them an exclusive claim to economic expertise.

Wendell Barry, Barbara Brandt, Andrew Schmookler, Kenneth Lux and many others are not trained as economists, yet they have made important contributions to our understanding of economic processes. As John Applegath has remarked: 'A priesthood that scores points by manipulating elaborate abstractions instead of carefully observing the behavior of actual human beings in various contexts, is viewed with great skepticism by those of us who think of ourselves as humanistic economists'.[31] The human economist fully expects that people from outside the profession will contribute prophetic voices to the school of thought that is the normal sphere of economists. Human economists welcome and are thankful for such insights, just as they welcome the insights of the professionally trained economists with their tradition and ability of deriving conclusions which may not at first glance be apparent.

Humanist economists are fully aware of the problem of evil and of the possibility of individual human beings making destructive, evil and/or erroneous choices. Mobs acting in a rage can do horrific things. But so can the professionally trained experts come to erroneous and/or evil and/or destructive choices. We are also quite aware that power corrupts the sophisticated and well-connected, the best and the brightest as well as the naive and poor. We are quite aware that self-serving and misleading pedants exist. We all know of experts who sell their expertise to the highest bidder, whether it be in the currency of money or power or influence. We are all aware of the dangers of excessive professionalization and the unbalanced view that often may be the result of a narrow and excessive specialization.

Systems and organizations

Humanist economists do believe that persons who have neither too much nor too little of economic goods, and who have some responsible, secure and meaningful control over their economic destiny, are more likely to be capable of making human-potential fulfilling decisions than those who are not so fortunately situated. This is why economic systems are so important. Not only do they perform the important role of advising how to allocate productive resources so that people can obtain a sufficient amount of economic goods, but they also play an important role in generating that type of society in which humans are most likely to be ennobled as humans, a role also to be kept in mind when evaluating the success of an economic system.

This is why humanist economists are suspicious of large organizations, whether they be government bureaucracy, private corporations or labor unions.[32] This is why humanist economists prefer the family farm to large agribusiness corporations and why humanist economists, when it is necessary to have large manufacturing plants, prefer the cooperation involved in worker-owned organizations to absentee ownership.

The humanist economist is very concerned whether the economy promotes a healthy and vibrant community, with its web of interpersonal and meaningful relationships. There can be unhealthy and destructive communities as well as healthy communities (see Daly and Cobb, 1989). Communities such as families, cities and churches are important not only for the sense of community and relationships they provide, but also because it is from the traditions and culture of our communities that we learn from infancy how to enquire about what it means to be truly human. Humanist economists, if they deserve that name, believe deep down that individual humans have within themselves the ability of making choices which will maximize their human potential and, that as much as possible and as many as possible, human beings should be given that opportunity.

This may indeed be naive and/or utopian. But I prefer to put myself in that camp rather than subscribe to that superficial and hollow future which an uncritical rational and mechanistic science holds out for human beings.

Notes

1. The adjective 'humanist' as used by the humanist school does not deny that humanism has about as many meanings as there are human beings, and perhaps properly so.

    The term 'humanism' here does not mean that 'secular rationalistic humanism' which is committed to an unquestioning belief in the progressive power and intelligence of unaided human rationality to the extent that it rejects both the concept of the spiritual world and the essential worth of Nature, the material but living world. According to David Ehrenfield, this secular rationalistic view of humanism underlies conventional economic theory. 'Modern conservative economics is the *ne plus ultra* of humanist arrogance, operating as it does in an artificially defined context which excludes as trivial or beneath contempt any consideration that cannot be translated into the crude and simple language of economics' (Ehrenfeld, 1978, p. 252). It is the position of this essay that such a secular rationalistic humanism ultimately leads to the definition of humans as '*homines economici*'.

    Many people have helped in writing this paper, including Donald Renner, Mark Davis, Helen Parris, Kenneth Polzin, John Applegath and many others who have taught me not only economics over the years but also what it means to be human. I am especially indebted to the many readers of the *Human Economy Newsletter* who corresponded with me while I was editor from 1984–94 as well as many former students. It will be clear to anyone who reads this chapter that it is indebted at key points to the writings of two modern scholars: the economist Herman Daly and the moral philosopher Alasdair MacIntyre.

2. This chapter attempts to (1) define humans as *homines sapientes*, as was done tradition-ally, rather than as *homines economici*, as is done in contemporary economic thought and (2) determine what this change in definition implies for economic theory. For two comple-mentary views of how society came to accept the definition of humans as *homines economici* and the implications for society in so doing, see the sociological study by Barry Schwartz (1986) on the role of economic theorists in this struggle to redefine human nature, and the historical study by William Leach (1993) on the role of the corporate marketers and merchandisers in redefining the citizen as a consumer.

3. As might be expected, both of these views of human nature have a long and many-pronged intellectual history. Alasdair MacIntyre (1988, p. 88) has noted that Aristotle inherited these two rival images of human nature from Plato and ultimately from Homer.

    An important figure because of his pivotal role in the transference of the *homo economicus* image of human nature from the Continent to England and thence to the founders of modern economic thought was the Dutch-born Jansenistic-educated British writer Bernard Mandeville. See Horne (1978) and Dumont (1977).

4. According to Neva Goodwin (1991), Alfred Marshall was the last major economist to have sight of both visions of humanity. She suggests that twentieth-century economists would have done better to keep both views of human nature within their discussion.

5. As Jerome Segal (1991, p. 287) has noted, 'Private and public action in the economic realm cannot be reasonably grounded unless it is placed within a larger understanding of human existence. This includes views of the nature of man, the nature of the good life, the point or purpose of human life, the existence and nature of God, and the nature of the broader human project'.

6. This spectrum is adapted from Daly (1993, p. 20).

7. I do not mean to imply that there are precise and clear boundaries between economics and other fields of studies. See the section 'The Boundaries of the Economic Process' in Georgescu-Roegen (1971, pp. 316–22).

8. To simplify, I focus upon the importance of economic goods and services to a high-quality life, omitting a discussion of how the economic system in its wholeness of production, power structure, access to and quality of work, distribution of wealth and income, and security contribute to a high-quality life.

    Daly and Cobb (1989) have explored how many of these economic topics have im-pacted upon the concept of community. Some of the work by the Society for the Advance-ment of Socio-Economics explores the relationship between economic systems and responsible communities. The *Human Economy Newsletter* has explored these issues over the past 15 years. *Humanistic Economics: The New Challenge* (1988) by Mark Lutz and Ken Lux is a concerted recent effort to explore these issues.

9. There is a large literature that supports each of these two conflicting views. This literature ultimately revolves around the importance of the entropy law and the possibility of technology keeping ahead of the ravages of the entropy law.

    The lead factual discussion in the empty-world view is Goeller and Weinberg (1978). It is significant that this article, which first appeared in *Science*, 1976, was reprinted in the *American Economic Review* special issue consisting solely of a list of all members and three significant-to-the-editors articles reprinted from other journals.

    The lead factual discussion in the full-world view appears to be Vitousek et al. (1986). Although this article is not as well known as the previous article, it has achieved a crucial role inasmuch as at critical points in their argument, economists who argue for reduced use of resources by the economic system refer to it for factual support for their position. See, for example, Daly and Cobb (1989, pp. 143–4).

10. Another reason which makes it possible to focus upon the question of importance of economic goods and services to a high quality life is because there is a group of econo-mists and ecologists who are wrestling with the question of the plenitude of the earth's resources, the members of The International Society for Ecological Economics and their journal *Ecological Economics*. It is nonetheless essential to the humanist economist to be

aware of this discussion for the reason that humans do need the earth to survive, are an integral part of the earth, and, in order to live a high-quality life, must live in spiritual and material harmony with the fragile but fertile planet Earth that in a real sense is a Mother.

11. Or as Herman Daly (1993, p. 23) has written: 'Human beings are both material creatures in absolute dependence upon their physical environment and rational beings who have purposes and strive to become better. These two aspects must be consistent with each other... Biophysically based conclusions about economic growth, or any other subject, should be in accord with morally based conclusions. A discrepancy indicates a flawed understanding of the natural world or a warped set of values'.

12. See Hausman and McPherson (1993, pp. 671–732) for one attempt to connect ethics and economics. Perhaps the following title by Kenneth Lux (1990), although no doubt oversimplified, does indeed say it all: *Adam Smith's Mistake: How a Moral Philosopher Invented Economics and Ended Morality.*

13. As Joseph Schumpeter (1954, p. 133) stated it: Utilitarianism is 'the shallowest of all conceivable philosophies of life that stands indeed in a position of irreconcilable antagonism to the rest of them'.

14. Although economic theory seems to be quite aware of the notion of 'limits', as one can read the phrases 'limited' capital or 'limited' resources often in economic literature, this is really an illusion, since the basic notion that humans are 'limited' i.e., not god-like, is foreign to the discussion. Such limits as are acknowledged in economic literature are temporary in nature and to be overcome in the future. There needs to be a more serious analysis of the concept of basic limits than now exists in the literature. Perhaps the most relevant work in this area is still J.W. von Goethe's *Faust*. There are two perceptive studies of Faust as it relates to modern economic systems. See Binswanger (1994, p. 89) or 'Goethe's *Faust*: The Tragedy of Development' in Berman (1982, pp. 37–87).

15. For a historical summary of humanistic economics, see either Smith (1993) or the chapter 'The History of Economics from a Humanistic Perspective' in Lutz and Lux (1979). Both of these studies agree that the modern founder of humanist economics was the Swiss/ English economist Jean Charles Léonard Simonde, or Sismondi (1773–1842). They also agree that much of the current renaissance in humanist economics can be traced back to E.F. Schumacher and his book *Small is Beautiful: Economics as if People Mattered* (1974).

16. For a study of how the neoclassical economic theory promotes addiction on a grand scale, see part 2, 'The Problem of Economic Addiction' in Brandt (1995).

17. Louis Dumont (1977, p. 5) makes a parallel observation when he writes: 'In ... traditional societies the relations between men are more important, more highly valued, than the relations between men and things. This primacy is reversed in the modern type of society, in which relations between men are subordinated to relations between men and things'.

18. Discussing the role which economists play in modern society, Warren Samuels (1974, pp. 314–5) has noted, 'Economics is also social control: economic ideology has largely replaced theology as the social device for achieving social cohesion, providing a set of moral rules, providing goals for individual internalization and identity-achievement, providing legitimation for the machinations of power players both in and out of government, and providing justification for "the ways of Mammon to man"'.

19. John Maynard Keynes (1949, p. 96) made a similar observation when he noted that he regarded the 'Benthamite tradition ... as the worm which has been gnawing at the insides of modern civilization and is responsible for its present moral decay'.

20. Some economists, such as Pareto (1971), have argued that *homo economicus* is one way of looking at human beings, but that there are other ways such as *homo faber, homo religiousus*, and the use of one *homo* does not preclude the other *homines* from existing. While this is no doubt true, it is still true that to the extent that *homo economicus* expands, the other *homines* must diminish, and, even more importantly, only one can be in first place. This reversal of primacy of place is what is at issue. It is also true that one cannot compartmentalize an individual human being into several distinct and separate *homines*. What I do as an economic person will affect what I am as a creative person or religious person.

For a reflective discussion of this and an insightful example in the person of the successful merchant John Wanamaker and his children of how *homo economicus* and *homo religiosus* have co-evolved in American society to the detriment of *homo religiosus*, see Leach (1993, pp. 191–224).

21. As Daly (1979, pp. 55–6) has written, 'the attempt to evade moral problems by further growth and techno-logical razzle-dazzle knows no limits'.
22. As Joseph Krutch (1959, p. 157) noted, 'This habit of mind sharpens one kind of awareness but tends to dull another because all such "explanations" are, in one sense, deceptive. What they come down to is no more than a more detailed description which distracts attention from what remains fundamentally inexplicable in the thing itself'.
23. Donald McCloskey (1995, p. 111) has written, 'Science in fact depends on ethics (I argue hopefully), which is one connection between the Good Economist and the Good Person'.
24. See the essay 'Consumers' Values in a Crazy World' by the humanist and humorous John Ise (1955) for a delightful parody of this type of person.
25. For example, Hyman (1994, p. 9): 'Economics: the study of the use of limited productive resources in a society to satisfy the unlimited desires of its members'.
26. Does the laissez-faire market economy which is prescribed by some neoclassical economists promote both the freedom of choice and the ability to discriminate between excellence and non-excellence necessary to achieve a fulfilled life? Several recent books address this issue. Andrew Schmookler (1993b) explores what freedom of choice the market gives us and what freedom of choice the same market takes away. Schmookler (1993a) shows how the market plays an important role in generating (manipulating?) the values which we use in making our choices.

The historian William Leach (1993, pp. 385–6) has investigated the impact of American corporate capitalism upon human nature between 1885 and 1930. He concluded that:

> Another corporate legacy passed on from the pre-1930s years is the concept of the human being as an insatiable, desiring machine or as an animal governed by an infinity of desires...
>
> At the same time, the conception of the desiring self, as expressed in capitalist terms and exploited by capitalism, offers a one-sided and flawed notion of what it means to be human. It rejects what is also 'human' about human beings: their ability to commit themselves, to establish binding relationships, to sink permanent roots, to maintain continuity with previous generations, to remember, to make ethical judgments, to seek pleasure in work, to remain steadfast on behalf of principle and loyal to community or country (to the degree that community or country strives to be just and fair), to seek spiritual transcendence beyond the self, and to fight a cause through to the end.

See also *The Costs of Living: How Market Freedom Erodes the Best Things in Life* by Barry Schwartz (1994).

27. Towards the end of his life, John Maynard Keynes (1949, pp. 99–100) made the following observation about evil and human nature: 'We repudiated all versions of the doctrine of original sin, of there being insane and irrational springs of wickedness in most men ... As cause and consequence of our state of mind we completely misunderstood human nature, including our own. The rationality which we attributed to it led to a superficiality, not only of judgment, but of feeling'.
28. For examples of what would be in such a chapter on consumer behavior, see the chapter 'Human Wants and Utility' in *Economics* by John Ise (1946).
29. In the section 'The First Tool of the Economist: The Mind of the Economist', Neva Goodwin (1991, pp. 158–9) writes:

> The normal way for the human mind to work is to take each new piece of information or new speculation and evaluate it for truth, or usefulness, or other merit, against the background of a life's experience... In contrast, the economic view of the human being, since Marshall's time, has operated as though starting from nearly complete ignorance on the part of the economist him/herself. ...The point of this ... is to suggest

that the way we have gone about developing our 'human sciences' may not be the way that can best take advantage of our starting point ourselves.

30. This is so much the case that the majority of PhD-granting institutions in Economics now prefer their undergraduates to be math majors.
31. Personal communication.
32. This is why humanist economics is even more opposed to Communism (centralized ownership of factors of production) than it is to neoclassical economic theory with its emphasis upon the market. Lenin was very aware of this opposition between communism and humanistic economics and it is no accident that several of his first major written works were against the humanist economics of his day in Russia. After that, he turned his attention to writing against the western market economists. See Lenin (1951) and, with respect to Sismondi, footnote 15.

For a historical description of the humanist movement in Russia in the late nineteenth-century (called the *narodniki* movement) as it struggled simultaneously against the cruel tyranny of the autocratic Tsar government, the permissive libertinism of the free market ideologists, and the economic determinism of the disciples of Marx, see Billington (1958).

References

Berman, Marshall (1982), *All That is Solid Melts into Air: The Experience of Modernity*, New York: Simon & Schuster.

Billington, James H. (1958), *Mikhailovsky and Russian Populism*, Oxford: Clarendon Press.

Binswanger, Hans Christoph (1994), *Money and Magic: A Critique of the Modern Economy in the Light of Goethe's Faust*, Chicago: University of Chicago Press.

Brandt, Barbara (1995), *Whole Life Economics: revaluing daily life*, Philadelphia: New Society Publishers.

Daly, Herman E. (1979), 'Ethical Implications of Limits to Global Development' in William Finnin, Jr. and Gerald Alonzo Smith (eds), *The Morality of Scarcity: limited resources and social policy*, Baton Rouge: Louisiana State University Press, 37–59.

Daly, Herman E. (1993), Introduction, *Valuing the Earth: Economics, Ecology, Ethics*, Herman Daly and Kenneth Townsend (eds), Cambridge, MA: MIT Press, 11–51.

Daly, Herman E. (1995), 'Some Implications of Process Philosophy for Economic Thought', Personal communication.

Daly, Herman and Cobb, John Jr. (1989), *For the Common Good: Redirecting the Economy towards Community, the Environment, and a Sustainable Future*, Boston: Beacon Press.

Dumont, Louis (1977), *From Mandeville to Marx: The Genesis and Triumph of Economic Ideology*, Chicago: University of Chicago Press.

Eberle, Don (1995), 'Even Newt Can't Save Us', *Wall St. Journal*, Feb. 3, A12.

Ehrenfeld, David (1978), *The Arrogance of Humanism*, New York: Oxford University Press.

Georgescu-Roegen, Nicholas (1971), *The Entropy Law and the Economic Process*, Cambridge, MA: Harvard University Press.

Goeller, H.E. and Weinberg, Alvin M. (1978), 'The Age of Substitutability', *American Economic Review*, **68** (6), 1–11.

Goodwin, Neva R. (1991), *Social Economics: An Alternative Theory, Vol. I, Building Anew on Marshall's Principles*, New York: St. Martin's Press.

Hausman, Daniel and McPherson, Michael (1993), 'Taking Ethics Seriously: Economics and Contemporary Moral Philosophy', *Journal of Economic Literature*, **31** (June), 671–731.

Horne, Thomas (1978), *The Social Thought of Bernard Mandeville: Virtue and Commerce in Early Eighteenth-Century England*, New York: Columbia University Press.

Hyman, David (1994), *Microeconomics*, Boston: Irwin.

Ise, John (1946), *Economics*, New York: Harper and Brothers.

Ise, John (1955), 'Consumers' Values in a Crazy World' in *The American Way*, Lawrence, Kansas: Allan Press.

Keynes, John Maynard (1949), *Two Memoirs, Dr Melchior, A Defeated Enemy, and My early beliefs*, New York: Augustus M. Kelley.

Krutch, Joseph Wood (1959), *Human Nature and the Human Condition*, New York: Random House.

Leach, William (1993), *Land of Desire: Merchants, Power, and the Rise of a New American Culture*, New York: Pantheon Books.

Lenin, V.I. (1951, 1894), *A Characterization of Economic Romanticism; Sismondi and our Native Sismondists*, Moscow: Foreign Language Pub. House.

Lewis, C.S. (1993), *The Abolition of Man*, New York: Collier Books, reprinted in Herman Daly and Kenneth Townsend (eds), *Valuing the Earth: Economics, Ecology, Ethics*, Cambridge, MA: MIT Press, 229–45.

Lutz, Mark A. (1995), 'Centering Social Economics on Human Dignity', Presidential Address to the Association for Social Economics, January 7, Washington, DC.

Lutz, Mark A. and Kenneth Lux (1979), *The Challenge of Humanistic Economics*, Menlo Park: Benjamin/Cummings Publishing Company.

Lutz, Mark A. and Lux, Kenneth (1988), *Humanistic Economics: The New Challenge*, New York: Bootstrap Press.

Lux, Kenneth (1990), *Adam Smith's Mistake: How a Moral Philosopher Invented Economics and Ended Morality*, New York: Random House

MacIntyre, Alasdiair (1977), 'Utilitarianism and Cost-Benefit Analysis: An Essay on the Relevance of Moral Philosophy to Bureaucratic Theory', in Kenneth Sayre (ed.), *Values in the Electric Power Industry*, Notre Dame: University of Notre Dame Press, 217–37.

MacIntyre, Alasdiair (1984), *After Virtue: A Study in Moral Theory*, Notre Dame: University of Notre Dame Press.

MacIntyre, Alasdiair (1988), *Whose Justice? Which Rationality?* Notre Dame: University of Notre Dame Press.

MacIntyre, Alasdiair (1990), *Three Rival Versions of Moral Enquiry*, Notre Dame: University of Notre Dame Press.

McCloskey, Donald N. (1994), *Knowledge and Persuasion in Economics*, New York: Cambridge University Press.

McCloskey, Donald N. (1995), 'He's Smart. And He's a Nice Guy, Too', *Eastern Economic Journal*, **21** (1), 109–12.

Pareto, Vilfredo (1971), *Manual of Political Economy*, trans. Ann S. Schwier, Ann S. Schwier and Alfred N. Page (eds), New York: A.M. Kelly.

Rhoads, Steven E. (1985), *The Economist's View of the World*, New York: Cambridge University Press.

Samuels, Warren (1974), 'The History of Economic Thought in Intellectual History', *History of Political Economy*, **6**, 305–24.

Schmookler, Andrew B. (1993a), *Fools Gold: The Fate of Values in a World of Goods*, New York: Harper Collins.

Schmookler, Andrew B. (1993b), *The Illusion of Choice: How the Market Economy Shapes Our Destiny*, Ithaca: State University of New York Press.

Schumacher, E.F. (1974), *Small is Beautiful: Economics as if People Mattered*, New York: Harper & Row.

Schumpeter, Joseph (1954), *History of Economic Analysis*, New York: Oxford University Press.

Schwartz, Barry (1986), *The Battle for Human Nature: Science, Morality and Modern Life*, New York: W.W. Norton & Company.

Schwartz, Barry (1994), *The Costs of Living: How Market Freedom Erodes the Best Things in Life*, New York: W.W. Norton.

Segal, Jerome M. (1991), 'Alternative Conceptions of the Economic Realm', in Richard M. Coughlin (ed.), *Morality, Rationality, and Efficiency: New Perspectives on Socio-Economics*, Armonk, NY: M.E. Sharpe, 287–309.

Smith, Gerald Alonzo (1993), 'The Purpose of Wealth: A Historical Perspective', in Herman Daly and Kenneth Townsend (eds), *Valuing the Earth: Economics, Ecology, Ethics*, Cambridge, MA: MIT Press, 183–211.

Vitousek, Peter M., Ehrlich, Paul R., Ehrlich, Anne H. and Matson, Pamela A. (1986), 'Human Appropriation of the Products of Photosynthesis', in *BioScience*, **36**, 368–73.

8 Nondeterminist Marxism: the birth of a postmodern tradition in economics

Jack Amariglio, Antonio Callari, Stephen Resnick, David Ruccio, and Richard Wolff

Explaining and exploring Marxian economics for the insights it can yield – never easy in the United States – is now more complicated than ever. In the economics profession generally, there remain, of course, the few who take Marxian thought seriously enough to criticize it and the few for whom it is simply evil. There remain as well the many for whom it is unknown or irrelevant to their professional lives since it is kept marginal to academic departments and is barely whispered about. But now we have a great fourth group, heavily overlapping the first three. It comprises those who declare that Marxism is finally over, passé, and ready to be retired to those early chapters of textbooks on the history of economic thought, itself a field in danger of passing entirely out of existence since all that is supposedly worth keeping in economics is already known and incorporated in the 'scientific core' of the discipline.

When challenged, these aforementioned academic modes of banishing Marxism and Marxists from core positions in the economics profession offer their justifications. Marxian economics, it is said, is just plain wrong. Its value theory is mathematically erroneous or, in Paul Samuelson's phrase, a pointless detour around neoclassical price theory, or merely a special case of a Sraffa-type theory of prices and income distribution. Its focus only on production and supply without any theory of demand is useless. It is a macro-level theory without proper microfoundations and, hence, absurd. Its primitive insights into business cycles have been superseded by much more complex Keynesian, new classical, Post Keynesian, new Keynesian, and other theoretical approaches. And, finally, its linear notion of economic development and history passing everywhere through identical stages culminating in a transition from capitalism to communism is theoretically untenable and empirically contradicted by the events over the past decade in Eastern Europe and the former Soviet Union. Marxism, so it is said, is a dead end whose brief appearance in history has been an unfortunate, costly, and tragic experiment in plainly wrong ideas and ideals.

And yet, in the face of these reactions and criticisms – indeed often in response to them – Marxian economics has continued to develop and is very much alive and productive. With just that touch of irony and dialectic Marx enjoyed, we might say that the new forms of Marxian economics – an infant analytic industry – were protected enough by denunciations, wholesale dismissals, and neglect of older forms to enable them to develop and debate basic concepts and logical procedures relatively free from serious scrutiny and textually-informed attack.

The developments within Marxian economics over the past 25 years or so have by now spawned discernible and often quite distinct alternative formulations – whole schools of Marxian thought. These range from Analytical Marxism and Marxist-Feminism to the nondeterminist (some would call it postmodern) Marxism that we ourselves have worked on for the past two decades.[1] These diverse approaches – these new traditions in Marxian economics – are clearly less known to our colleagues in the economics profession. And, we think that an engagement with the theoretical breakthroughs and forms of discussion emerging in these traditions is now in order. To avoid such an engagement would simply permit the stale repetition of fulminating against and rejecting a Marxian economics (an orthodoxy, no doubt) that has mostly passed from the scene: an exercise in beating the proverbial dead horse.

The postmodern revolution
In the remainder of our paper, we shall focus on describing the innovations in just one of these new Marxian traditions, the one we believe we know best: nondeterminist Marxism. In one sense, this new Marxian economics participates in the postmodern revolution in thought and practice that has shaken so many disciplines to their roots across this century.[2] This participation takes several forms.

In psychology, Sigmund Freud's analysis of the unconscious and its consequent interpretation by Jacques Lacan displaced the notion of a unified 'rational' subject in favor of a decentered, multiple, fully endogenous, and 'overdetermined' subjectivity. This displacement, embraced in nondeterminist Marxian economics (one of its distinguishing characteristics, we note), focuses attention on how individuals are socially constituted (in part by the economy) as multiple, decentered subjects or selves. Individuals thus conceived in this new psychology behave differently (as producers, consumers, buyers, and sellers) from the prescriptions of neoclassical economics. They interact with the economy (and society altogether) in different ways as well. Gone is the modernist notion of the centered individual – the economic agent of most economic theory – with consistent tastes and rationality. Gone, as well, is pushing subjectivity to the margin, as an exogenous 'first cause' untainted by the actions and decisions which it is said to motivate. Gone is the unidirectional determining effect of economic agency on institutional arrangements. Gone, therefore, is the entire apparatus of nineteenth century utilitarian philosophy – still the hallmark of most neoclassical economic theory – with its enduring commitment to the mythology of unified, singular, centered individuals (or at least where economic activity is concerned).

The postmodern revolution has been also largely concerned with the notions of causality, as various disciplines, practices, movements – from art to architecture – have struggled to avoid being collapsed into a moment of some world-historical cause. In the natural sciences as well, a major development of the twentieth century has been the rejection of determinism: models of complex systems in which one subset of elements ('independent' variables) functions as cause while another subset ('dependent' variables) functions as effect. Instead, the thrust of theoretical innovation across the disciplines has been toward approaches in which causes are seen also as effects, and vice versa.

The logic of overdetermination

Influenced by and participating in the ubiquitous rejection of determinism, for nondeterminist Marxian economics, the determinist logics of analysis have given way to 'overdetermination'.[3] In this conception, all aspects of any relational system are simultaneously each others' causes and effects. Thus, for example, while the focus of nondeterminist Marxian economics is upon class – as an aspect of society whose repression by other economists we seek to undo – there is no claim that class is a cause rather than an effect of economic structure and change.

In our own work, and in that of others working in the nondeterminist tradition, economic events, such as prices, cycles, income distribution, and capital accumulation, are not reduced to the effects of class. Rather, our commitment to the logic of overdetermination means that we aim to study, empirically as well as theoretically, the multifarious ways in which class and these other economic events simultaneously constitute and condition one another. Indeed, overdetermination also entails continuously exploring and integrating the interaction of non-economic and economic events and relationships.

Postmodernism, as it has enlivened nondeterminist Marxism, also entails a central recognition of difference. And this theoretical appreciation of the centrality of difference, among other things, has contributed to what we regard as a unique epistemological position – a different view about knowledge, its status, and its effects – within the field of economics. Theories, languages, individuals, and so forth, are viewed as irreducibly different from one another. Moreover, in the realm of theoretical frameworks, for example, they are each conceived to have different criteria of what is true or plausible or persuasive. Thus, in the field of economics, all schools of economic thought are to be treated as collections of irreducibly different approaches or discursive formations or analytical systems. From this Marxian epistemological perspective, there is no resolving these differences according to one universal standard since each approach, framework, and system erects its own standards of truth. Thus, from the point of view of nondeterminist Marxism, schools of economic thought become sites at which alternative structures of meaning engage, confront, and contend with one another in a process of mutual transformation. Economics is then an arena in which emerge fundamentally different ways of posing and answering questions about what an economy is, how it works, and where it is going. To study economics is to engage the differences, to learn from all of them, and to alter them in accord with the ever-changing needs and circumstances of social life as it is *differently* understood within any society.

In contrast, many of our colleagues, Marxist as well as non-Marxist, wish to reaffirm determinist frameworks and narrow disciplinary boundaries. Disregarding or even repudiating the postmodern revolution, many economists continue to 'show' how economic events and economic knowledge all reduce, in the last analysis, to effects of foundational determinants. For many neoclassicals and those influenced by them, these determinants continue to be primarily preferences, technology, and initial endowments. Old debates among economists continue firmly situated on determinist terrain; modernist notions of cause and effect seem to die hard. For example, microfoundationalists (methodological individualists or humanists) battle macrofoundationalists (methodological structuralists) over whether micro is the final determinant of macro, or vice versa. The analytical move beyond determinism per se, established fully in nondeterminist Marxian economics as, by now, in many disciplines outside of economics, has barely entered the domain of discourse in conventional economics. The commitment to overdetermination in nondeterminist Marxian economics has yielded concrete analytic and empirical fruits already. Old Marxian notions of capital accumulation as *the* determinant of capitalist dynamics have been overturned – for example in the work of Bruce Norton (1988, 1992, 1995) – in favor of showing the varying circumstances in which capitalism may or may not promote accumulation, when accumulation may or may not end a cyclical downturn, when profit maximization may and when it may not contribute to accumulation, and so on. Norton's work, conducted as a sustained critique of the monopoly-capital and Steindl schools within Marxian economics, challenges entirely the longstanding view that capitalism and its historical development cannot be understood without grounding its 'dynamic' in the forms and processes of capital accumulation. Norton's (1995, p. 745) view is informed by the observation that, at least since the 1970s, 'domestic market concentration is now less readily associated with inevitable pricing power; manufacturing industries are less readily taken to represent "the economy" as a whole; within manufacturing, giant firms are less readily taken as representative agents standing in for all significant enterprises'. For Norton, 'perhaps corporations are no longer easily construed as omnipotent with respect to everything except demand'.

Norton shows, along these lines, that the capitalist firm is itself the site of a plethora of forces and pressures, and is not, as has been touted in much of the Marxian literature, reducible to an essential constituent drive to accumulate capital. Indeed, in a creative use of the concept of overdetermination, Norton has indicated that *disaccumulation* may at various points in time characterize the 'motivation' of the capitalist firm, as such firms may in fact transform themselves and enhance their profitability by becoming (at least partly) banks, retailers – not exploiters of wage labor – and so forth.

The idea that there are subtle and endless possibilities, depending on the overdetermined context, for the constitution and direction of capitalist firms reappears again in Stephen Cullenberg's writings on profit rates and their tendencies. In reviewing the traditional Marxian debates over the direction of profit rates under conditions of mature competition, Cullenberg (1994) puts forward what he calls a 'decentered approach' to both the enterprise and the economy. Like Norton, Cullenberg argues in his recent book that 'each capitalist enterprise is uniquely constituted with respect to both its internal and external conditions of existence. That is, each capitalist enterprise has a unique management structure, forms of control, labor process, personalities of management and workers, history of labor relations, and so forth' (Cullenberg, 1994, p. 94). Cullenberg unearths the deep discursive structures underlying the traditional Marxian debates on the tendency for the profit rate to either rise or fall with changes in the technical and social conditions of capitalist firms. Cullenberg's overdeterminist approach, in which the profit rate is shown to exist at all moments in contradiction and with absolutely no inevitable, historical tendency, frees Marxian economic analysis from the structuralism of Hegelian Marxism, but also from the pervasive humanism of Cartesian-inspired approaches to the behavior of capitalist entrepreneurs. Cullenberg insightfully separates most prior Marxian explanations into two major camps: one, the Hegelian, for which a falling rate of profit denotes the necessary effectivity of systemic macro laws; the other, the Cartesian, for which a rising rate of profit (as with Okishio) is derived from the micro behavior of each individual entrepreneur. Cullenberg's work, ultimately, is built upon his stance that a nondeterminist Marxism can break new ground and can transcend the repetitious contentions between these camps over the correct and determinate essential tendency of profit rates.

New Marxian vistas

On the vexing issues, so prevalent in past Marxian considerations on the relations between value, price, and money, nondeterminist Marxism has opened up new and often surprising vistas. For example, nondeterminist Marxian economics does not reduce prices to values or labor inputs; instead, as in several papers by Wolff, Roberts, and Callari (1982, 1984), it has constructed a value-and-price theory in which values and prices simultaneously cause each other. This approach yields insights unobtainable from the old Marxian economics of the 'transformation problem'. Moreover, this new Marxian theory of prices and values – developed by sorting out and distinguishing Marxian from Ricardian procedures in linking values and prices – is neither vulnerable to Böhm-Bawerk's nineteenth-century critique of Marx, nor does it follow the neoclassical procedure of collapsing values and prices into synonyms and then reducing them finally (as a new unity) to mere effects of preferences, technology, and endowments as their determining essences.

Similarly, the movement away from the typically reductionist forms of Marxian explanation can be seen in John Roche's (1985) analysis of the complex interaction between money, value, and capitalist crises. Roche's take on overdetermination leads him to show the impossibility of dichotomizing the sphere of circulation – the realm of money and price – and the sphere of production – the so-called 'real' sector of value determination. Roche notes that at every moment, value, money, and price overdetermine each other's existence and that 'real' crises never simply reflect or express, but are constituted by as they themselves constitute the determination of monetary values and/or ruptures in the process of circulation. In a later, startling rethinking of traditional Marxian economic theory, Roche (1988) locates in part the failure of Marxists to see the manifold interdeterminations of money, price, and crises in the use of the labor theory of value as an 'equilibrium' approach, shared, to Marxism's detriment (especially in making sense of Marx's sophisticated theories of crises), with mainstream theories of market economic behavior.

Together, the innovations in economic theory brought about by nondeterminist Marxism lead to original ways of developing Marxian value theory – thus sharpening and highlighting the distinctive contributions offered by a Marxian approach to economic analysis – and at the same time, to new forms of engagement with other 'heterodox' understandings of economic activities and institutions. One example is the social construction of economic subjectivities. According to nondeterminist Marxists (see for example Amariglio and Callari, 1993), the section on commodity fetishism in volume 1 of Marx's *Capital* can be read profitably not as economic determinists often do, as a theory of 'false consciousness', but, rather, as Marx's critique of the classical political economists' presumption of the naturalness and universality of the forms of rationality, and so on, required of economic agents who engage in commodity exchange.

The section on commodity fetishism can be read as well as a statement of Marx's alternative conception of the contingent historical and social constitution of the subjectivities associated with market exchange. In this, the contributions of nondeterminist Marxists coincide with those of both institutionalist economists who, drawing on the work of Karl Polanyi and others, have emphasized the 'social embeddedness' of markets and the existence of nonmarket forms of exchange, and of radical economists who have drawn attention to the significance of political power in the overdetermination of economic relationships.

Similarly, when nondeterminist Marxists investigate race and gender as important factors in the discursive and social construction of the conditions of existence of abstract labor, thereby emphasizing the role of race and gender in the basic concepts of Marxian value theory, they acknowledge their indebtedness to (and, at the same time, the role of Marxism itself in helping to produce) newly emergent antiracist and feminist traditions within economics.[4] The nondeterminist Marxian approach to knowledge – the idea that all forms of knowledge, both of economists and of economic agents, is irreducibly discursive and fragmentary – coincides, notwithstanding substantial differences in other dimensions of their respective approaches, with the notion of 'fundamental uncertainty' emphasized by Post Keynesian economists, the role of 'subjective' knowledge in Austrian economics, pragmatism as it has passed into economic methodology, and the focus on rhetoric and metaphors in the work of Donald McCloskey (1985, 1994), Arjo Klamer (1990, 1995), and Diana Strassmann (1993; Strassmann and Polanyi, 1995).[5]

In each case, openings within Marxian economics pioneered by nondeterminists have served both to create new points of confluence and conversation with other dissident traditions within economics and to underscore its own radical break from and alternative to the concepts and protocols – the notions of value, science, and so on – of mainstream economics.

Analysis of class

The innovations in economic theory brought forth by nondeterminist Marxism are not limited to changes in theories of accumulation, profits, value, price, and money. Indeed, in much of this emerging framework there has been a paradigm shift in the meaning and import of the concept of economic class and the resulting notions of class structure and social formation. Much of this work, concentrating on the various fundamental and subsumed class forms through which surplus labor is produced, appropriated, and distributed, may be more familiar to our colleagues.

But we wish to stress our strong belief that a simultaneous commitment to class and overdetermination can produce an entirely novel way to conceive of society. No longer must we understand the mode of production to determine, in the last instance, the dominant class nature of the society in question. For nondeterminist Marxism, the hegemonic role of class in society has been removed. Instead, any society is understood as an overdetermined complexity, a shifting amalgamation of interacting and contending class and nonclass processes. So, for example, the United States today can be conceived to exist as a social formation comprising capitalist, feudal, ancient (self-employed), communist, and still other class processes. Individuals within such a formation are understood over time and at different moments of their lives to participate in diverse class and nonclass processes. Women, for example, during the same day may occupy a feudal class position within a family household, and a capitalist class position outside of it. On weekends, they may add a third class position as a self-employed ancient. Their different class lives depend, in turn, upon radically different nonclass processes. One kind of culture and politics helps to constitute their feudal existence within households, while another creates their capitalist lives outside of the domestic site.

For Katherine Gibson and Julie Graham (Gibson-Graham, 1996), one of the important obstacles to seeing and analyzing these multiple class processes is the representation of the capitalist economy that is often presumed in traditional modes of economic thinking. Marxist economists, especially, have tended to focus their attention on the 'systemic logic' and 'laws of motion' of capitalism, to the exclusion of the presence and effects of noncapitalist class processes. Incorporating the insights of nondeterminist Marxism with those of feminism and poststructuralism, Gibson and Graham have begun to challenge existing discourses of the economy and to produce new ones. In their view, the fact that capitalism is seen as dominating or determining most if not all economic and social events in the world today is because of the way capitalism itself is constructed as a concept: it is understood to be a large, integrated, singular, economic system in comparison to which all other economic events (particularly forms of noncapitalism) are considered to be small, partial, and incomplete. What Gibson and Graham do is radically transform the existing model of capitalism – seeing it as a fragmented and partial set of economic processes and institutions, without any necessary unifying drive or logic – and to create a theoretical space for the proliferation of noncapitalist – ancient, communal, feudal, slave, and so on – class processes in contemporary economic and social institutions. They also build on this decentering of the economy, first, by calling attention to the gendered nature of the metaphors which structure many theoretical and policy discussions in economics and, second, by examining not only forms of exploitation but also distributive class processes, thus creating new objects of theoretical analysis and political transformation.

Because the respective existence and reproduction of diverse class processes and positions depend on being able to secure specific and likely competing nonclass processes, each has only a contingent and uncertain life. Indeed, the concept of overdetermination means that the very dynamic of each fosters its other, while simultaneously producing effects undermining that very causation. Hence, because of their sheer number and nonpermanent status, the class nature of the United States, or of any society, remains always an object of and for theoretical and political struggle.

Three examples
As in the past, perhaps the discursive power of any Marxian tradition resides in this struggle, the struggle to tell persuasive stories about the class nature of actual societies. So we conclude our paper with three such stories. But we remind our readers that these are intended mostly to illuminate the codetermination of class and nonclass central to the nondeterminist approach.

As one case study in this tradition, Richard McIntyre (1996) has focused attention on the class structure of the United States. His question is a basic one: Is the United States capitalist? While generations of Marxist and other radical economists have generally presumed the capitalist nature of the American economy and society, McIntyre's view is that, even today, many US economic establishments do not involve the extraction of surplus value by industrial capitalists from wage-laborers. Instead, he argues, building on his own work on the notion of uneven development and that of Frank Annunziato (1990), Satyananda Gabriel (1990a), and others concerning the class nature of individual employment, a large number of enterprises and jobs in the United States involve forms of self-employment that include the individual or 'ancient' appropriation and distribution of surplus labor. And the ancient and other noncapitalist class processes are not in the process of disappearing. Indeed, from the perspective of nondeterminist Marxism, the United States continues to exhibit as complex and diverse a class structure as any which the 'articulation of modes of production' has made visible in the third world.

A second example is from Carole Biewener (1987, 1990), who has focused her attention on the socialist experiment in France during the 1980s. She shows that the identification of socialism alternatively with nonclass processes of democracy in the workplace, collectivization and nationalization of property, increased social welfare, and much else did little to alter the capitalist class process, i.e., the production and appropriation of surplus value. That is, Biewener demonstrates that the left Keynesian policies of the Mitterand regime – committed socialists, without a doubt – were fundamentally blind to class and to its complicated interrelations with a whole host of nonclass processes, many of which were mistaken for class. The outcome, now well established, is that a basic shift in France's class structure did not occur under the socialists. The best that was achieved was capitalism with a sometimes happy face.

An even less happy story is our slightly longer one regarding US capitalism over the past 20 years or so. Whatever differences exist among economists in explaining the reasons for today's wage stagnation, unequal income distribution, and underclass steeped in a culture of crime and hopelessness, they commonly reject any link between such nonclass events and Marx's notion of class exploitation. It is precisely that connection, however, that Marx contributed to economics to make sense of the hard times of his capitalist day. We intend to do the same here.[6]

The decade of the 1970s ended and that of the 1980s began with difficult problems faced by industrial capitalist enterprises. In class terms, industrial enterprises could not appropriate enough surplus value to satisfy the nonclass demands placed upon that surplus. Securing these demands meant distributing the surplus to acquire those nonclass processes of capital accumulation, research and development, managerial supervision, credit, and so forth that together formed the conditions of existence of enterprises' surplus value. The threat of crisis loomed, because if these nonclass demands were unmet, then continuation of the class process itself would be undermined.

The next two decades, starting with the policies of Reagan in the 1980s and continuing through the Bush years, was a successful story of how capitalism – including the role of the state – changed the two sides of this class equation. This success can be measured in two ways. On the one hand, more surplus value was generated by increasing the rate of exploitation of US workers. On the other hand, distributions of portions of that surplus in the form of monopoly payments to unionized workers and OPEC and of taxes to the state were reduced, while attempts were made to expand distributions destined for capital accumulation and research and development. US industrial capital effectively restructured its source of profits – the class process – as well as its distributions to secure nonclass processes that constituted in part these profits.

The costs have been heavy however. They account for much of the difficult times too many Americans have undergone and continue to suffer through. One such cost, recognized by Marxism, was that of continued downward pressure on the real wage of productive labor, eventually producing a fall in the value of labor power. We think the last twenty years or so produced one of those conjunctures in capitalism when, to use Marx's words, a change in the 'historical and moral element' results, in this case, in a lowered 'bundle of means of subsistence' for workers in capitalist enterprises. Surplus value rose because the value of labor power fell to this lowered real wage for productive labor. This kind of class cost harks back to the capitalism of an older, more severe time, a period when labor was especially subservient to capital.

The success of capital in achieving this reduced value of labor power was also a failure of capitalism: the crisis of industrial capital was displaced onto the worker. The consequences help to explain the weary life experienced by so many in our factories, our cities, and our families. They also pushed an increasing number of them to seek out new, noncapitalist class structures in our cities and households.

A rise in capitalist class exploitation outside households helped create tensions, struggles, and disruption within them. We and others have argued this point for the United States over the last two decades. Reduced earnings for male workers pressured women to produce more surplus labor for their husbands (and children) in households. Hence class exploitation rose both outside and inside American households. Reduced earnings for men also helped push women into the labor force to maintain family earnings. Typically, this meant that women now held two jobs, working at least a 'second shift'. It also meant added downward pressure on wages for both men and women.

We think these changes accounted for a major class structural shift experienced by many American households. Out of the disruption and fragmentation of, in Marxian terms, traditional feudal households, in which wives performed feudal surplus labor for their husbands, emerged new ancient (single adult) households in which women and men individually in their separated households produced surplus labor for themselves as individuals. The impact both positive and negative of this household transition will be with us for decades to come.

A fall in the value of labor power also led individuals to seek new ways to find untapped sources of income in order to survive in these hard times. Our cities became sites, not only of employed capitalist labor, but increasingly of a large mass of ancient (self-employed) producers producing and selling a vast array of goods and services, from occasional handiwork to crack and prostitution.

From our perspective, the costs of this capitalist restructuring – presented most often as a success story – are an enhanced rate of class exploitation now connected to an out-of-control state, a disintegration of many family structures, and exploding inner cities. These costs are truly terrifying. But this same restructuring has meant undermining feudal exploitation of women, creation of communal forms of household and nonhousehold production, greater independence and autonomy for some workers, especially ancients (the self-employed), new and different types of families, and much else. These changes give us hope. What we as nondeterminist Marxists seek is the incessant proliferation of stories in which both terror and hope – success and failure – occupy the same discursive space.

Notes

1. To view a few of our main contributions to a nondeterminist Marxian economics, readers can consult Resnick and Wolff (1987a, 1987b); Amariglio (1987); Amariglio, Resnick, and Wolff (1993); Amariglio and Ruccio (1994); Callari (1986); Callari, Cullenberg, and Biewener (1995); and Ruccio (1986, 1992).
2. For more explicit discussions of the debt and contribution of Marxian economics as well as economics more broadly to postmodernism, see Amariglio (1990); Amariglio and Ruccio (1994); Ruccio (1991); Callari and Ruccio (1996); Garnett (1995); and Pietrykowski (1996).
3. The concept of overdetermination has passed into economic discourse largely through the publication of Resnick and Wolff's *Knowledge and Class*.
4. For some examples, see Bergeron (1996), Curtis (1986, 1988), Fraad, Resnick, and Wolff (1994), Feiner (1995), Feiner and Roberts (1990a, 1990b), Gabriel (1990b), and Levin (1995). For other attempts to mine Marxism, feminism, and antiracist writings for their employment in contemporary economics, see Grapard (1995) and Amott and Matthaei (1991).
5. These similarities and interconnections are explored in part in Amariglio and Ruccio (1994, 1995), Burczak (1994), Milberg (1988, 1991), and Wilson (1995).
6. See also the story put forward by Richard McIntyre and Michael Hillard (1991).

References

Amariglio, Jack (1987), 'Marxism against Economic Science: Althusser's Legacy' in P. Zarembka (ed.), *Research in Political Economy*, **10**, Greenwich, CT: JAI Press, 159–94.

Amariglio, Jack (1990), 'Economics as a Postmodern Discourse' in W. Samuels (ed.), *Economics as Discourse*, Boston: Kluwer Academic Publishers, 15–46.

Amariglio, Jack and Callari, Antonio (1993), 'Marxian Value Theory and the Problem of the Subject: The Role of Commodity Fetishism' in E. Apter and W. Pietz (eds), *Fetishism as Cultural Discourse*, Ithaca: Cornell University Press, 186–216.

Amariglio, Jack, Resnick, Stephen and Wolff, Richard (1993), 'Division and Difference in the "Discipline" of Economics' in E. Messer-Davidow, D. Shumway and D. Sylvan (eds), *Knowledges: Historical and Critical Studies in Disciplinarity*, Charlottesville: University Press of Virginia, 150–84.

Amariglio, Jack and Ruccio, David (1994), 'Postmodernism, Marxism, and the Critique of Modern Economic Thought', *Rethinking Marxism*, **7** (Fall), 7–35.

Amariglio, Jack and Ruccio, David (1995), 'Keynes, Postmodernism, Uncertainty', in S. Dow and J. Hillard (eds), *Keynes, Knowledge, and Uncertainty*, Aldershot, UK: Edward Elgar, 334–56.

Amott, Teresa and Matthaei, Julie (1991), *Race, Gender, and Work: A Multicultural Economic History of Women in the United States*, Boston: South End Press.

Annunziato, Frank (1990), 'Commodity Unionism', *Rethinking Marxism*, **3** (Summer), 8–33.

Bergeron, Suzanne (1996), 'The Nation as a Gendered Subject of Microeconomics', in I. Bakker (ed.), *Rethinking Restructuring: Gender and Change*, Toronto: University of Toronto Press, 111–25.

Biewener, Carole (1987), 'Class and Socialist Politics in France', *Review of Radical Political Economics*, **19** (Summer), 61–76.

Biewener, Carole (1990), 'Loss of a Socialist Vision in France', *Rethinking Marxism*, **3** (Fall–Winter), 12–26.

Burczak, Theodore (1994), 'The Postmodern Moments of F.A. Hayek's Economics', *Economics and Philosophy*, **10**, 31–58.

Callari, Antonio (1986), 'History, Epistemology, and Marx's Theory of Value' in P. Zarembka (ed.), *Research in Political Economy*, **9**, Greenwich, CT: JAI Press, 69–93.

Callari, Antonio, Cullenberg, Stephen and Biewener, Carole (eds) (1995), *Marxism in the Postmodern Age: Confronting the New World Order*, New York: Guilford Publications.

Callari, Antonio and Ruccio, David (1996), Introduction, in A. Callari and D. Ruccio (eds), *Postmodern Materialism and the Future of Marxist Theory: Essays in the Althusserian Tradition*, Middletown, CT: Wesleyan University Press, 1–47, forthcoming.

146   Beyond neoclassical economics

Cullenberg, Stephen (1994), *The Falling Rate of Profit: Recasting the Marxian Debate*, London: Pluto Press.

Curtis, Fred (1986), 'Class, Race and Income Distribution: Analyzing "White" South Africa', in P. Zarembka (ed.), *Research in Political Economy*, **9**, Greenwich, CT: JAI Press, 33–67.

Curtis, Fred (1988), 'Race and Class in South Africa: Socialist Politics in the Current Conjuncture', *Rethinking Marxism*, **1** (Spring), 108–34.

Feiner, Susan (1995), 'Reading Neoclassical Economics: Toward an Erotic Economy of Sharing' in E. Kuiper and J. Sap (eds), *Out of the Margin: Feminist Perspectives on Economics*, London: Routledge, 151–66.

Feiner, Susan and Roberts, Bruce (1990a), 'Hidden by the Invisible Hand: Neoclassical Economic Theory and the Textbook Treatment of Race and Gender', *Gender and Society*, **4** (2), 159–81.

Feiner, Susan and Roberts, Bruce (1990b), 'Slave Exploitation in Neoclassical Economics: Criticism and an Alternative Direction' in R. America (ed.), *The Wealth of Races: The Present Value of Benefits from Past Injustices*, New York: Greenwood Press, 139–49.

Fraad, Harriet, Resnick, Stephen and Wolff, Richard (1994), *Bringing It All Back Home: Class, Gender and Power in the Modern Household*, London: Pluto Press.

Gabriel, Satyananda (1990a), 'Ancients: A Marxian Theory of Self-Exploitation', *Rethinking Marxism*, **3** (Spring), 85–106.

Gabriel, Satyananda (1990b), 'The Continuing Significance of Race: An Overdeterminist Approach to Racism', *Rethinking Marxism*, **3** (Fall–Winter), 65–78.

Garnett, Robert (1995), 'Marx's Value Theory: Modern or Postmodern?', *Rethinking Marxism*, **8** (Winter).

Gibson-Graham, J.K. (1996), *The End of Capitalism (As We Knew It): A Feminist Critique of Political Economy*, London: Basil Blackwell, forthcoming.

Grapard, Ulla (1995), 'Robinson Crusoe: The Quintessential Economic Man?', *Feminist Economics*, **1** (1), 33–52.

Klamer, Arjo (1990), 'Toward the Native's Point of View: The Difficulty of Changing the Conversation' in Don Lavoie (ed.), *Economics and Hermeneutics*, London and New York: Routledge, 19–33.

Klamer, Arjo (1995), 'The Conception of Modernism in Economics: Samuelson, Keynes and Harrod' in S. Dow and J. Hillard (eds), *Keynes, Knowledge and Uncertainty*, Aldershot, UK: Edward Elgar, 318–33.

Levin, Lee (1995), 'Toward a Feminist, Post-Keynesian Theory of Investment' in E. Kuiper and J. Sap (eds), *Out of the Margin: Feminist Perspectives on Economics*, London: Routledge, 100–119.

McCloskey, Donald (1985), *The Rhetoric of Economics*, Madison: University of Wisconsin Press.

McCloskey, Donald (1994), *Knowledge and Persuasion in Economics*, Cambridge: Cambridge University Press.

McIntyre, Richard (1996), 'Mode of Production, Social Formation, and Uneven Development: Or, Is There Capitalism in America?' in A. Callari and D. Ruccio (eds), *Postmodern Materialism and the Future of Marxist Theory: Essays in the Althusserian Tradition*, Middletown, CT: Wesleyan University Press, 231–53.

McIntyre, Richard and Hillard, Michael (1991), 'A Kinder, Gentler Capitalism? Resurgent Corporate Liberalism in the Age of Bush', *Rethinking Marxism*, **4** (Spring), 104–14.

Milberg, William (1988), 'The Language of Economics: Deconstructing the Neoclassical Text', *Social Concept*, **4**, 33–57.

Milberg, William (1991), 'Marxism, Poststructuralism, and the Discourse of Economics', *Rethinking Marxism*, **4** (Summer), 93–104.

Norton, Bruce (1988), 'Epochs and Essences: A Review of Marxian Long Wave and Stagnation Theories', *Cambridge Journal of Economics*, **12** (2), 203–24.

Norton, Bruce (1992), 'Radical Theories of Accumulation and Crisis: Developments and Directions' in S. Feiner and B. Roberts (eds), *Radical Economics*, Boston: Kluwer Academic Publishers, 155–98.

Norton, Bruce (1995), 'The Theory of Monopoly Capitalism and Classical Economics', *History of Political Economy*, **27** (4), 733–49.

Pietrykowski, Bruce (1996), 'Deconstructing Consumer Behavior: Developing a Postmodern Approach to Economic Analysis' in M. Bianchi and D. Gualerzi (eds), *The Active Consumer*, forthcoming.

Resnick, Stephen and Wolff, Richard (1987a), *Knowledge and Class*, Chicago: University of Chicago Press.

Resnick, Stephen and Wolff, Richard (1987b), *Economics: Marxian versus Neoclassical*, Baltimore: Johns Hopkins University Press.

Roche, John (1985), 'Marx's Theory of Money: A Reinterpretation', *Review of Radical Political Economics*, **17** (1&2), 201–11.

Roche, John (1988), 'Value, Money, and Crisis in the First Part of Capital', *Rethinking Marxism*, **1** (Winter), 126–43.

Ruccio, David (1986), 'Essentialism and Socialist Economic Planning: A Methodological Critique of Optimal Planning Theory' in W. Samuels (ed.), *Research in the History of Economic Thought and Methodology*, **4**, Greenwich, CT: JAI Press, 85–108.

Ruccio, David (1991), 'Postmodernism and Economics', *Journal of Post Keynesian Economics*, **13** (Summer), 495–510.

Ruccio, David (1992), 'Failure of Socialism, Future of Socialists?' *Rethinking Marxism*, **5** (Summer), 7–22.

Strassmann, Diana (1993), 'Not a Free Market: The Rhetoric of Disciplinary Authority in Economics' in Marianne A. Ferber and Julie A. Nelson (eds) *Beyond Economic Man: Feminist Theory and Economics*, Chicago: University of Chicago Press, 54–68.

Strassmann, Diana and Polanyi, Livia (1995), 'The Economist as Storyteller: What the Texts Reveal' in Edith Kuiper and Jolande Sap (eds), *Out of the Margin: Feminist Perspectives on Economic Theory*, London: Routledge, 129–50.

Wilson, Lucas (1995), *Deweyan Pragmatism and the Critique of Modernist Economic Methodology*, PhD dissertation, University of Massachusetts.

Wolff, Richard, Roberts, Bruce and Callari, Antonio (1982), 'Marx's (not Ricardo's) "Transformation Problem": A Radical Reconceptualization', *History of Political Economy*, **14** (4), 564–82.

Wolff, Richard, Roberts, Bruce and Callari, Antonio (1984), 'A Marxian Alternative to the Traditional "Transformation Problem"', *Review of Radical Political Economics*, **16** (2&3), 115–35.

9 Foundational economics

Fred E. Foldvary

The elements of foundational economics

Scientific theory consists of a related set of warranted propositions. A theorem may be deduced from and hence warranted or justified by other theorems, but ultimately a body of theory is warranted by a set of postulates which are not deduced from other theorems, and hence form a set of foundational propositions from which all other theorems are derived. Foundational economics (FE) studies such foundations of economic theory and also how theory is derived from the foundation. The foundational postulates can be considered to be axioms, hence axiomatic propositions. The axioms are not regarded as 'self evident', but are made evident from observed data. Axiomatic propositions are thus empirically warranted, and '*a priori*' only in preceding the theory derived from them.

The axiomatic-deductive method, deriving theory from axiomatic propositions, was used, however imperfectly, in classical economics. Currently, the Austrian and geo-economic schools consciously use this methodology, but neither has set forth a list of explicit foundational propositions. Leland Yeager (1954, p. 235) compares the axiomatic-deductive methodology of Henry George, who developed the basic theory of the geo-economics school, and Carl Menger, founder of the Austrian school of economics. Both held the view that 'The facts that economists induce from the behavior of themselves and other people serve as axioms from which a useful body of economic theory can be logically deduced'. Yeager adds, 'George and Menger conceived of economic theory as a body of deductions from basic principles having a strong empirical foundation. The methodological individualism of George and Menger stems from a realization that the economist's 'inside' knowledge of human motives and decision-making is a leading source of empirical generalizations'.

Neoclassical microeconomic textbooks and models also typically use axiomatic deduction to develop and explain theory, and microeconomic foundations have been analyzed by some for macroeconomic theory. In contrast, postmodern thought rejects the concept of universally applicable foundations, although postmodern theory may be using the method implicitly.

A principle of Foundational Economics as presented here is that any body of theory must unavoidably be founded on axiomatic propositions. Another principle of FE is that a proposition is warranted either by confirmed observations or by rigorous logical deduction from other warranted propositions. FE applies the Socratic questions, 'what do you mean?' and 'how do you know?', to propositions to determine their semantic clarity and substance, and to determine their warrants in logic and evidence. Foundational analysis can thus be used to deconstruct propositions to distinguish between unwarranted or unclear assertions, partially warranted conjectures and hypotheses, and fully (though not with certainty) warranted theorems (see Chapter 1 for a discussion distinguishing these). Note that in foundational terminology, 'theory' or 'theorem' refers only to fully warranted propositions whose key terms have clear and distinct definitions.

The objective warranting or justification of propositions is challenged by postmodern and pragmatic thought which rejects universal, objective, and certain 'Truth' (often capitalized to contrast it with small-t 'truth'). In the foundational approach presented here, 'truth' as a noun is a derivative of 'true' as an adjective. Hence, 'truth' means the quality of being true. Under the 'correspondence' principle, propositions are 'true' if they are in accord with perceived reality or derive validly from propositions in accord with reality. Hence, the ultimate soundness of propositions derives from confirmed observation, i.e. observations which can either be confirmed by others (as in repeatable experiments) or unrepeatable events which have been observed and which have explanations that are in accord with theory. Propositions based on events for which witnessed reports are reasonably contested fall under the category of conjectures. The foundational approach thus does not distinguish between 'true' and 'True', or between 'truth' and 'Truth', but recognizes that propositions regarded as warranted, hence true, may always be challenged. As to certainty, both human memory and senses are fallible, so any evidence beyond one's own existence is not certain. Warranting by evidence consists of high probability in relationship to other observations, rather than absolute certitude, with the realist presumption that normal observations are most likely in accord with the mapped reality. Some simple logical deductions are indeed certain, e.g. if A is a subset of B, then it is certain that the existence of A implies the existence of B. But complex reasoning is highly uncertain, since, for example, there may be hidden premises which are not easy to uncover.

The discovery and warranting of axiomatic propositions

With respect to axiomatic propositions, Frank Knight (1956, p. 164) went so far as to say: 'We surely 'know' these propositions better, more confidently and certainly, than we know the truth of any statement about any concrete physical fact or event... We know them in the same way that one knows one is writing sentences and not simply making dark markings on a white surface'.

The following methodology is postulated for obtaining and warranting axiomatic propositions:

1.   A proposition can be taken from a another field of science or else discovered through observation, including personal experience. C.I. Lewis (1946, p. 171) noted that 'Empirical truth cannot be known except, finally, through presentations of sense'. Tamara Horowitz (1985, p. 230) states that 'A person has enough experience to know a proposition if and only if that person's experience suffices for him to discover that the proposition is true given only further ratiocination'.

2.   Since, as Popper (1952) wrote, no source of knowledge has authority, a proposition is examined by the 'internal dialogue' of introspection and reflection, asking the epistemological question, 'how do I know?' and the semantic question 'what do I mean?' to clarify the key terms. The scientist considers (a) whether the proposition is peculiar to one's local circumstance and subjective views or has a universal application, and (b) whether it is based upon arbitrary notions or whether its content is based on evidence.

3.   Since a scientist recognizes that observations and reasoning can be mistaken, he engages in an 'external dialogue' with others, who again ask the two questions. This is akin to what Popper (1965) called 'critical rationalism': criticizing the theories of others. Dialogue is a check against error.

In the foundational approach, the truth of a proposition does not depend on any agreement. As stated by Uskali Mäki (1995, p. 1305), a coherence view of justification, in which beliefs are justified by coherence with other beliefs, is 'in conflict with forms of what is customarily called foundationalism'. Although a profession may endow propositions with scientific imprimatur when they have persuasive arguments (McCloskey, 1985), foundationalism is based on a realist philosophy which rejects 'socially constituted reality' (except for a socially created culture), since foundationalists regard logic and evidence as ontologically objective, i.e. as existing apart from our personal views. Coherence methodology also suffers from the contradiction of incorporating constraints on rhetoric which themselves are not a product of coherence. It should be noted that McCloskey (1995) in response to Mäki thinks that coherence and correspondence are not mutually exclusive and are not the only ways of attaining knowledge.

But how we come to know reality, the epistemological question, is an individual procedure. Foundationalism adheres to methodological individualism, hence the judgment of how much a proposition is warranted is an individual matter. Epistemologically, with respect to 'how do you know', a proposition acquires a scientific imprimatur by an agreement among some scientists on the warranting. But imprimatur is not a warrant. If there is disagreement among analysts, the proposition has the status of a theory within a school that considers it warranted, and as a conjecture within the discipline considered as a whole.

4. After the scientist is satisfied with step 3, or when it yields diminishing returns, the scientist repeats step 2 to determine whether any objections have proven fatal to the proposition. If not, it is accepted by him or her as true, but always subject to further arguments that may challenge it.

Steps 1 through 4 are not one-time events, but are continuously traversed by students and those (few) scientists who choose to question fundamental assumptions. Each scientist must obtain his own science; each mind must acquire and warrant knowledge individually. Science is ontologically objective but epistemologically subjective, since each individual is an equal judge of how well propositions are warranted in logic and evidence. An intersubjective agreement thus does not warrant theory but only creates a school of thought within which it is thought warranted. What prevents warranting from degenerating into idiosyncracy is the requirement to use logic and confirmed observation. Although ultimately the judging of warrantedness is individual because thinking is so, logic can expose weak and false warrants.

Foundational economics includes the following elements:

1. FE analyzes particular bodies of theory (e.g. of a school of thought) to determine their foundational propositions and how their theory derives from them. FE also judges the soundness or warrantedness of theory and its foundations, as well as the clarity of the meaning of the key terms. In analyzing foundations as well as theory, FE uses lateral logic in determining whether the premises or options are comprehensive, i.e. if there are missing elements which then skews the soundness of the theory.

2. FE endeavors to determine the foundational propositions and taxonomy of economic science, apart from the particular bodies of theory of various schools. The foundation consists of ethical as well as economic propositions. FE then determines the structure of methodology, theory and data based on the foundation.

3. The subfield of synthetic theory construction constructs a systematic and comprehensive synthesis of the sound theories of various (ideally, all) schools of thought, based on the axiomatic propositions determined in (2). Synthetic theory construction is closely related to comparative economic theory (CET) (described in Chapter 1).

The structure of theory
Foundational analysis as presented here posits the following structure for the theory of any scientific field. It is emphasized that the structure applies to theory and not theorizing; as McCloskey (1985) has shown, economists do not necessarily follow the methodology they espouse in actually doing

economics. For example, although logically theory rests on its foundational postulates, in discovering the theory, a scientist might actually come up with the axiomatic propositions after working out much of the theory, when the foundation may become clearer.

1.   There is a set of axiomatic propositions from which the entire body of theory can be derived. The axioms are universal to the field; in economics, the foundation includes ethical premises. The theory can also include auxiliary propositions and data which are not universal, hence not axiomatic, but particular to time, place, and culture.

2.   There is a taxonomy that divides aspects of a field into meaningful subsets. The taxonomy itself is not axiomatic but is derived, and the taxonomy is not absolute, since it can depend on the context of the theory. Examples of taxonomy include the division of factors into land, labor, and capital goods; the division of expenditure into consumption and investment; and the division of economic sectors as households, firms, and government. F.A. Hayek (1942 [1948], p. 67) stated that much social science consists in classifications of types of behavior, providing 'an orderly arrangement of the material', which is 'a kind of logic'.

3.   The key terms of the propositions and taxonomy, especially when controversial or having multiple meanings, are given clear and distinct definitions, in answer to 'what do you mean?'. These definitions must be in accord with the context of the propositions in which they are put.

4.   Pure theory, applicable to the universe of the field, is derived from the foundational propositions, and such theory applies to the whole domain of the science. In economics, pure theory applies to all economies regardless of culture or history.

Many economists have analyzed such pure theory. Terence Hutchison (1938) stated that the propositions of 'pure theory' are necessary. James Buchanan (1979, p. 42) writes, of economics, that in the logic of choice, 'certain laws can be deduced, even if conceptually refutable hypotheses cannot be derived'. John Neville Keynes (1917 [1963]), p. 142), father of John Maynard Keynes, wrote, 'In the abstract or pure theory of political economy we concern ourselves entirely with certain broad general principles irrespective of particular economic conditions'. He added, 'concrete economics comes in to supplement the pure theory... the premises and conclusions are adapted to suit special circumstances, and both premises and conclusions are constantly tested by direct appeals to experience'.

5.   Pure theory itself has a taxonomy of conditional and unconditional propositions. An unconditional theorem follows directly from other theorems or foundational propositions, and thus always applies to the field. A conditional theorem is derived both from unconditional propositions and from propositions which may not always be empirically in existence, hence the

theorem is conditional or contingent on the conditions and only applies empirically if the conditional premises are true in practice. For example, the premise that firms maximize profits is not an axiom but an auxiliary proposition from which theory conditional on it derives; whether firms do in practice attempt to maximize profits is an empirical matter, not a universal absolute.

6. For phenomena particular to time, place, and culture (such as the cause of the Great Depression), specific theory is derived and discovered based partly on pure theory and partly on data specific to the phenomenon. Pure conditional theorems may be applied to discover specific theory if the conditional premise is found to apply empirically. Specific theory can be devised by abduction along the lines suggested by Charles Sanders Peirce (see Lawson, 1994), generating hypotheses for particular facts.

Specific theory itself can be either unconditional or conditional. Specific theory typically begins as conjectures or hypotheses which then become better warranted from more testing or evidence gathering. Besides hypothesis testing, specific theory can be warranted from a convergence method that uses data to better warrant a conjecture, which is then applied to the same or additional data, eventually converging into a warranted proposition (Handy and Harwood, 1973).

As Buchanan (1969 [1987]), p. 38) stated, 'As we move beyond this pure logic, ... [s]pecific motivation is imputed to the decision maker...'. John Stuart Mill (1836 [1984], p. 54) noted that 'practical men require specific experience'. Thomas Meyer (1993, p. 7) also draws a distinction between two types of theory: one is 'abstract theory that is concerned with high-level generalizations, and looks towards axiomatization. The other, empirical science theory, focuses on explaining past observations and predicting future ones'.

7. Theory, both universal and specific, is used in observing and interpreting empirical phenomena. A field of study includes both theory and a body of empirical observations and descriptions. Data is theory-laden in being understood within the context of one's theoretical background, but data then also provides material for discovering or speculating on new propositions as well as providing further warrants to propositions. Foundational analysis accepts all data types, including statistics, case studies, interviews, and archival data.

8. Induction plays a role in developing both specific theory and the foundational propositions. As Lewis wrote (1946, p. 361), 'we have no alternative but to accept...in some form or other, the Rule of Induction'. Henri Poincaré (1952, p. xxvi) states that 'The method of the physical sciences is based on the induction which leads us to expect the recurrence of a phenomenon when the circumstances which give rise to it are repeated'. Inductive and probabilistic theory as well as abduction can be one stage in formulating a hypothesis or conjecture.

To sum up, this 'structure of science' is an integrated pluralism of methodology: axiomatic deduction for pure theory, particular description of observed phenomena, induction probabilistic generalizations, abduction and hypothetical deduction for falsifiable generalizations, and interpretive understanding of all these. Each mediates the others; none can claim exclusivity. John N. Keynes (1917 [1963]) recognized that a variety of methodologies were appropriate. But it is not enough to simply accept these various methodologies, floating about the house of science with no relationship to one another. The structure presented here integrates the methodologies into a unified, systematic whole. To use a metaphor, science is a body for which axiomatic propositions supply the skeleton, description the senses, induction and abduction the nervous system, interpretive understanding the brain, pure theory the organs, and hypothetical-deduction the muscle. They form an organic whole.

Philosophers of foundational thought

Most schools of thought do not merely set forth a body of theory, but also constitute a culture within their field. Members of a school become inculcated in a tradition which has a history, key personages (often a founder), and a distinctive language. Austrians, for example, look to Menger, Mises, and Hayek for inspiration, cite them frequently, and use terminology such as 'catallaxy' and 'capital structure'. Certain themes such as subjectivity and spontaneous orders are emphasized. In contrast, for example, Marxists look to Marx for textual backing, inspiration, topics, and vocabulary.

Foundational economics is cultureless in this sense, since it attempts to examine all schools of thought and since it examines a foundation for all economic phenomena. Perhaps, though, if it develops as a distinct literature, foundationalism may develop a culture.

The French Physiocrats of the 1700s had considered economics to follow natural laws, and Sir Dudly North and David Ricardo had used deductive theory, but Joseph Schumpeter (1954, p. 575) credits Nassau Senior (1790–1864) as the first economist to explicitly attempt to provide an axiomatic basis for economic theory, 'a venture in pure theory' (p. 576), although it was, says Schumpeter, defective. Senior's four axioms were (1) the economizing principle (people desire to obtain wealth with minimum sacrifice), (2) population growth (population is limited only by moral or physical restraints), (3) increasing returns on labor, (4) decreasing returns in agriculture (Senior, 1939).

Thomas Reid (1815, 1969), writing 'Of First Principles in General', stated that 'there are other propositions which are no sooner understood than they are believed. The judgment naturally follows the apprehension of them necessarily, and both are equally the work of nature, and the result of our original powers. There is no searching for evidence, no weighing of arguments; the proposition is not deduced or inferred from another...'. These propositions 'when they are used in matters of science, have commonly been called axioms and ... first principles... self-evident truths'. All reasoning must have a foundation, 'a fixed point to rest on' (p. 596).

Edmund Husserl (1973, p. 352) wrote, 'The universal truths, in which we merely display what belongs to pure essential generalities, precede all questions bearing on facts and the truths which concern them'. 'What is easy to make clear in the example of mathematical thinking and mathematical natural science is valid in a completely general way for every objective sphere' (p. 353). Karl Popper (1983, p. 79) stated that 'There exists at least one true law of nature', and (1965, p. 122) that 'every description uses...universals'.

Patrick O'Sullivan (1987, p. 12) calls first principles 'reflexively self-justifying propositions' which are true because their denial would involve a 'performative contradiction' (p. 13).

Lionel Robbins (1935 [1979], p. 39) wrote: 'The propositions of economic theory, like all scientific theory, are obviously deductions from a series of postulates. And the chief of these postulates are all assumptions involving in some way simple and indisputable facts of experience... They are the stuff of our everyday experience... [I]t is on postulates of this sort that the complicated theorems of advanced analysis ultimately depend'.

Frank Knight (1956, p. 158) thought that the epistemology of such propositions is 'explained by the fact that our minds lack any power of really creative imagination or original intuitive knowledge of superempirical reality: ... Any statement which "must" be true under all conditions is simply a statement of a fact about the world which is so universal and fundamental for experience that we cannot "think it away" or imagine a situation in which it would not be true'.

Axiomatic propositions can be regarded as forming 'natural law', i.e. universally valid propositions, such as regularities of nature or the rules of an ethic. Though Ludwig von Mises (1957 [1985], p. 45) of the Austrian school did not prefer the term, he pointed out the sound idea of 'a nature-given order of things to which man must adjust his actions if he wants to succeed'.

Other economists have had the contrasting view that 'Economic theory cannot be of much use unless it is prepared to adapt to real changing conditions... The evolutionary nature of economic events requires that economic reasoning itself be evolutionary' (Carson, 1990, p. 28). But is this statement itself a proposition using economic reasoning? Does it too adapt to changing conditions? Will it evolve into something else? It is apparently meant as a general proposition about all economic theory, and hence it is self-negating. The proposition that there are axiomatic propositions, in contrast, is at least not self-contradictory.

Mises termed the deductive methodology and its theory 'praxeology': 'The starting point of all praxeological thinking is not arbitrarily chosen axioms, but a self-evident proposition, fully, clearly, and necessarily present in every human mind' (1962, p. 4). The central proposition for Mises, and Austrian economics in general, is human action: 'To act means: to strive after ends, that is, to choose a goal and to resort to means in order to attain the goal sought' (pp. 4–5). The Misesian 'axiom' of human action is actually a pure theorem derived from the social-science or praxeological proposition of purposeful behavior and more basic economic propositions.

For Mises, these propositions are not innate ideas nor a precipitate of experience, but are based on the 'logical structure of the human mind' (p. 16). 'The negation of what it asserts is unthinkable... [Praxeology] partakes of the apodictic certainty provided by logical reasoning that starts from an a priori category' (p. 18).

Mises took apriorism to an extreme by asserting its apodictic certainty. George Selgin (1990, p. 14) notes that 'Although supposedly irrefutable, this axiom is not merely "analytic", i.e., non-empirical or vacuous'. It is not independent from experience, but is based on inner reflection, not merely from sense data alone.

When Mises developed the idea of human action, he had not only learned previous economic texts but had personal experience in action, which necessarily gave him data on action. Hence, Mises' assertion that experience plays no role in formulating the propositions must be rejected, and with that, the apodictic certainty of pure theory. An earlier Austrian, Wieser, saw the origin of the insights relevant to axiomatic propositions in experience. The human consciousness contains a 'treasury of experiences' (quoted in Fabian and Simons, 1986, p. 82), but the scientist must clarify the meaning of the concepts of everyday language (p. 83). 'Wieser insisted that subjective value theory is concerned strictly with empirical fact, though it appears deductive...in that it deals with *typical* phenomena in the guise of ideal types' (White, 1977, p. 7).

Mises, of course, knew Wieser's work, and states that Wieser's 'common experience' 'is not the experience with which the empirical sciences are concerned' (1976, p. 21). 'What Wieser calls "common experience" is to be sharply distinguished from experience acquired "through observations collected in the manner of historical or statistical studies"' (p. 22). Mises insists that Wieser's notion is a 'presupposition of every experience' (ibid.).

Another Austrian economist, Hayek, rejects positivist objectivism but accepts empirical falsification. 'Hayek's critique of scientism in the human sciences is a call to his readers to make the interpretive turn' (Madison, 1989, p. 172). Human action must be understood as purposeful and meaningful. However, there is a problem. 'What has been described as the "fundamental dilemma" for modern Austrians lies in the "later" Hayek's attempt to combine two different philosophies of social science: the Austrian praxeological school with its axiomatic rejection of empirical testing, and the hypothetical-deductive approach of Popperian falsifiability' (Shand, 1984, p. 4).

The integrated methodological pluralism described above overcomes this dilemma by subsuming both interpretation and falsifiability as complementary methods under the umbrella of axiomatic propositions themselves based on experience and reason. Caldwell (1988, p. 235) is one economist who has called for pluralism, by which he means an evaluation and appreciation of all research programs, but his pluralism is a 'meta-methodological position' (p. 240) that takes what economists do as a given. This is a call for tolerance, but provides no guidance. In the foundational structure presented here, pluralism is an integrated structure of theory made up of interdependent methodologies, integrating the universal with the specific and the falsifiable with the interpretive. It is internally pluralist, but externally a unified whole. It is not mere pluralism but *e pluribus unum*.

The propositions of economics
The remainder of this chapter focuses on the field of economics to show how axiomatic propositions form its basis and generate its pure theory. Following are some of the axiomatic propositions which I regard as foundational for economic theory, which would be added to other propositions which apply to all social science. The propositions listed here do not necessarily exhaust the axioms of economics. The point here is not to lay down a complete foundation of economic theory as such, but to show how propositions do form such a foundation.

Propositions about physical resources and technology
1. Available natural resources are finite.
2. Natural resources are heterogenous
3. A finite output can be produced with given inputs.
4. The output from production depends on the process.
5. Eventually, increases of a variable input applied to a fixed input yield diminishing returns.
6. A production process exhibits either decreasing, constant, or increasing returns to scale (ratio of output to inputs).

Propositions about human behavior and thought
7. All persons have ends.
8. A person's total desires or ends have no limit.
9. The marginal utility of a good will eventually diminish.
10. Persons can determine the value of an end relative to other ends.
11. Some ends can be satisfied by means of economic goods.

12. Persons will economize in achieving ends (a.k.a. 'maximizing').
13. The desires of human beings include self-gratification (ends connected with their own survival, happiness, and power).
14. Human beings can sympathize with others and thus obtain utility when the utility of others is increased.
15. Human beings learn, i.e. obtain, retain, and apply new information.
16. The value of any economic item is determined subjectively.
17. People tend to have a time preference, preferring goods at present to those in the future.

Propositions about knowledge

18. The future is uncertain.
19. Empirical knowledge is incomplete.
20. Human cognition is limited.

Ethical propositions

Besides these propositions, economics also rests on an ethical foundation, since the concept of the market as a process of voluntary exchange implies rules that the agents follow, by which voluntary and involuntary acts can be distinguished (High, 1985). For there to be a universal theory of the market process, there needs to be a universal ethic (Foldvary, 1980), a moral standard which would be derived from premises based on human nature. 'A market is therefore the totality of the voluntary economic acts of agents' (Foldvary, 1994). A non-arbitrary and universal ethic also makes possible a standard for policy which is independent of culture.

The foundational axioms of this universal ethic consist of two propositions about human nature: (1) human beings are independent (biologically, not socially or economically); (2) human beings are equal (in moral worth). These premises were recognized by John Locke (1947 [1690], p. 123): 'The state of nature has a law of nature to govern it which obliges every one; and reason, which is that law, teaches all mankind who will but consult it that, being all equal and independent, no one ought to harm another in his life, health, liberty, or possessions...'.

From these premises and the criteria for a non-arbitrary ethic one can derive the following ethical rules:

1. All acts, and only those acts, which coercively harm others are evil, other than direct self-defense.
2. All acts, and only those acts, which are welcomed benefits are good.
3. All other acts are assigned a moral value of 'neutral'.

The maximizing maxim

The twelfth proposition on economizing drives much of economic theory. As stated by Machlup (1946, p. 521), 'The proposition that the firm will attempt to equate marginal cost and marginal revenue is logically implied in the assumption that the firm will attempt to maximize its profit (or minimize its loss)'.

A common fallacy regarding the economizing proposition is that it includes the presumption that people have knowledge about the 'costs, incomes, and yields with respect to all their options' (Plattner, 1989, p. 8). As an axiom, the proposition presumes nothing about the amount of knowledge people have, nor about their capacity to analyze data. It only states that they will economize in achieving their ends, whatever their state of knowledge. Any additional assumptions constitute either specific theory (for falsifiable hypotheses) or premises for conditional pure theory.

Another misconception is to impute a 'selfish' motive into the economizing principle and create the caricature 'homo economicus' that humanist and other economists justifiably object to, hence applying proposition #13 to the exclusion of #14. As noted by Rima (1994, p. 190), 'political economists from Smith onward came to rely on deductive logic to articulate the vision of an economy that is comprised of self-interested individuals whose actions bring about beneficial results for all market participants'.

Buchanan and Tullock (1962 [1965], p. 17), in developing the Virginian theory of public choice, recognize that economic theory concerning a person's choices does not depend on 'self-interest in all aspects of his behavior'. Normally, economic theory assumes the principle of 'non-Tuism', that the subjects are not gift giving; the interests of others in an exchange are 'excluded from consideration' (p. 18). Non-Tuism hence is an important auxiliary postulate in addition to the economizing proposition, and theory using it is conditional on that premise.

However, Adam Smith, whose 'invisible hand' theory regarding self-interested activity is well known, also provided a theory of the 'visible hand' of benevolent activity in his work, *The Theory of Moral Sentiments* (1790 [1982]). Smith stated that there is an element of human nature by which a person is interested 'in the fortune of others', though one 'derives nothing from it except the pleasure in seeing it' (p. 9). This element he identified as 'sympathy', by which Smith meant 'our fellow-feeling with any passion whatever' (p. 10). The benevolent provision of services and funds is also part of the market process and plays an important part in the provision of public goods (Foldvary, 1994).

Subjective values

The sixteenth proposition was not universally accepted in economics, and it is instructive in showing how economic paradigms derive from the axiomatic propositions. The classical school postulates that value is equal to the costs of production, a premise which seems to be generally valid except in the case of monopolies and goods no longer being produced, hence fixed in supply. The Marxist school obtained its value theory from classical thought, and orthodox Marxism still has it in its theoretical foundation. Since labor is the principle cost in the production process (the machines too are made by labor), the value of output is that of the labor, according to the Marxist labor theory of value. If workers do not get this value in wages, they are exploited, according to orthodox Marxism.

In the second half of the 19th century, the 'marginalist' revolution took place in economic thought. The Austrian economist Menger, as well as two others, Walras and Jevons, challenged the classical proposition. The value of a good, they argued, is not determined by its costs; the consumer does not care about the costs of production. The buyer is concerned with the value to him of the marginal or additional unit of a good. The price he is willing to pay for this determines the price of the good. Menger states this in the most thoroughly subjective way. The marginal value of a good, says Menger, is subjective, and from this proposition and those regarding ends he derives the pure theorem that 'The value of a particular good or of a given portion of the whole quantity of a good at the disposal of an economizing individual is thus for him equal to the importance of the least important of the satisfactions assured by the whole quantity and achieved with any equal portion' (Menger (1871 [1976], p. 139). The classicists had the process backwards. Goods tend to sell for the costs of production because at such a price, a consumer will value the good enough to make it worth producing. Goods which people do not want enough of may not get sold at the costs of production.

This change in an axiomatic proposition was so fundamental to the theory of value that economists consider the classical school to have died with it and a new paradigm, that of neoclassical economics, replaced it. Later, neoclassical microeconomics divided into the mathematical neoclassical school and the more radically subjectivist and interpretive Austrian school. However, orthodox Marxism kept the labor theory of value, making its theory radically different from the neoclassicals and Austrians.

However, we can dig deeper into the issue of what separates these two fundamentally different schools of thought. The division may be normative at heart, rather than a difference in the perception of value. We can designate the cost-of-production as cost-value and the subjective value of a good as exchange-value. The issue may not be which value is the 'true' value; there are two types of values, and the question now becomes which value should be that which the laborer receives as wages: the cost-value determined by the price of the good, or the marginal value of the labor (of the next worker hired), as subjectively determined by the employer? What seems to be an axiomatic difference may be a normative difference. Moreover, since capital goods are in turn produced by labor, capital, and land, ultimately goods are produced by land and labor, and the Marxist norm is logically reducible to the Henry George norm that the rent of land be distributed among all the people. Marxists may be, at bottom, geo-economists with a deficient axiomatic foundation.

Conclusion

Theory rests on axiomatic foundations. Just as a house is better constructed when its foundation is sound, theory that derives from explicit foundational principles is clearer and better warranted than that in which the foundation is implicit and unexamined. Combined with Comparative Economic Theory, Foundational Economics offers a methodology for evaluating theory and to selectively synthesize the thought of various schools of economics into a more comprehensive and useful science.

References

Buchanan, James M. (1969, 1987), 'Is Economics the Science of Choice?', in Robert Tollison and Viktor Vanberg (eds), *Economics: Between Predictive Science and Moral Philosophy*, College Station: Texas A&M University.

Buchanan, James M. (1979), *What Should Economists Do?*, Indianapolis: Liberty Press.

Buchanan, James M. and Tullock, Gordon (1962, 1965), *Calculus of Consent*, Ann Arbor: University of Michigan Press.

Caldwell, Bruce J. (1988) 'The Case for Pluralism', in Neil de Marchi (ed.), *The Popperian Legacy in Economics*, Cambridge: Cambridge University Press.

Carson, Robert B. (1990), *What Economists Know*, NY: St. Martin's Press.

Fabian, Reinhard and Simons, Peter (1986), 'The Second Austrian School of Value Theory' in Wolfgang Grassl and Barry Smith (eds), *Austrian Economics: Historical and Philosophical Background*, New York: New York University Press.

Foldvary, Fred (1980), *The Soul of Liberty*, San Francisco: The Gutenberg Press.

Foldvary, Fred (1994), *Public Goods and Private Communities*, Aldershot, UK: Edward Elgar.

Geiger, George R. (1994), *The Philosophy of Henry George*, NY: The Macmillan Company.

George, Henry (1879, 1975), *Progress and Poverty*, NY: Robert Schalkenbach Foundation.

Handy, Rollo and Harwood, E.C. (1973), *Useful Procedures of Inquiry*, Great Barrington: Behavioral Research Council (American Institute for Economic Research).

Hayek, F.A. (1948), 'The Facts of the Social Sciences', in *Individualism and Economic Order*, Chicago: University of Chicago Press, 57–76 (First read before the Cambridge University Moral Science Club, 1942).

High, Jack (1985), 'Is Economics Independent of Ethics?', *Reason Papers*, **10** (Spring), 3–16.

Horowitz, Tamara (1985), 'A Priori Truth', *Journal of Philosophy*, **82**, 225–39.

Husserl, Edmund (1973), *Experience and Judgment*, translated by James S. Churchill and Karl Ameriks, Evanston: Northwestern University Press.

Hutchison, Terence (1938, 1960), *The Significance and Basic Postulates of Economic Theory*, 2nd edn, New York: Augustus M. Kelley.

Keynes, John Neville (1917, 1963), *The Scope and Method of Political Economy*, 4th edn, New York: Augustus M. Kelly.

Knight, Frank H. (1940, 1956), '"What Is Truth" in Economics?', *Journal of Political Economy*, **48**, reprinted in *On the History and Method of Economics*, Chicago: University of Chicago Press.

Lawson, Tony (1994), 'A Realist Theory for Economics', in Roger Backhouse (ed.), *New Directions in Economic Methodology*, London: Routledge.

Lewis, Clarence Irving (1946), *An Analysis of Knowledge and Valuation*, La Salle: Open Court.

Lewis, Clarence Irving (1955, 1970), 'Realism or Phenomenalism?' in John D. Goheen and

John L. Mothershead, Jr. (eds), *Collected Papers of Clarence Irving Lewis*, Stanford: Stanford University Press.

Locke, John (1947 [1690]), *Two Treatises of Government*, New York: Hafner Press.

Machlup, Fritz (1946), 'Marginal Analysis and Empirical Research', *American Economic Review*, **36**, 519–54.

Madison, G.B. (1989), 'Hayek and the Interpretive Turn', *Critical Review*, **3**, 169–85.

Mäki, Uskali (1995), 'Diagnosing McCloskey', *Journal of Economic Literature*, **33** (3), 1300–318.

McCloskey, Donald (1985), *The Rhetoric of Economics*, Madison: University of Wisconsin Press.

McCloskey, Donald (1995), 'Modern Epistemology Against Analytic Philosophy: A Reply to Mäki', *Journal of Economic Literature*, **33** (3), 1319–23.

Menger, Carl (1871, 1976), *Principles of Economics*, trs. James Dignwall and Bert Hoselitz, New York: New York University Press.

Meyer, Thomas (1993), *Truth versus Precision in Economics*, Aldershot, UK: Edward Elgar.

Mill, John Stuart (1836, 1948), 'On the definition and method of political economy', in *Philosophy of Economics*, reprinted in *Essays on Some Unsettled Questions of Political Economy*, 3rd edn, London: London School of Economics.

Mises, Ludwig Von (1962), *The Ultimate Foundations of Economic Science*, Kansas City: Sheed Andrews and McMeel.

Mises, Ludwig Von (1976), *Epistemological Problems of Economics*, NY: New York University Press.

Mises, Ludwig Von (1957, 1985), *Theory and History*, Auburn, AL: Ludwig von Mises Institute.

O'Sullivan, Patrick J. (1987), *Economic Methodology and Freedom to Choose*, London: Allen & Unwin.

Plattner, Stuart (1989), Introduction, *Economic Anthropology*, Stuart Plattner (ed.), Stanford: Stanford University Press.

Poincaré, Henri (1952), *Science and Hypothesis*, New York: Dover Publications.

Popper, Karl R. (1965, 1970), 'Three Views Concerning Human Knowledge' in Charles Landsman (ed.), *The Foundation of Knowledge*, Englewood Cliffs: Prentice Hall, 93–123, reprinted in *Conjectures and Refutations*, New York: Basic Books.

Popper, Karl R. (1983), *Realism and the Aim of Science*, Totowa, NJ: Rowman and Littlefield.

Reid, Thomas (1815, 1969), *Essays on the Intellectual Powers of Man*, Cambridge: MIT Press.

Rima, Ingrid H. (1994), 'The Role of Numeracy in the History of Economic Analysis', *Journal of the History of Economic Thought*, **16**, 188–201.

Robbins, Lionel (1979), 'The Nature of Economic Generalizations', in *Philosophy and Economic Theory*, reprinted. (First Published in *The Nature and Significance of Economic Understanding*, London: Macmillan, 1935.)

Schumpeter, Joseph A. (1954), *History of Economic Analysis*, New York: Oxford University Press.

Selgin, George (1990), *Praxeology and Understanding*, Auburn: Ludwig von Mises Institute.

Senior, Nassau (1836, 1939), *An Outline of the Science of Political Economy*, New York: Rinehart.

Shand, Alexander H. (1984), *The Capitalist Alternative: An Introduction to Neo-Austrian Economics*, New York: New York University Press.

Smith, Adam (1790, 1982), *The Theory of Moral Sentiments*, Indianapolis: Liberty Classics.

White, Lawrence H. (1977), *The Methodology of the Austrian School of Economics*, Occasional Paper Series #1, New York: Center for Libertarian Studies.

Yeager, Leland B. (1954), 'The Methodology of Henry George and Karl Menger', *American Journal of Economics and Sociology*, **13**: 233–45.

10 Dialogues in economics

In this chapter, the authors were invited to comment on the other essays, in keeping with the theme, 'Dialogues in Economics', of the Eastern Economic Association conference for which the panel was assembled.

Kris Feder

On Austrian economics

Individual geo-economists have been associated with diverse schools, including neoclassical, Austrian, and even socialist. Henry George himself held to an ideology that has been called libertarian, and a methodology similar to the Austrian. There are notable parallels between his concerns and those expressed by Peter Boettke. The economics of George, like that of The Austrian School, is, as he put it, 'not heterodox in certain fundamental respects', yet with regard to the research project undertaken, 'is every bit as heterodox as any of the alternative schools'.

Boettke argues that neoclassical economists have over-emphasized syntactic clarity at the expense of semantic clarity, and thus have been unwilling to analyze the complex and subtle practical problems which their mathematical models cannot handle. George too criticized the 'learned professors' (1898, p. 205) for failing to solve, or even honestly to confront, the foremost economic problems of the real world, such as 'the concomitance of progress and poverty', cyclical instability, misallocation of resources, trade barriers, and monopoly. George complained not of excessive formalism, but of the sloppy use of natural language and wholesale abandonment of natural laws and general principles. The economists' 'incomprehensible jargon', he suspected, was not a symptom of ineptidude but a deliberate strategy to divert the public from clear thinking about politically dangerous issues – principally the one he himself had raised in *Progress and Poverty* (pp. 203–9). Geo-economists have reiterated similar charges over the years (Brown, 1924; Feder, 1994; Gaffney and Harrison, 1994).

George also shared both the Austrian preference for methodological individualism (Yeager, 1954) and Boettke's view of the task of economic science: to explain market regularities as outcomes of rational choices of individuals subject to constraints (1898, pp. 74–100). Boettke calls this a 'neoclassical' task, but it is far older. It is explicit, for example, in Nassau Senior's *Outlines* (1836, *passim*), as well as in George:

> ... this disposition of men to seek the satisfaction of their desires with the minimum of exertion is so universal and unfailing that it constitutes one of those invariable sequences that we denominate laws of nature, and from which we may safely reason. (1898, p. 87)

Boettke and other contributors to this volume warn against twisting this economizing axiom into the shallow 'economic man' caricature. Evidently that interpretation is not a neoclassical contribution either, for George warned of it too. Nearly a century ago he noted with dismay 'how completely the idea has prevailed that the foundation of political economy is the assumption of human selfishness' (1898, p. 88).

Boettke writes that 'money, within the Austrian analytical framework, represents ... the key social institution of coordination that allows us to bridge the gap between solipsism and social order'. He cites 'Menger's depiction of the evolution of a medium of exchange'. While George believed that institutions of land tenure were more important targets for reform than monetary institutions, he too wrote of the spontaneous evolution of money. A glance at his table of contents for Book V, Chapter V of *The Science of Political Economy* makes the point:

THE GENESIS OF MONEY.
SHOWING THAT THE LAW OF GRATIFYING DESIRES WITH THE LEAST EXERTION PROMPTS THE USE FROM TIME TO TIME OF THE MOST LABOR-SAVING MEDIUM AVAILABLE.

As George stated, 'Money not an invention, but developed by civilization – It grows with the growth of exchanges...' (1898, p. xxxiii).

One result of the mainstream dependence on formal equilibrium modeling, Boettke observes, is that 'the prime mover of economic progress – the entrepreneur – has been systematically weeded out of formal economic theory'. George would also have lamented this neoclassical drift. Subsuming entrepreneurial activity under the category 'labor', he recognized its vital economic function:

> ... any form of labor, that is to say, any form of human exertion in the production of wealth above that which cattle may be applied to doing, requires the human brain as truly as the human hand .... Labor ... is ... the means by which the spiritual element which is in man ... begins to exert its control on matter and motion, and to modify the material world to its desires. As land is the natural or passive factor in all production, so labor is the human or active factor. As such, it is the initiatory factor. All production results from the action of labor on land, and hence it is truly said that labor is the producer of all wealth. (1898, pp. 411–12)

This perspective is reflected in George's policy proposals. He would remove institutional impediments to trade, innovation and competition and abolish not only taxes on ordinary wages but also on entrepreneurial profits. The land tax he advocated would be set at the market-determined rent and would not vary with the effort or entrepreneurial success of the title holder.

Another of Boettke's general research interests is 'how institutions shape the individual's perception of what improving their lot in the world means'. Henry George wrote at length on this question (for example, 1879, pp. 454–543).

Some of the specific difficulties which Boettke identifies in his 'consequentialist' critique of the neoclassical 'obsession' with mathematics are of special interest to geo-economists. One telling example pertains to the economic analysis of pollution. Boettke observes that 'the policy recommendation that emerged out of the Pigovian framework required a level of detailed knowledge of the circumstances that were it to exist would render the policy recommendation redundant'. Knowledge of the costs and benefits of pollution is insufficient, so 'we do not know how to calculate the required taxes and subsidies'. Geo-economist Mason Gaffney has made much the same criticism:

> Nonpoint pollution goes right to a chink in the armor of conventionally trained economists (like myself) who are overtrained towards becoming protagonists of the price system. ... [W]e can't meter runoff – how frustrating. It comes from areas – how disorienting. Its damages are spread unequally over other areas, differentially populated – how non-homogeneous. Standard-brand economists are ill-equipped and undisposed to face such problems. (1987, p. 1)

Gaffney offers a geo-economic analysis and a 'tractable solution' to the 'intractable problem'. He outlines a set of positive policies that, together, would effect a fundamental cultural shift toward 'land stewardship, a new-old ethic to supplant the cowboy ethic in which western man has wallowed over several centuries of territorial expansion' (p. 22).

These and other parallels suggest that the Austrian and geo-economic schools of thought may offer largely complementary analytic frameworks (see also Yeager, 1954 and 1984). They differ with regard to their primary research questions, but even here there is a complementarity of interests. At the top of Boettke's agenda is 'the problem situation of time and ignorance', a problem which geo-economists must also tackle to further their analysis of the land problem. The immobility and long life of buildings, and the longer life of land, imply that the valuation of real estate is crucially dependent upon expectations regarding an uncertain future. Land speculation, prominent in geo-economic thought, cannot be understood merely by means of perfect-information equilibrium models.

If the present dialogue continues, and if the Austrian research program in 'time and ignorance' proceeds as Boettke hopes, it could offer geo-economists just the sort of analytic language they need to carry forward their own inquiry. In return, Austrians and their allies might give thought to what geo-economists argue is the tragic flaw of conventional libertarianism: the unexamined assumption that land can be subjected to private property rights on the same ethical basis as produced wealth.

> There can be to the ownership of anything no rightful title which is not derived from the title of the producer and does not rest upon the natural right of the man to himself. ... This right of ownership that springs from labor excludes the possibility of any other right of ownership. ... [T]he recognition of private property in land is a wrong. For the right to the produce of labor cannot be enjoyed without the right to the free use of the opportunities offered by nature .... When nonproducers can claim as rent a portion of the wealth created by producers, the right of the producers to the fruits of their labor is to that extent denied. (George, 1879, pp. 335–6)

Charles J. Whalen

Shared beliefs and research suggestions
Fred Foldvary has given both those who are reading and contributing to the present volume a rare yet vital opportunity – a chance to break out of our comfortable patterns of thought and reflect on a wide range of economic perspectives. This opportunity is indeed rare: most academic discussions take place within a small community of like-minded individuals, all familiar with the same literature and interested in similar issues. At the same time, broad dialogues are essential. As Keynes stated in the Preface to his *General Theory*, it's astonishing what foolish things we can believe if we think too long alone, particularly in economics.

What struck me most when reading the contributions of my colleagues in this volume was the degree to which our perspectives rest on shared beliefs. In the interest of paving the way for future discussions, I will use the space allotted to me here to bring attention to some of this common ground. This exploration will be followed by a brief discussion of suggestions for future collaborative inquiry.

Shared beliefs
Institutionalists are often considered activists, while Austrians are libertarian. But Peter Boettke's chapter suggests that institutionalists and Austrians actually have a great deal in common. Both share a recognition of the economic importance of time, uncertainty, knowledge and learning. Both are critical of the neoclassicals for taking human ends as given, rather than recognizing that both means and ends are subject to frequent re-examination and adjustment. Both also share an interest in constructing an economic theory that offers not just coherence but also correspondence with reality.

The shared beliefs of institutionalists and Austrians make a rejection of general competitive equilibrium inevitable. They agree that neoclassical theorists ignore nearly all that is essential for an understanding of economic life by choosing to treat market institutions and social practices as mere 'frictions' that have no place in mainstream analyses. It is obvious to both of these heterodox schools that private-sector economic reality is far from perfectly competitive.

John R. Commons, a founding member of the institutionalist tradition, expressed great interest in the ideas of Henry George early in his career. My reading of Kris Feder's chapter suggests that the modern-day descendants of Commons and George can find common ground in the notion that natural resources should be treated as the common heritage of all. Similar common ground exists with respect to both a belief in the importance of private property (as it relates to the products of human effort) and the suggestion that equity and efficiency are not necessarily incompatible. It appears to me that institutionalists are more mindful of the socially-constructed and fluid nature of categories such as 'public' and 'private' – and of the powerful impact that economic change and distribution can have on 'efficiency' – but perhaps these concerns can be accommodated by the Georgists. Future institutionalist-Georgist dialogues may want to devote attention to such matters.

The concept of efficiency seems also to have the ability to place a wedge between institutionalists and members of the Virginia school. The latter appears to have much more faith in 'economic markets' than an institutionalist could muster (not to mention the institutionalist rejection of the concept of a 'free' market). Nevertheless, two fundamental areas of shared agreement were revealed by my reading of Charles Rowley's chapter. We concur in the belief that 'political markets' are often inefficient; and we also seem to agree that evaluating the operation of real-world markets can only be done through detailed empirical analyses.

Institutionalists have perhaps even more in common with feminist and humanist economists than they do with the traditions discussed so far. The compatibility of institutionalism and feminism has already been discussed in my own chapter, and the connection between institutionalism and the pragmatic, volitional and humanistic economics described by Gerald Smith is self-evident. I would even submit that humanistic and institutional economics (I prefer the broader term 'political economy') are one and the same. Smith's excellent discussion of ethics, values, human nature and the importance of allowing for the maximization of an individual's human potential seems in total harmony with the institutionalist viewpoint.

Chapter 9 by Fred Foldvary is a bit different from the others in that it seeks to integrate various contending schools of thought at the level of methodology. But it should be noted that I find his synthesis in agreement with the methodological thinking of institutionalists. Both institutionalism and Foldvary's foundationalism point to an empirical economics that has a place for both induction and deduction (see Whalen (1996) and Doug Brown's chapter in Clark (1955)).

Research suggestions

The one element that seems to unify all the perspectives presented in this volume is a belief in the need for an economics that is historically and empirically grounded rather than mechanistic. Economics cannot escape being both a *social* science and a discipline rooted in *moral philosophy*. Members of these traditions should build on this and other shared beliefs and engage in collaborative research. In particular, I have in mind two realms of inquiry that seem especially worthy of our joint attention.

One matter that deserves attention is an inquiry into the nature and limits of individualism – a philosophical exploration of the relationship between the individual, market and state. What is the connection between capitalism and freedom? Under what general conditions might collective action play a useful role in furthering the agenda of those interested in expanding individual liberty? Do markets fail to detect and account for certain human values? Is it possible for us to devise a unified conception of private property? Part of the reason why conventional economics has lost touch with reality is because it ignores these questions; heterodox economists should address them squarely.

The second area of joint research flows from our recognition of the fact that both the state and the market are flawed social institutions. Together we must study these institutions and improve not only our knowledge of how they function and evolve but also our understanding of their various strengths and weaknesses. This work would allow us to help revitalize not only our profession but also our society. To not engage in such work is to allow America and the world to drift aimlessly into the 21st century.

Wesley Mitchell once wrote that whether economics is a subject of thrilling interests or a dismal pseudo-science depends on ourselves. Most orthodox economists are satisfied with the latter. Working together, heterodox economists can transform the discipline into the former.

Fred E. Foldvary

On Austrian economics

Austrian economists have analyzed ways in which state intervention, imposing restrictions as well as costs and subsidies, skews prices and profits, creating distorted signals which reduce the productivity of market economies. Austrian analysis of markets is positive and poses a challenge to heterodox schools critical of free markets. These critics typically conflate the concept of the pure market with actual 'capitalist' economies which are mixed systems of intervention as well as government-operated industries.

In addition to Peter Boettke's inclusion of deficiencies in Austrian economics, the school can be criticized for having a weak theory of public goods and their financing. Kris Feder's dialogue addresses how the geo-economic method of using revenue from natural-resource rents can fill this gap. Even if Austrians do not accept the geo-economic normative premises, on positive grounds, the financing of public goods from their generated rents is market-compatible and is in fact being implemented by markets (Foldvary, 1994). Here indeed is a good candidate for comparative analysis and synthetic theory construction. No doubt Austrian analysis can also be further enriched by dialogue with other schools, Austrians already having links to institutionalist as well as Virginia-school approaches.

On geo-economics

Kris Feder's 'Geo-economics' is an example of a part of economics that is often given only cursory treatment by orthodox textbooks and academic literature. This omission is an example of the lack of comprehensive treatment of topics by orthodox economics. Debates on tax reform, for example, focus on tapping streams of income or output, ignoring the possibility and advantage of using rents unrelated to human effort, thus eliminating disincentives, tax wedges, and excess burdens.

There are a few points where I would treat the topic a bit differently. My view of the normative premise of geo-economics is that the benefit of natural resources, i.e. the right to the yield, is regarded as common property, but the possession of the resources themselves, with rights of use and exchange, can be properly private. The bundle of rights constituting ownership is thus split between private rights of possession and common rights to yields. The rights of yield furthermore need to distinguish land rents due to the efforts of the local community, which can be proprietary, and rents due to natural factors and regional externalities. Those yields which can be identified as due to the efforts of local owners properly belong to those owners.

Professor Feder differs from the standard-textbook treatment of the supply of land as fixed, since landowners have reservation prices, and the supply of land offered to a market increases with increasing price. But land prices are the capitalized value of land rent, and what is capitalized is economic rent rather than any explicit financial rental payments. Assume some territory T with land of uniform quality and only one product. All lots will have the same economic rent, even though some owners will not wish to sell their land at the current capitalized price. Land does not have a leisure/production tradeoff as labor does; its economic rent is continuous. The economic rent will be a function of the amount of available land in T and the demand for land. The supply curve with economic rent at the vertical axis is indeed vertical. This result generalizes to land with various uses. The supply of land offered for explicit financial rentals and for sale will indeed be upward sloping, but not the supply of land as a function of economic rent.

On speculation, the problem is not just holding land out of use but also the opposite problem, excessive construction during a real-estate boom. When anticipated profits include a land-gain component, construction becomes malinvested when the cycle turns and the demand for commercial and residential buildings falls. Austrians also point out that such malinvestment occurs when interest rates are artificially reduced due to credit expansion caused by money creation in excess of the growth of savings. Austrian and geo-economic cycle theory can thus complement one another to create a more comprehensive synthesis, an application of the synthetic theory construction described in Chapter 1.

On portfolio effects, while the taxation of land rent would increase capital goods and reduce their productivity and yield relative to other factors, much investment also is applied to improving technology and creating new products, hence capital yields may not decrease in actuality. By reducing interest rates, the community collection of land rent would increase not only capital formation but also technological innovation.

Geo-economics, focused on land and to some degree on labor, is deficient in its treatment of capital goods and interest. Here, a synthesis with Austrian theory, which is strong in capital and interest and weak in its analysis of land, would be mutually advantageous. Combining the Austrian financial theory of business cycles with the geo-economic real theory focusing on the role of real estate (Foldvary, 1991) also has prospects for a fruitful synthesis. Geo-economists could also learn much from the Virginia school as to why, if geo-economics offers prosperity, politicians have been shunning the concept. Henry George was quite aware of the public-choice elements, but contemporary geo-economists have yet to fully integrate modern public-choice theory along with institutional analysis into their body of theory. Other schools would also contribute insight on the persistence of dysfunctional fiscal policy.

On Virginia political economy
The 'self-interest' proposition of the Virginia school does not claim that all public choices of all persons are based on narrow self-gratification, but rather is a premise on which theory conditional to it is derived, to be tested against the evidence, which the Virginia school concludes is consistent with its theory, which hence has significant explanatory power. Humanists may well urge a public-interest motivation for government agents, but the Virginia school in its positive analysis studies the situation as it is, within contemporary institutions and culture. The self-interest premise is also a method of

maintaining theoretical consistency between the private and government sectors; indeed, it is an antidote to the predilection of some reformers to treat government as a benevolent despot which need only be given the correct economic and ethical prescriptions. In urging 'better' values, the humanists and other reformers would do well to adopt the Virginia school's examination of alternative institutions for their incentives and constraints, which would alter behavior within the current culture, and perhaps change the culture to the more humane direction they desire.

Institutionalist economics
I agree with Charles Whalen that there is much common ground in the schools presented here, and I second his call for continued dialogue. Institutional thought had great influence in the US, and the school has a long and distinguished history, as outlined by Whalen in his chapter, that other schools can learn much from.

The institutional school as presented here offers theory that is complementary to both orthodoxy and to other heterodox schools, such as broadening economics by endogenizing culture and institutions. However, it is not clear to me whether institutional thought adds to or alters the foundational premises of economics (as I analyze them in Chapter 9). Whalen presents characteristics of institutional premises as holistic, processual, and envalued, but does not provide specific contents of such premises, i.e. as propositions, perhaps because there is as yet insufficient institutional analysis as to what they are (or perhaps anti-foundational analysis showing that the foundational approach is an illusion!).

I also find some gaps in institutionalist business cycle theory, in which a boom produces fragile financial structures and unsustainable debt. It is not clear why in a market economy banks would overlend, why interest rates would not rise to reduce borrowing, unless a central bank is accommodating the demand for borrowed funds. Institutionalism may well investigate the institution of central banking to determine the role played by state regulation, as for example analyzed by Austrians, and also determine the institutional structure of key investment areas such as real estate, where speculation is tied to public works as well as to redistributive tax policy, as analyzed by geo-economic theory (Foldvary, 1991). Cycle theory is a good candidate for the bridge-building to other schools that Whalen advocates. A synthetic endogenous cycle theory can then enrich and perhaps supplant the neoclassical theory that posits exogenous shocks as triggers to macroeconomic fluctuations.

With its inclusion of the institution of the state and its regulations and taxation, it is curious that Whalen refers to the current policy path as laissez-faire or 'free market'. Further bridges to both the Austrian and geo-economic schools may help institutionalists to better appreciate the institutional concept that industrial economies are mixtures of market and substantial state intervention which severely skews outcomes from what genuine laissez faire or free-market policy would bring about.

On feminist economics

Ulla Grapard criticizes neoclassical orthodoxy for basing its behavioral premises on masculine nature, ignoring for example reproductive labor such as child care and home production. But the fundamental theory of labor may be subsuming aspects such as home labor, so the lacunae may be more on the applied side than on pure theory. Feminists thus can validly point out that much labor analysis is theory conditional on, or specific to, our culture and institutions rather than universal.

It would be more persuasive to have explicit textual examples of faulty treatment of gender when such is being claimed. For example, Grapard states that in the social contract theory of Locke, among others, women are relegated to the role of caregiver in the home, but one of the foundations of Locke's (1690, p. 123) ethical philosophy is that human beings 'are all equal'. We can charitably interpret Locke's term 'mankind' as including all humanity unless there is textual evidence for a male bias.

According to Grapard, feminist economics rejects the assumption that men and women have a biologically determined nature. Feminists rightly reject unwarranted assumptions on sexual roles as universal, but the premise that there is no genetically determined behavioral human nature is itself not demonstrated. Feminist economics could, however, rightfully point out that any psychological and biological sexual differences are irrelevant for the basic premises on which economic theory is based.

Feminists criticize the 'separative model' of human nature in neoclassical economics, that actors have independent utility functions. The model is alleged to be illusory because human beings are dependent; children depend on parents and most men depend on their wives' unrenumerated labor. This labor should indeed be counted as economic, but it is not clear how these facts contradict independent utility functions; they derive from the 'independence' of human beings as biologically distinct beings rather than from any economic or social independence. Each human being has a separate mind and subjective values and feelings; that values are to a large degree socially derived is beside the point.

Feminist economists can also enhance their theory by examining other heterodox theory. One of Grapard's examples on gender is the crisis in child and elder care, stemming from relying on undervalued non-paid labor. Geoeconomics can shed further light on this problem, since the tax wedge of conventional taxation both reduces wage income and employment opportunities, while artificially increasing the cost of commercial care, problems which geo-economic policy can alleviate in a more fundamental way than conventional policy which only treats the effects of low wages by further intervention that then reduces after-tax wages even further.

On humanist economics

Human nature is a central concept of humanist economics, and Gerald Smith posits a *homo sapiens* who strives for 'excellence of being', in contrast to a *homo economicus* who strives for the power to remake the world and for whom economic goods determine the quality of life. But the premise of subjective values or desires, which Austrian and other economists agree with, implies that each human being has individual subjective ends, and so there is no universal end or ultimate human goal. Hence, a third view would posit a *homo subjectivus* who can be both a self-interested goods-seeking *homo economicus* and a community-conscious non-materialistic *homo sympaticus*. Moreover, many economists posit *homo economicus* as a premise for conditional theory without implying that people behave that way or have such values exclusively. Also, the subjectivity of values does not imply that there is no moral judgment; in ethics, acts are designated as good, evil, or neutral; indeed, such judgment can be derived from subjective values (Foldvary, 1980).

Nevertheless, humanist economics reminds us that there is more to human life and utility than the goods and self-gratification typically considered by economists, and that greed (along with ignorance and apathy) is a foundational cause of social ills (Foldvary, 1995). Also, humanist economics can criticize *homo economicus* as the predominant premise of economic theory, or as a premise that most behavior adheres to it, especially the notion that 'rational' behavior is self-seeking.

Gerald Smith presents two alternatives for natural resources: abundance (empty world) or resources vulnerability to early exhaustion (full world). But a third approach is that these are not meaningful as economic categories; resources are scarce, but available at a price, which increases as they become used up. A normative implication would be that growth need not be destructive if users pay the price, including the social costs, of using the resources. Sustainable growth is thus possible even with the constraint of maintaining renewable resources, since as the price increases, users economize more and discover substitutes as technology improves and knowledge increases.

Whereas Smith states that 'the laissez-faire market economy' is generally prescribed by neoclassical economists (Note 34), most in fact seem to favor mixed economies, including government provision of public goods (see Foldvary, 1994) and conventional taxation and, to some extent, welfare-state programs.

The greatest of all humanist principles may be the Austrian *homo subjectivus*, who has subjective values and experiences subjective costs and benefits. Subjectivity endows *homo sapiens* with supreme sovereignty over his values. The second great humanist principle is human moral equality. The logical economic and moral implication of these two foundational human principles, though recognized long ago by John Locke, has yet to be fully appreciated.

On nondeterminist Marxism

Postmodern thought rejects a universal standard of truth, which would then make any comparative theory problematic, since there would then be no school-independent criteria to judge by. But the proposition that there is no universal scientific methodology would apply to itself, which then depletes it of universal impact.

While nondeterminist Marxism provides complementary theory in studying economic classes, a topic omitted by most other schools, it retains Marxist concepts such as 'surplus value', 'surplus labor', and the 'exploitation' of labor. Could postmodern analysis deconstruct such concepts as the subjective interpretations of an academic tradition? Insights from other schools might bring to the Marxist analysis a greater role for the afflictions of workers from imposed costs by the state and from protected monopolies. Marxists might also ponder further the Austrian analysis of entrepreneurial profits arising from uncertainty and ignorance, and the geo-economic proposition that the surplus not earned by either competitive labor or competitive enterprise consists of economic rent mainly from natural resources. There is much gold yet to be mined in the study of heterodox thought.

Conclusion

I hope the reader has enjoyed this journey through heterodoxia and the examination of the curious phenomena of the sharply heterogenous nature of economic science that Warren Samuels aptly describes in the Foreword. It is hoped that these essays provide students of economics with a more comprehensive and deeper knowledge of economic theory, as well as a greater sensitivity to the views and values of fellow economists. It is hoped also that this work will spur further investigation of comparative and foundational theory.

May the dialogue continue!

References

Brown, H.G. (1924), 'The Single-Tax Complex of Some Contemporary Economists', *American Economic Review*, **14**, 164–79.

Clark, Charles M.A. (1955), *Institutional Economics and the Theory of Social Value*, Boston: Kluwer Academic Publishers.

Feder, Kris (1994), 'Public Finance and the Cooperative Society' in Michael Hudson, G.J.

Miller and Kris Feder, *A Philosophy for a Fair Society*, London: Shepheard-Walwyn, 123–62.

Foldvary, Fred (1980), *The Soul of Liberty*, San Francisco: Gutenberg Press.

Foldvary, Fred (1991), 'Real Estate and Business Cycles', paper presented at the Conference on Henry George, Lafayette College, June 13.

Foldvary, Fred (1994), *Public Goods and Private Communities*, Aldershot, UK: Edward Elgar.

Foldvary, Fred (1995), 'Ignorance, Apathy, and Greed as Root Causes of Social Problems'. Working Paper #E95-08 (April), Virginia Tech.

Gaffney, Mason (1987), 'Nonpoint Pollution: Tractable Solutions to Intractable Problems', paper delivered at Conference on 'Political, Institutional and Fiscal Alternatives to Accelerate Nonpoint Pollution Programs', Milwaukee, December 9.

Gaffney, Mason and Harrison, Fred (1994), *The Corruption of Economics*, London: Shepheard-Walwyn.

George, Henry (1879, 1971), *Progress and Poverty*, New York: Robert Schalkenbach Foundation.

George, Henry (1898, 1981), *The Science of Political Economy*, New York: Robert Schalkenbach Foundation.

Locke, John (1690, 1947), *Two Treatises of Government*, New York: Hafner Press.

Senior, William Nassau (1836, 1951), *Outlines of the Science of Political Economy*, 6th edn, New York: Augustus Kelley.

Yeager, Leland B. (1954), 'The Methodology of Henry George and Carl Menger', *American Journal of Economics and Sociology* **13**, 233–8.

Yeager, Leland B. (1984), 'Henry George and Austrian Economics', *History of Political Economy*, **16** (2), 157–74.

Whalen, Charles (1996), *Political Economy for the 21st Century*, Armonk, NY: M.E. Sharpe.

Wieser, Friedrich von (1967, 1927), *Social Economics*, trans. A. Ford Hinrichs, New York: Augustus M. Kelley.

Index

a priori xv, 156, 161
abduction xviii, 153–4
abstraction 4, 26, 30–31, 121
AEA *see* American Economic Association
altruism 18, 108–9
    see also sympathy
Amariglio, Jack xvii, 107, 111, 134, 139, 145
amateur 127
American Economic Association 26, 103
ancient (self) employment 41, 141–2, 144
anti-feminist 108
apriorism 156
Arrow, Kenneth 68, 72–3
ASSA (Allied Social Science Associations) 103
Austrian school
    and axiomatic-deduction 13, 32, 148, 156–7
    and axiomatic propositions 13, 32, 156
    and capital goods 13–14
    as a culture 154
    and cycle theory 14, 170
    and dialogue 169
    disagreement within 33
    and the entrepreneur 13
    and geo-economics 163, 165, 170–71
    and heterogeneity xiv, 13
    and historicism 28–9
    and human action 13, 32, 156
    and humanist economics 18
    and institutional economics xiv, 16, 27–8, 32–3, 89
    and intervention 1, 13, 168
    and knowledge 13, 140
    and land 15
    and malinvestments 170
    and marginalism 13, 160
    and markets 13–14, 27–8, 32, 168
    and methodology 13, 27, 32, 156–7
    and money 14, 29, 164
    and natural law 155
    and neoclassicism xiv, 13–14, 23, 29–32, 35
    and profits 174
    and public finance 169
    and realism 30–32
    and regulation 171
    as a school 8, 32, 63
    and subjective values 13, 19, 32, 160, 173–4
    and synthesis 35
    as theory 27
    and uncertainty 13, 19
    and universality 32
    and value theory 32, 160
    and the Virginia school 16
    what's wrong with 23, 32–5, 166, 169
    see also Austrians, Boettke, Böhm-Bawerk, Hayek, Menger, Mises, praxeology, Selgin, White, Wieser
Austrians 29–30, 33–35, 94, 154, 157, 160, 166–171
authentic fulfillment 120–21, 125
authority 10, 74, 105–6, 113, 147, 150
axiomatic
    analysis xiv, 3, 5, 148–61
    deductive 5, 13, 148
    propositions 3, 8, 12, 64, 101, 148–61, 164
    see also foundational
Ayres, Clarence 84–5, 89, 95–6

banking 6, 10, 16, 45, 171
Becker, Gary 24, 67, 68, 70, 78, 108, 109
benevolent 68, 109, 159, 171
bi-paradigmatic 19
bi-theoretic 19
Biewener, Carole 142
biological 6, 101–2, 104, 113, 172
biologically determined 17, 104, 172
biology 17, 89, 102, 104

Boettke, Peter xiv, 12–13, 20, 22, 163–6, 169
Böhm-Bawerk 29, 139
Buchanan, James 61–2, 65, 68, 71, 152–3, 159
bureaucracy 50, 53, 59, 61, 74, 79–82, 128
business cycle *see* cycles

Callari, Antonio xvii, xx, 134, 139
capital
    access to 44
    accumulation 136–8, 143
    and Austrian theory 170
    endowments 93
    as a factor 53, 55
    flows 58
    formation 46, 56, 170
    fixed 44
    gains 45, 51–2
    industrial 143
    investment in 46
    and labour 144
    and land 46
    limited 130
    markets 44, 79
    mobility 50, 92
    monopoly 137
    people and 50
    productivity of 46
    in socialism 53
    structure 154
    taxation of 46
    yields 170
Capital (Marx) 139
capital goods 5–6, 9, 13–15, 43–4, 46, 53, 55–6, 93, 143, 152, 160, 170
capitalism xv, xviii, 21, 41, 53–4, 57, 59, 68, 72, 80, 82, 91, 97, 99, 111, 114, 131, 134, 137, 141, 143, 144, 146, 147, 168
capitalist
    class 9, 141, 142–4
    crises 139
    development 91
    dynamics 137
    economy 84, 141–2, 169
    entrepreneurs 138
    exploitation 1
    firms xviii, 138, 142–3

ideal 54
labor 144
    restructuring 144
    systems xviii, 53–4, 90, 142
    terms 131
Cartesian 138
categorizing 104
Center for Study of Public Choice 61–2, 65
ceremonial 17, 89
CET 1–3, 9, 11, 151
Chicago
    challenge to Virginia 65
    microeconomics 26
    political economy 8, 16, 67, 70, 72
    school 62, 72, 80
    University of 62–4, 85
children 17, 101, 108–11, 131, 144, 172
class xviii, 9, 19, 53, 63–4, 73, 84, 99, 107, 112, 136, 140–47
    exploitation 143–4
classical economics
    anti-classical 56
    and geo-economics 41, 45
    and Marxism 139, 160
    New Classical 8, 134
    period of 120
    and political economy 58, 61
    school 1, 3–4, 8–9, 15, 28–9, 148
    and value theory 159
Coase, Ronald xiii, 26, 34, 39, 61–2, 71, 73–4, 80
coherence 87, 150, 166
collective action 47, 50, 57, 77, 81, 84, 97, 168
commodity fetishism xviii, 139–40
common 4, 14, 18, 21, 28–9, 41–2, 47, 49, 51–2, 54–5, 77, 80, 86, 94, 95, 97, 101, 122, 127, 132, 156, 159, 166–7, 169, 171
Commons, John 84–5, 89, 91, 95–7, 167
Communism 132, 134
community xii, xvi, 11, 15, 17, 43, 47, 51, 54–5, 59, 88, 97, 100, 102–6, 111, 122, 128–9, 131–2, 166, 169–70, 173
comparative xiii, xiv, xx, 1–3, 5, 7, 11, 16, 19, 21, 68, 89, 93, 98, 109, 151, 161, 169, 174
    analysis xx, 68, 169

theory xiii, xiv, xx, 1–3, 5, 7, 11, 19, 151, 161, 174
compassion xvii, 122–3, 126
complementary 2, 12, 14, 16–17, 129, 157, 165, 170–71, 174
comprehensive xx, 1, 3, 5, 10, 12, 15, 17–20, 79, 151, 161, 169, 170, 174
conjecture 11, 151, 153
conjectures xviii, 11–12, 149, 153, 162
constitutional 58, 64, 71–2, 81
contradiction 139, 150, 155
conventional xiii, 14–17, 19, 32, 80, 85, 86, 92–4, 96, 120, 122–6, 128, 137, 166, 168, 172, 173
convergence 25, 69, 153
corporations 89, 91, 128, 138
correspondence 1, 51, 123, 149, 150, 166
critical rationalism xvi, 10, 20, 63, 66, 105, 129, 145, 150, 162, 166, 168
CSWEP 103
Cullenberg, Stephen 138
culture 6–7, 16, 20, 63, 86–7, 92, 98, 101–2, 107, 110, 111, 124, 128, 133, 141, 143, 150, 152–4, 158, 170–72
cycles
  business xvi, xvii, 5, 7, 14, 24, 44, 50, 53, 57–9, 70, 84, 85, 89–91, 97, 109, 134, 137, 163, 170, 171
  voting 76

de Bono 10, 20
decentering 141, 138
deconstruction
  and feminist thought 107
  and foundationalism 149
  as methodology 6
deduction xviii, 148–9, 154, 168
definitions 1, 3, 4, 8, 9, 11, 14, 63–4, 100, 148–9, 152, 158
democracy viii, xv, 16, 28, 47, 49, 65–9, 71, 74–7, 80, 107, 142
description 3, 6–8, 32, 88, 112, 131–2, 154–5
determinate x, xiii–xiv, xviii, 12, 24, 27, 39, 43, 138
determinist xiii, xvii, 8, 19, 136–7, 139
  see also nondeterminist, overdetermination
development xviii, 1, 7, 22, 28, 39, 44, 46, 50, 55–6, 63, 83–5, 89, 91, 94–5, 99, 107, 109–12, 130, 132, 134, 136, 137, 142–3, 146
Dewey, John xvii, 83, 85, 96
dialectic 63, 135
dialogue xx, 20, 100, 103–4, 150, 163, 165–7, 169, 171, 174
  external 14, 47, 62, 71, 77, 79, 92, 138, 150
  internal 5, 14, 79, 97, 138, 150
discursive 137–8, 140, 142, 144
domestic lives 105, 108, 110, 113, 137, 141
Downs, Anthony 69, 73, 75, 79–80
dual-economy 90
dynamic xvi, 22, 83, 87, 89–90, 96, 137, 142

economic class x–xi, xiii–xviii, xx, 1–11, 13–14, 16–24, 24–32, 34, 38–9, 41, 43–4, 46, 48–59, 61, 63, 65–75, 77, 79–116, 119–42, 145–8, 151–2, 154–67, 169–74
economizing 4, 18, 72, 154, 158–60, 164, 173
efficiency xv, 10, 15, 22, 41, 43–4, 46, 48, 50–53, 55–6, 66–70, 72, 74–5, 77–80, 93, 121, 133, 167
Ely, Richard 83–4
empirically grounded 168
entrepreneur 13, 31, 138, 164–5, 174
  see also profit: entrepreneurial
envalued 5, 171
environment 16, 32, 48, 56, 68, 73, 78–80, 87, 98, 107, 130, 132
epistemological xvi, xviii, 29, 32–3, 84, 123, 136, 137, 150, 162
equal 14, 15, 26, 41–4, 49, 51–4, 72, 75, 89, 120, 125, 126, 151, 158–60, 172, 174
equilibrium x, xiii, xviii, 6, 13, 16, 24, 27, 30–31, 33, 44, 51, 63, 67, 70, 76–7, 87, 93, 139, 164–5, 167
equity 41, 46, 50, 52–3, 56, 167
essentialist 24, 101, 102
ethic xv, 14, 18, 67, 155, 158, 165
ethical viii, 9, 41, 56, 131–2, 151–2, 158, 166, 171, 172
ethics 3, 40, 82, 98, 130–33, 161, 167, 173

evil 1, 125, 127, 131, 134, 158, 173
evolutionary viii, xii, xvi, xviii, 8, 16,
    20, 39, 83–4, 86–7, 89, 94–6, 155
excellence 18, 115, 121, 124–7, 131,
    173
exploitation 1, 19, 141, 143–4, 146, 174
externalities 46–7, 50, 52, 66, 67, 70–
    73, 81, 169

factors xiii, xvii, 5–6, 9, 24, 33, 43, 53,
    56–7, 89, 92, 124, 132, 140, 152,
    164, 169, 170
family 4, 17, 87, 91–2, 108–9, 111, 128,
    141, 144
FE 148, 149, 151
Feder, Kris xiv–xv, xvii, 14–15, 41, 43,
    45, 58–9, 163, 167, 169, 174–5
female xvi, 17–18, 101, 102
    and male nature 104, 108
feminine 101–2
    as opposite to masculine 107
feminist economics
    and deconstruction 107
    and economics xvi, 8, 17–19, 100–
        114
    on Grapard's chapter xvi, 17, 172
    on human nature 18, 104–5, 172
    and institutional economics 18, 94,
        167
    labor theory 172
    on male domination xvii, 1
    and Marxism (nondeterminist) 140
    on masculine economic man 104–5
    on sexual roles 104, 172
    on women's issues 172
    see also feminists
feminists
    as a community 104
    in economics 17–18, 100–107
    on gender's role 1, 17, 104
    on gendered science 104–5
    on objectivity 105
    political theorists 107
    and postmodern thought 107
fiscal policy 15, 170
Foldvary, Fred xiii–xiv, xviii, xx, 1, 18,
    148, 166–8
formal 24, 26, 30–32, 34, 164
formalism x, xiii–xiv, 26, 31, 93, 163
foundational

anti- 19, 101, 137, 171
cause 172–3
deconstruction 149
economics xviii, xx, 1, 3, 8, 10, 17,
    19, 148, 151, 154, 161
human principles 12–13, 124, 172, 174
methodology 149–53, 161
philosophers 154
propositions 6, 9, 17, 23, 101, 124,
    137, 148, 150–53, 157–8, 161,
    171–3
theory 148–53, 161, 174
foundationalism 8
    and axiomatic-deduction 148
    and coherence 150
    and correspondence 149
    as culture 154
    elements of 150–51
    and empirical economics 168
    and truth 149–50
foundations xvii–xviii, xx, 2–3, 5, 9, 12,
    14, 18, 20, 25, 38–9, 41, 84, 97,
    104, 106
    of constitutional democracy 71
    of economic theory 13, 18, 30, 32, 41,
        84, 86, 88, 90, 101, 104, 106,
        124, 134, 137, 148–53, 157
    ethical, of economics xviii, 14, 151–2,
        158
    for feminist analysis 94, 101
    of Locke's thought 172, 174
    of Marxism 160–61
    of political economy 51, 95, 164
    of reasoning 150, 155
    in selfishness 164
    of social ills 173
    of theory 148–52, 155–8, 161
France 94, 142–3, 145, 154
free market *see* market: free
freedom xv, 41, 68, 80, 99, 122, 125,
    131, 133, 162, 168
Friedman, Milton 24, 63, 68, 80
fullness of life 122, 126

Gaffney, Mason 9, 20, 43–5, 48–51, 54,
    56, 58–9, 163, 165, 175
Galbraith, John 25, 85–6, 88–90, 92, 96
game theory xiii, 6, 13
gender xvi, xviii, 6, 17–18, 92, 97, 100–
    113, 140–41, 145–6, 172

geo-Austrian 19
geo-economics 1, 8, 9, 14–16, 18–19,
    41–60, 148, 161, 163, 165, 166,
    169, 170–74
    see also Georgist; Feder; Gaffney;
    George; Tideman
Geo-Economics Society 57
George, Henry xiv–xv, 15, 20, 41–8, 51–
    2, 54–9, 148, 161–7, 170
George Mason University 62
Georgist 8, 43, 45, 46, 49–52, 55–9,
    167
    see also geo-economics; George,
    Henry
German 28, 35, 83
Gordon, Wendell 89
government xv, 1, 5, 6, 9, 10, 14–16,
    18–19, 28, 42, 46–57, 62, 66–8,
    70–76, 78–81, 91, 93, 95, 97, 99,
    128, 130, 132, 152, 169–71, 173
graduate 24–6, 34, 35, 39, 61, 65, 81,
    96, 103
Grapard, Ulla xiii, xvi, 17, 19, 100–101,
    105, 145, 172
greed 121, 173, 175
Gruchy, Allan 85–7, 90

Hayek, Friedrich 19, 25, 33, 68, 72, 145,
    152, 154, 156–7
Hegelian 138
Henry George Theorem 15, 48, 51, 57
heterodox xi–xviii, xx, 2, 12, 20–21, 23,
    29, 32, 35, 94, 139, 163, 167–8,
    171–2, 174
heterodoxia 174
heterogeneity xiv, 13–14, 157, 174
Hicks, John xi
historical school 35, 83
historicist 8, 29
holism xviii, 4–5, 16–17, 86–8, 99, 171
homo economicus 17, 20, 101, 105, 107,
    115, 119–24, 126, 128–31, 159,
    173
homo sapiens xvii, 18, 115, 119, 121,
    124, 129, 173, 174
homo subjectivus 173, 174
homo sympaticus 20, 173
human action xiv, 13, 21, 32, 39, 156
human behavior 4, 33, 38, 63, 85, 101,
    106, 157

human beings 14, 20, 32, 115, 119, 123–
    5, 127, 128, 130, 131, 158, 172
human nature 17, 18, 100–102, 104–5,
    115–16, 121, 125–6, 129, 131, 133,
    158–9, 167, 172, 173
humanistic xvii, 32, 35, 120–21, 127,
    129, 130, 132–3, 167
humanists 1, 18, 121, 137, 170, 171
Husserl, Edmund 155, 161
hypothesis xvii, 11, 22, 30, 68, 153,
    162

IAFFE viii, 102–3, 112
ideological xi, 2, 9, 64, 80
ideology 9, 64, 65, 69, 77, 112, 113,
    130, 132, 163
ignorance 1, 27, 29, 30, 32, 34, 39, 72,
    73, 77–8, 131, 165, 173–5
imprimatur 150
individualism xiv, 5, 13, 32, 56, 94, 148,
    150, 161, 163, 168
induction xviii, 153, 154, 168
information 7, 10, 22, 27, 29–31, 45, 66,
    72–4, 79–81, 106, 116, 126, 131,
    158, 165
institutional xiv–xvi, 1, 8, 11, 16–17, 20,
    23, 27, 32–3, 39, 52, 64, 66–7, 73,
    75, 78–9, 83–8, 93–9, 102–3, 106,
    111–14, 135, 164, 167, 170–74
institutionalism xv, 16, 17, 23, 83–97,
    111, 113, 167–8, 171
institutionalists xvi–xvii, 3, 16–18, 83–
    97, 166–8, 172
institutions xii–xvi, 6–7, 16–17, 20–21,
    26–8, 33, 39, 41, 49, 54, 63–4, 67–
    8, 83, 87–9, 91, 95–6, 98, 102, 125,
    132, 139, 141, 164, 165, 167–8,
    170–72
instrumental xvii, 17, 35, 89
interest group xi, xiii, xx, 4, 7, 13–15,
    18, 28–9, 39, 44–5, 48–9, 52, 58,
    64, 66, 71–4, 77–8, 84–5, 95, 97,
    110, 112, 122, 124–5, 159, 165–7,
    170–71
interpretive
    Austrian school 160
    community xii, xvi, 103, 106, 111
    turn 156
    understanding xviii, 6, 154, 157
intersubjective 32, 151

intervention 1, 9, 10, 13, 16, 68, 71, 73,
    91, 168, 169, 172, 173
invisible hand 28, 159

justice 41, 52, 133
justification 60, 71, 101, 108–9, 130,
    149, 150

Keynes, John Maynard
    and Austrian theory 29
    and Benthamism 130
    and classical theory 29
    as economist 63
    and foolish beliefs 166
    and human nature 131
Keynes, John Neville 152, 154
Keynesian
    and Cambridge school 63
    macroeconomics 8, 90
    and market failure 1
    New Keynesian 30
    policy 53, 86, 142
Knight, Frank xv, xix, 26, 63, 149, 155
knowledge
    attaining 102, 123–4, 126, 150
    of costs and benefits 26, 165
    in economics xvi, xviii, 6, 13, 18, 25–
        8, 31, 33–5, 100–102, 105–6,
        116, 123–4, 126, 136–7, 140,
        148, 158, 166
    of institutions 168
    limitations of 13, 28, 123, 140, 158
    of people 13, 26, 123, 126, 140, 159
    of reality 102, 105–6, 116, 123, 140,
        155
    situated 46, 106, 112, 127, 137
    subjective 123, 140
    of technology 96, 173
    of theory 31, 100, 105–6, 123–4, 126,
        174
    warranting of 33, 105–6, 123, 151

labor
    abstract 140
    and capital 144
    capitalist 138, 144
    as cost of production 160
    division of 9, 101, 108, 145, 152, 160
    economics 4, 6, 18
    as entrepreneurship 164

exploitation of 1, 138, 142, 174
    as a factor 5, 9, 14–15, 41, 43, 53, 87,
        92, 152, 161–2, 164
    Henry George on 1, 40–43, 161, 164,
        166
    hiring 45
    invisible 105, 111
    legislation 84
    marginal value of 160
    non-paid 105, 109–10, 172
    power 143–4
    reproductive 17, 101, 108, 110, 172
    rights to fruit of 42, 45, 51, 54, 160,
        166
    saving 164
    Senior on 154
    surplus 54, 140, 142, 144, 174
    theory of value 87, 139, 160
    unions 128
    unremunerated 105
    wage of 143–4
    and women *see* women: and labor
    see also wages
laissez-faire 93, 95, 131, 171–3
land
    as factor 5–6, 9, 15, 41–3, 152, 160–
        61, 164
    and geo-economics xv, 1, 15, 41–58,
        161, 164–6, 169–70
    owners xv, 42–8, 52, 54, 169
    prices xv, 43–4, 46–7, 49, 169
    rent 1, 9, 15, 42–59, 161, 169–70
    rights 41–3, 49, 51, 53–5, 110, 166
    speculation *see* speculation: land
    supply of 43–4, 169–70
    tax *see* taxation: of land value or rent
    tenure 42, 50, 55–6, 58, 164, 166
    see also real estate; rent
lateral reasoning 10, 151
libertarian 162, 163, 166
liberty 32, 39, 41, 52, 54, 61, 81, 88, 93,
    158, 161–2, 168, 175
Locke, John 14, 41, 42, 108, 158, 172,
    174
    see also proviso, Lockean
logic 6, 9, 11, 12, 25–7, 30, 1, 33, 77,
    81, 112, 124, 136, 141, 149–53,
    159
LVT (land-value taxation) *see* taxation:
    of land value or rent

macroeconomic 5, 15, 17, 44, 45, 57, 91, 99, 116, 119, 148, 171
mainstream xvi, xviii, xx, 15, 18, 20, 23, 30–31, 33–5, 66, 83, 88–9, 92, 94–6, 100, 103, 106, 108, 139, 140, 164, 167
majoritarian 16
male xvi, 1, 17–18, 101, 104, 108, 111, 144, 172
malinvestment 170
market
  and Austrian economics 13, 27–8, 30–33, 35, 168
  capital 44, 79
  concentration 137
  creation of 9, 92
  defined 9, 14, 158
  economic x, xvi, 6, 22–4, 27–8, 30–31, 35, 43–7, 49, 53, 55–6, 65–73, 77–9, 167
  economy 9–10, 131, 133, 168, 171–3
  and ethics 9, 158
  evaluating 10, 63, 73, 131, 167
  exchange 55, 140
  failure 1, 10, 15–16, 30, 45–6, 53, 55, 65–8, 70–76, 79–80, 86, 168
  free 9–10, 14, 46, 68, 113, 131–2, 147, 167–72
  global 92
  institutional thought on xvi, 83, 86–7, 92–5, 167–8
  and institutions xvi, 87, 167–8, 171
  and intervention 10, 168
  and land 165, 169
  laissez-faire 131, 172–3
  and Marxist thought 63, 132, 137–40
  mixed 169, 172
  place 71, 73, 105, 108
  political xvi, 15–16, 50, 53, 65–80, 167
  process xvi, 9, 13–14, 28, 31–3, 158–9
  and public goods 159, 169
  pure 169
  regularities 23, 163
  and self interest 159
  social aspect of 92–3, 140
  values 27, 43–4, 55–6, 95
  as voluntary exchange 158

  work 103, 109
Marshall, Alfred 24–5, 29, 129, 131
Marshall, Ray 91–2
Marxism xvii, xx, 1, 8, 16, 19, 23, 64, 87, 89, 94, 112, 134–47, 154, 160, 161, 174
masculine model 101
mathematical xiv, 9, 12, 13, 24, 25, 27, 34, 112, 126, 155, 160, 163
mathematics xiii, 6, 8, 13–14, 24–6, 34, 38, 126, 165
matrix xii–xiv, 11
maximizing xiii, 4, 24, 27, 31, 44, 50, 65, 67, 69, 79, 108, 116, 122, 124, 126, 128, 153, 158, 159
McCloskey, Donald 3, 12, 21, 26, 39, 106, 112–13, 123, 131, 133, 140, 150–51
McIntyre, Richard 142
median voter 69, 75–7, 81
Menger, Carl 13, 15, 21, 28, 29–30, 39, 148, 154, 160, 162, 164, 175
metaphors 8, 140, 141
methodological xiv, xviii, 5, 13, 15, 17, 32–3, 35, 63–4, 84, 86, 88, 94, 99–100, 106, 137, 147–8, 150, 157, 163, 168
  holism 4–5, 16–17, 86–8, 171
  individualism xiv, 5, 13, 32, 137, 148, 150, 163
  pluralism 157
  structuralists 137
methodology xi, xx, 1, 4, 5, 8, 12–14, 18–21, 29, 34, 39, 41, 63–4, 88, 94, 96, 99, 113, 140, 147–8, 150–51, 154, 156, 161–3, 167, 174, 175
mezoeconomics 5–6
microeconomics 1, 5–6, 31, 57, 97, 126, 132, 160
Mill, John Stuart 41, 108, 153
Miller and Mair 2–3
Mises, Ludwig von 13, 21, 33, 39, 63, 68, 154–6, 162
  see also praxeology
Mitchell, Wesley 84–5, 89, 95–6, 168
mixed systems 169
modernist 135, 137, 147
money 6, 14, 16, 28, 29, 39, 50, 84–5, 89, 92, 96–8, 109, 110, 127, 132, 139, 140, 147, 164, 170

moral philosophy 132–3, 161, 168
Mueller, Dennis 1, 21, 63–4, 81
multi-paradigmism 19
Myrdal, Gunnar 85–6, 93, 96

natural language 24, 27, 34, 163
natural law 155
natural opportunities 14, 41–2, 51–2
natural resources 7, 14, 41, 46–7, 49, 53,
     55, 57, 89, 93, 116, 157, 167, 169,
     173–4
natural rights 42, 166
Neoclassical x–xviii, xx, 1, 3, 8–9, 11–
     20, 22–4, 27, 29–31, 33–5, 39, 56,
     59, 61–3, 66, 83, 85, 87–96, 100–
     101, 105, 107, 109, 111, 114, 119–
     21, 124, 130–32, 134–6, 139, 146–
     8, 160, 163–5, 167, 171–3
New Classical *see* classical: New
     Classical
Niskanen, William 79
Nobel Prize 61, 65, 86
non-Tuism 159
nondeterminist xvii, xx, 8, 13, 19, 134–
     42, 144–5, 174
     see also postmodern
nonmarket 43, 72, 140
normative 9, 13–14, 28, 32, 41, 49, 64,
     98, 116, 160, 169, 173
Norton, Bruce 137–8

objectivity 99, 105–7, 111–12, 126
orthodoxy xiv, 3, 14–15, 17, 63, 84–6,
     89, 92, 135, 160, 168–9, 171–2
overdeterminist xvii–xviii, 19, 135–42,
     145

pan-theoretic 19
paradigm x–xiii, xv, 13–16, 19, 32, 41,
     56–9, 65, 100, 105, 140, 159–60
Pareto xiii, xv, 30, 39, 67, 70–72, 75–6,
     130, 133
parliamentary 67, 69, 78–9
pathological 66
Peirce, Charles xvii–xviii, 83–4, 95, 98
Physiocrats 154
pluralism 154, 157, 161
policy xi, xv, 1, 9–11, 14–19, 25–6, 28,
     32, 35, 52–3, 56–9, 69, 73, 75–8,
     80, 82–7, 94–5, 98–100, 102–4,

107, 110–11, 132, 141, 158, 164–5,
     170–73
political economy ix, xi, xv, 1–2, 7, 8,
     15–16, 21, 35, 38, 40–41, 55, 58,
     61, 63–5, 80–83, 88, 91, 93, 95, 99,
     111, 113, 133, 145–7, 152, 161–2,
     164, 167, 170, 175
political markets xv, 65–70, 72–8, 80,
     167
pollution 48–9, 52–3, 56, 116, 165, 175
Popper, Karl 113, 150, 155, 157
portfolio effects 45–6, 170
positivist x, xvii, 13, 105–6, 156
Post Keynesian 20, 39, 96–7, 99, 134,
     140, 147
post-modern 1, 8
postmodern xvii, xx, 13, 19, 106–7, 111,
     112, 134–7, 145, 146–9, 174
poverty xvi, 1, 7, 15, 20, 50, 53, 55–6,
     58–9, 110, 120, 161, 163, 175
pragmatism 30, 83, 84, 95, 98, 113, 140,
     147
praxeology 6, 13, 156, 162
prediction 88
prices xvi, 13–14, 19, 27, 40, 44, 46, 49,
     56, 58, 87, 90, 91, 95, 98, 134, 136,
     139, 168–9
     see also value: as price
principal–agent 76, 79
privileges 45, 53–4
process x, xiv, xvi–xvii, 3–4, 6, 9–11,
     13, 17, 26–7, 32–3, 39, 56, 66, 76,
     84, 86, 92–4, 96, 111, 116, 126,
     129, 132, 137–9, 142–3, 157–60
processual 16, 87–8, 90, 171
profit
     of capital 143
     entrepreneurial 165, 174
     fall of 91
     intervention skewing 168
     and land gains 170
     maximizing xiii, 27, 31, 96, 108, 126,
          137, 153, 159
     rates 138
     and rent seeking 49
     stabilizing 90
     theory of xvi, 107, 140
property xv, 14, 24, 41–2, 45, 47–9, 51–
     5, 58–9, 66, 73, 74, 76, 92, 97, 108,
     110–11, 142, 166, 167–9

private xv, 41–2, 45, 49, 51–3, 97,
    166–8
proviso, Lockean 14, 42
psychology 20, 86, 104, 135
public choice 7, 15, 16, 21, 24, 49, 57,
    61–5, 68, 72, 74–6, 80–82, 88, 159,
    170
public finance 7, 15, 48, 50, 52, 55, 57–
    8, 80, 174
public goods vii, 7, 14, 15, 20, 34, 42,
    48, 55, 58, 59, 66, 70, 71, 73–5, 77,
    122, 159, 161, 169, 173, 175

qualitative 89, 96

race xviii, 86, 104, 107, 112, 114, 140,
    145–6
radical economists 8, 100, 140, 142
rational xi, xvii, 2–4, 23, 35, 42, 51–2,
    63, 67–8, 72–3, 77–9, 101, 128,
    130, 135, 163, 173
real estate 165, 170–71, 175
    see also land; rent: of land
real-world 15, 86, 88, 93, 95, 167
realistic 13–14, 16, 32, 88, 90
redistribution 51, 53, 67, 74–5, 78
Reid, Thomas 154
rent
    of land xv, 1, 9, 15, 16, 42–59, 161,
        165–6, 169–70, 174
    tax of *see* taxation: of land value or
        rent
    (transfer) seeking 1, 16, 49, 70–71,
        74–5, 78
resources xvii, 3, 4, 7, 14, 27, 41–3, 45–
    7, 49, 53–7, 59, 70, 73–5, 80, 89,
    91–4, 102, 110, 111, 113, 116, 119,
    121, 125, 128–32, 157, 163, 167,
    169, 173, 174
revised sequence 92
rhetoric x, 6, 21, 33, 106–7, 112–13,
    140, 146–7, 150, 162
Ricardian xv, 8, 28, 139
Ricardo, David 29, 147, 154
rights xv, 14, 24, 41–3, 49, 51, 54, 55,
    73–4, 76, 89, 92, 107, 108, 110,
    166, 169
rigor 34
Robbins, Lionel 3–4, 155
Robinson, Joan 9, 21, 88, 99

Robinson Crusoe 101, 112, 146
Roche, John 139
Rowley, Charles xv, xx, 15–16, 61, 167
Russia 132

Samuels, Warren x, 2, 9–11, 27, 130,
    174
Samuelson, Paul 25, 134
schools x–xx, 1–5, 8–12, 16–21, 23, 32,
    46, 63, 64, 94, 100, 103, 111, 119–
    20, 125, 135–7, 148, 151, 154,
    160–61, 163–72, 174
    defined 1, 63–4
Schumpeter, Joseph 130, 154
self-gratification 1, 18, 158, 170, 173
self-interest xi, 15, 18, 48, 64, 66, 112,
    122, 124, 159, 170
selfishness 164
Selgin, George 156
semantic 25, 34, 149, 150, 163
Senior, Nassau 154, 163
separative model 105, 172
sex 101–2
sexual 101, 108, 113, 172
simultaneously xvii, 13, 35, 69, 132,
    136, 139, 142
Smith, Adam 31, 41, 61, 63, 83, 105,
    108, 130, 159
Smith, Gerald xvii, 18, 105, 115, 167,
    173
social
    construction xvi, xvii, 112, 139, 140
    embeddedness 27, 1, 33, 140
    ills 173
    relations 92, 104, 107
socialism xv, 40, 41, 53, 54, 57, 59, 81,
    142, 145–7, 163
socially constituted xii, xv, xviii, 17, 44,
    50, 102, 106, 107, 109, 135, 150,
    158, 167, 172
sociobiology 104
speculation
    land 44–5, 48, 165, 170–71
    scientific 11, 131
Sraffa theory 134
state (government) 53–5, 70–73, 75, 83,
    87–8, 90, 92–6, 143–4, 168, 171–4
statistics 6, 61, 81, 85, 89, 153
Stigler, George 68–9
Stiglitz, Joseph 70, 73–4

structure of science 154
subjective 13, 18, 19, 23, 27–9, 39, 92,
    101, 107, 135, 140, 150, 151, 154,
    156, 158–60, 172–4
substitutive 2, 12, 14, 16–17, 19, 119
surplus
    labour *see* labor: surplus
    value 19, 63, 142–3, 174
sympathy 20, 158–9
syntactic clarity 25, 34, 163
synthetic
    economics xiv, 3
    theory 11–12, 17–19, 59, 94, 151,
        169–71

tastes 105, 135
taxation
    analysis of 10, 14, 75
    burden of 15, 42–6, 52–5, 67, 169,
        171–3
    calculation of 26, 52, 75, 165
    and fiscal policy 53, 69, 72, 75, 143,
        169, 172–3
    of labor and production 1, 15, 44–6,
        48, 50–51, 165, 171
    of land value or rent xv, 1, 15–16, 18,
        42–57, 165, 170
    opposition to 122
    of pollution 49, 56, 165
    shift of 15, 42, 46, 51–2, 165
    and special interests 50
    violate self-ownership 42
taxonomy 3, 5, 6, 9, 15–17, 110, 151–2
technology xvi, 22–3, 89, 96, 122–3,
    129, 137, 139, 157, 170, 173
theory
    absolute xii
    anatomy of 5, 151–3
    comparative xiii–xiv, xx, 1–21, 136
    defined 11, 148–9
    game xiii, 6, 13, 109
    laden xii, 29, 153
    pure 13, 33, 81, 152–4, 156, 157, 159,
        172
    realism 32
    specific xvi, 7, 47, 69, 77, 100, 102,
        106, 142, 153, 157, 159, 165,
        171, 172
Thomas Jefferson Center 61–2
Tideman, Nicolaus 50–51

time
    historical 87, 106, 144
    and ignorance 27, 30, 32, 34, 39, 165
    and interest 7
    passage of 28, 44, 47, 64, 71, 85, 90,
        138, 141, 165
    preference 158
    and theory 7, 89, 91, 94, 96, 109, 124,
        152–3, 165–6
transactions 29, 45, 87, 89, 108
transfer seeking 16
    see also rent seeking
truth x, xi, xii, 1, 3, 19, 84, 105, 106, 123,
    126, 131, 137, 149–50, 161–2, 174
Tullock, Gordon 4, 61–2, 65, 68, 70–71,
    73–5, 79, 159

unanimity 71
uncertainty 13, 16, 19, 51, 58, 63, 80,
    84, 87, 98, 140, 142, 145–6, 149,
    158, 165–6, 174
United Kingdom 63, 67, 78, 83, 107,
    129
United States 45, 54–6, 71, 78–9, 83,
    89, 93, 98, 134, 141–2, 144
universal
    and absolute 105
    application 34, 150
    consent 71
    ethic 158
    premises 13
    principle 32
    rationality 140
    rights 41
    scientific methodology 174
    standard 137, 174
    suffrage 66
    theory 27, 155, 158
    Truth 1
    truths 19, 155
universalist economics 19–20
urban 7, 46, 48–50, 55–9
utility
    comparisons 105
    economic 4–6, 9, 67, 74, 92, 120,
        157–8, 173
    economics as science of 4
    functions 4, 67, 70, 105, 109, 172
    maximization 16, 27, 31, 67, 96, 108–
        9, 115, 120, 124–6

public 84
see also value

Vachris, Michelle xv, 61
value
   economic xv, 9, 18, 27, 42–52, 55, 57,
      71, 74, 77, 79, 87, 95, 105, 110,
      120, 131, 139–40, 143–4, 157–
      60, 172
   free (independent) 5, 18, 87, 106
   of knowledge 86, 88
   labor theory of *see* labor: theory of
      value
   laden (envalued) 5, 88, 171
   moral xvi–xviii, 16, 18, 86, 122, 130,
      140, 158, 167–8, 171, 173–4
   as price 42–52, 55, 57, 160, 169
   subjective 13, 19, 156–60, 172–4
   surplus 19, 63, 142–3, 174
   theory 45, 134, 139–40, 146, 156,
      159–61
Veblen, Thorstein 83–6, 88–9, 92, 94–6
Veblenian dichotomy 89
vertical reasoning 9, 10, 43, 170
Virginia school xx, 1, 8, 15–16, 18–19,
   24, 61–5, 68, 80, 159, 167, 169–71
voluntary 14, 53, 67, 73, 74, 158

wages
   fair earnings of 45, 160
   lowering of 91, 144, 173
   raising of 46, 52, 56, 58
   taxes on 165, 173
   see also labor
Walrasian 29

want creation 87, 92, 96
warranting 3, 11–12, 14, 58, 87, 148–51,
   153, 161
wealth xvii, 3, 4, 14, 41, 42, 45, 46, 50–
   55, 65, 67, 74, 75, 78, 83, 86, 122,
   129, 133, 146, 154, 164, 166
welfare xv, xvii, 7, 18, 28–30, 53–5, 58–
   9, 66–8, 72–3, 80–82, 86, 110, 116,
   142, 173
Weltanschauung *see* world view
Whalen, Charles xv, 16–17, 83, 166, 171
White, Lawrence 156
Wieser, Friedrich von 156
Wisconsin 21, 58–60, 84, 113, 146, 162
Wittman, Donald 65–70, 76, 80
Wolff, Richard xvii, 134, 139
women
   biological nature of 101, 104, 108,
      172
   as caregiver 172
   as category 102, 104, 107
   and development economics 110–11
   in economics 103–7
   in economy xvii, 17, 101, 104–6,
      108–11, 141
   invisible 107, 110–11
   and labor 105, 108–11, 141, 144
   lack of rights 108–11
   voices of 105–6
   see also female; feminine; feminist
      economics; labor: reproductive;
      labor: non-paid
world view 1, 63, 129

Yeager, Leland 148, 163, 165